MW01009484

THE PERMISSION SOCIETY

ALSO BY TIMOTHY SANDEFUR

The Right to Earn a Living:
Economic Freedom and the Law

The Conscience of the Constitution

Cornerstone of Liberty:
Property Rights in 21st-Century America
(coauthored with Christina Sandefur)

THE
PERMISSION SOCIETY

How the Ruling Class Turns

Our Freedoms into Privileges

and What We Can Do About It

TIMOTHY SANDEFUR

To Robert *(signed)* and Brenda Burns —
Thank you for helping us defend freedom!

(signature)

ENCOUNTER BOOKS

NEW YORK · LONDON

© 2016 by Timothy Sandefur

All rights reserved. No part of this publication may be reproduced, stored in a retrieval system, or transmitted, in any form or by any means, electronic, mechanical, photocopying, recording, or otherwise, without the prior written permission of Encounter Books, 900 Broadway, Suite 601, New York, New York, 10003.

First American edition published in 2016 by Encounter Books, an activity of Encounter for Culture and Education, Inc., a nonprofit, tax exempt corporation.
Encounter Books website address: www.encounterbooks.com

Manufactured in the United States and printed on acid-free paper. The paper used in this publication meets the minimum requirements of ANSI/NISO Z39.48—1992 (R 1997) (*Permanence of Paper*).

FIRST AMERICAN EDITION

LIBRARY OF CONGRESS CATALOGING-IN-PUBLICATION DATA

Names: Sandefur, Timothy, author.
Title: The permission society : how the ruling class turns our freedoms into privileges and what we can do about it / by Timothy Sandefur.
Description: New York : Encounter Books, [2016] | Includes bibliographical references and index.
Identifiers: LCCN 2016002491 (print) | LCCN 2016015051 (ebook) | ISBN 9781594038396 (hardcover : alk. paper) | ISBN 9781594038402 (Ebook)
Subjects: LCSH: Liberty – United States. | Abuse of administrative power – United States. | Political culture – United States.
Classification: LCC JC599.U5 S334 2016 (print) | LCC JC599.U5 (ebook) | DDC 323.4/90973—dc23
LC record available at https://lccn.loc.gov/2016002491

CONTENTS

TO MY PARENTS, MARK AND JULIE,
AND TO DANNY

INTRODUCTION

NOT HAVING to ask permission is one of the most essential parts of freedom. To be free means to be able to make one's own decisions – to take "the open road," as Walt Whitman put it, "wherever I choose"[1] – without first seeking some kind of approval from a superior. Freedom does not mean the right to do whatever pleases, regardless of harm to others – "for who could be free," asked John Locke, "when every other man's humour might domineer over him?" Instead, freedom means a person's ability to "dispose, and order as he lists, his person, actions, possessions, and his whole property," without having to obey "the arbitrary will of another."[2] Freedom means the ability to follow one's own will: to do as one chooses with oneself – with one's own abilities and property – without being required to ask leave of somebody else.[3]

This is the difference between rights and permissions. We have freedom when we can make the operative choices about our lives – about what to say, what our religious beliefs are, what jobs to take, or what to build on our property. To the degree that we must ask someone else to let us act, we do not have rights but privileges – licenses that are granted, on limited terms, from someone who stands above us.

Under the rule of monarchy, subjects enjoyed no freedoms except those that the ruler chose to allow. Someone wishing to travel, preach, start a business, publish a book, or engage in any number of other activities was first required to obtain permission from the authorities. Under such rules, the people enjoyed only privileges, not rights. Their freedoms took the form of forbearance on the part of the ruler, which could be revoked at any time. When America's founders broke with the mother country, they sought to reverse this polarity. The government of the new United States would not give permissions *to* people but would have to ask permission *from* the people. The founding fathers pledged their lives, fortunes, and sacred honor to the proposition that all human beings are fundamentally equal, with none enjoying any special right to rule another. Government existed not to give people rights, but to protect the rights that were already theirs.

Sadly, today America is gradually losing this principle of freedom and becoming instead what I call the Permission Society – a society in which our choices are increasingly subject to government pre-approval. Whether it be building a house, getting a job, owning a gun, expressing one's political beliefs, or even taking a life-saving medicine, laws and regulations at the federal, state, and local levels now impose permit requirements that forbid us to act unless we first get permission from the government. Thanks in particular to ideas that originated with the early twentieth-century Progressive movement, today's leading politicians, judges, intellectuals, and activists now believe that we are not free unless and until the government says we are.

This book examines this dangerous trend and how we can fight back. I look at some of the different ways permit requirements affect our daily lives: from the most famous such rule – the "prior restraint," which forces people to get permission before they may speak – to rules that require property owners to pay the government money or give it land in exchange for permission to build homes, to laws that force business owners to get permission *from their own competitors* before they may start operating, to laws that require government approval to take life-saving medications.

These laws expand the power of the state, stifle innovation and entrepreneurship, and do violence to the basic principle of equality on which our nation's institutions rest. Our Constitution promises more – and Americans deserve better.

CHAPTER ONE

CHARTERS OF LIBERTY
GRANTED BY POWER

IN 1792, in a short essay called "Charters," James Madison succinctly explained what he thought was the essential difference between the United States Constitution and the constitutions of every other nation in history. "In Europe," he wrote, "charters of liberty have been granted by power. America has set the example ... of charters of power granted by liberty. This revolution in the practice of the world may, with an honest praise, be pronounced the most triumphant epoch of its history."[1]

The "charters of liberty ... granted by power" that Madison had in mind were the celebrated documents of freedom that kings and parliaments had issued throughout the ages, many still honored today: Magna Carta of 1215, the English Petition of Right of 1628, the English Bill of Rights of 1689. Documents like these had made the British constitution – unwritten though it was – the freest in the world prior to the American Revolution. A British subject enjoyed more room to express his opinions, more liberty to do as he liked with his property, more security against government intrusion, and greater religious toleration than the subject of any other monarchy in the known world.

Yet for Madison and his contemporaries, that was not enough.

He and his fellow patriots considered "charters of liberty ... granted by power" a poor substitute for actual freedom because however noble their words, such charters were still nothing more than pledges by those in power not to invade a subject's freedom. And because those pledges were "granted by power," they could also be revoked by the same power. If freedom was only a privilege the king gave subjects out of his own magnanimity, then freedom could also be taken away whenever the king saw fit.

Whether Parliament could repeal the charters of British freedom was a point of controversy among lawyers and political thinkers up to, and after, the muskets began firing at Lexington and Concord. The British judge William Blackstone, whose four-volume *Commentaries on the Laws of England* was published in the 1760s and became a landmark in legal history, was proud that Great Britain was foremost in the world in terms of respecting the rights God gave all people. Yet at the same time, he believed that Parliament's power was "supreme" and "absolute"[2] and that, if it chose, it could change the rules of monarchical succession, alter the country's religion, and "do everything that is not naturally impossible."[3] Parliament's "omnipotence" was so vast that it had power over "[a]ll mischiefs and grievances, operations and remedies, that transcend the ordinary course of the laws."[4] Other thinkers, most notably John Locke, had argued that individual rights took precedence over government power, so that the people always retain the right to overthrow tyrannical rulers. But Blackstone rejected this idea because it "would jeopardise the authority of all positive laws before enacted." As long as the British government exists, he wrote, "the power of parliament is absolute and without control."[5]

The idea that Parliament's "absolute" power included a right to revoke protections for individual rights repelled America's founders. They believed that people are inherently free and that government answers to them, not the other way around. James Wilson, a signer of the Declaration of Independence who served alongside Madison at the Constitutional Convention, pointed out that if

Blackstone was right in thinking that freedom is given to people by all-powerful rulers, then the "undeniable and unavoidable" consequence would be that "the right of individuals to their private property, to their personal liberty, to their health, to their reputation, and to their life, flow from a human establishment, and can be traced to no higher source." That would mean that "man is not only made *for*, but made *by* the government: he is nothing but what society frames: he can claim nothing but what the society provides."[6] The fundamental problem with the monarchical idea of charters of liberty granted by power was that freedom could then only consist of those rights the king chose to grant and only for so long as he chose to grant them.

This was not just a theoretical problem. Monarchs often revoked "charters of liberty" after granting them. Even the glorified Magna Carta was repudiated not long after it was issued, and many kings refused to acknowledge its authority. Perhaps the most notorious example of the fragility of such charters came from France. In 1598, King Henry IV issued the Edict of Nantes, promising religious toleration to Protestants. For decades, Protestants and Catholics had murdered one another, most infamously in the St. Bartholomew's Day Massacre of 1572, during which unknown thousands were slaughtered. Henry himself was spared only when he converted to Catholicism. (Three decades later, he was assassinated anyway, after more than a dozen attempts on his life.) Although the Edict proclaimed Catholicism the national religion, it also allowed Protestants to "live and abide in all the cities and places of this our kingdom ... without being annoyed, molested, or compelled to do anything in the matter of religion contrary to their consciences," so long as they complied with the secular laws. This, Henry proclaimed, would "leave no occasion for troubles or differences between our subjects."[7]

The Edict remained in place for nearly a century – until 1685, when King Louis XIV revoked it and proclaimed Protestantism illegal. Faced with new rounds of persecution, as many as 400,000

French Protestants fled to Britain, Sweden, and the North American colonies. Among them was Apollos Rivoire, whose son, taking the Anglicized name Paul Revere, became a leading Boston patriot. The revocation of the Edict terrified the Protestants of Great Britain, too; that country's king was also a Catholic, and they feared he might imitate the French monarch.

British kings often betrayed their past promises. In the years after 1660, King Charles II and his successor, James II, sought to reorganize the North American colonies and bring them more directly under the Crown's control. This, they hoped, would ensure that the colonists produced more profit for the mother country. Charles II decreed that what is now Maine, New Hampshire, Vermont, Massachusetts, Rhode Island, and Connecticut would be reorganized as a new "Dominion of New England" governed by a single man who answered solely to the king. New York and New Jersey were soon added.

In 1684, Charles's agent, Edmond Andros, and Andros's aide, Joseph Dudley, arrived to take control of the new Dominion. They dismissed the Massachusetts colonial assembly and instituted autocratic rule, jailing those who resisted and rejecting the colonists' assertions of British liberties. "You have no more privileges left you than not to be sold as slaves," Dudley told one prisoner who asserted his right to a fair trial under Magna Carta.[8] Andros and Dudley's autocracy ended only when James II was overthrown in the Glorious Revolution of 1688. New England colonists, learning of the rebellion, immediately arrested the pair and sent them back to England. Only three years after the Dominion had been proclaimed, it was dissolved and the old colonies restored.

Almost a century later, good Massachusetts men like John Adams still seethed at the memory. George III's ministers, Adams wrote in 1775, were "but the servile copyers of the designs of Andross [and] Dudley [sic]."[8] Adams had good cause for this allegation: in the Declaratory Act of 1766, Parliament had asserted that it had authority to legislate for the colonies "in all cases whatsoever."[10] Some colonists viewed that act as essentially repealing Magna Carta. When it came time to declare independence, Adams and the other revolutionaries listed among Parliament's malefactions "taking away our Charters, abolishing our most valuable Laws,... altering fundamentally the Forms of our Government,... suspending our own Legislatures, and declaring themselves invested with power to legislate for us in all cases whatsoever."[11] Americans had learned that royal "charters of liberty" were pie crust promises, which crumbled all too easily.[12]

Even after the Revolution, the founders were so skeptical of paper pledges of rights that the Constitution's authors initially demurred when Americans demanded that it be amended to include a Bill of Rights. In their view, such "parchment barriers" typically proved useless in times of crisis, because those in power could so easily revoke them, ignore them, or argue them away. Better to focus instead on designing a government that would include checks and balances and other structural protections to prevent the government from acting tyrannically. Even when they agreed to add a Bill of Rights, they remained convinced that freedom could never be secured solely through written promises.

To them, freedom was not a privilege the state provides but a birthright the state must protect. George Mason put this point succinctly in June 1776, when he wrote in the Virginia Declaration of Rights that "all men are by nature equally free and independent and have certain inherent rights," which include "the enjoyment of life and liberty, with the means of acquiring and possessing property, and pursuing and obtaining happiness and safety."[13] Government does not give people these rights – people already have them, and the people "cannot, by any compact, deprive or divest their posterity" of these rights. Thomas Jefferson would make the point even more concisely a month later, when he wrote in the Declaration of Independence that "all men are created equal" and are "endowed" with "inalienable rights," which include "life, liberty, and the pursuit of happiness." Government exists "to secure these rights," not to grant them, and if it turns instead to destroying those rights, "it is the right of the people to alter or to abolish" that government.

Freedom Is Not Permission

These phrases are not mere rhetoric. They express a profound and elegant political philosophy. To understand it, we must begin with a basic presumption or default position. Logicians, lawyers, and laymen use such presumptions as the foundation for any argument. Presumptions of the "when in doubt do x" variety serve as starting points for any sort of discussion or agreement, so that we know where to go in the event that the agreement or argument fails. These sorts of "default rules" surround us every day. Many sub-scription services, for example, require people to opt out of annual renewal; unless they unsubscribe, the company presumes at the end of the first year that users want to pay for a second. These defaults are not set in stone, of course – the subscriber can decline the second year if he wants – but as a rule of thumb, it makes things easier by placing the burden on the subscriber to refuse a second year, rather than on the company to ask again after the first.

As this example suggests, choosing who bears the burden can have important consequences. If we start from a flawed initial position, we risk a dangerous and costly error. A subscriber who forgets to cancel might be surprised to see the second year's charge appear on his bill.

Choosing an initial presumption is extremely important in the realm of politics or law, where the stakes are much greater. When we establish a presumption or a starting point for a political or legal argument, we are choosing what the *normal* rule will be, in the absence of good reason to deviate or in the event that we make a mistake. The obvious example is criminal law: courts presume a defendant to be not guilty and place the burden on prosecutors, which means that if the prosecutor fails to persuade the judge, or makes a mistake, the accused person is free to go.

In discussing politics, there are two possible candidates for an initial presumption. We might presume in favor of totalitarianism – everything is controlled by the government, and citizens must justify any desire to be free – or we can presume in favor of liberty and require anyone who proposes to restrict freedom to justify that restriction. Either everything is allowed that is not forbidden, or everything is forbidden that is not allowed. As Professor Richard Epstein observes, there is no third, middle-ground option, because there is no obvious midpoint between the two extremes: people will bicker endlessly about what qualifies as exactly halfway.[14] So we must start by presuming either in favor of freedom or against it.

Yet these two candidates for starting points are not mirror images, and their differences are crucial. The differences are both procedural and substantive.

As a matter of procedure, starting with a presumption in favor of freedom is preferable because each step people take away from a state of liberty can be justified in theory by measuring whether they are better off. When two people sign a contract, they bind themselves, and in that sense are less free. But they consider themselves better off, and that is good enough, as long as they harm nobody else. It is not so easy to justify the reverse – a movement from a state of total unfreedom to one that is freer – because each step affects far more people. The totalitarian state is frozen solid, so that every action inflicts consequences on everyone else, and the slightest deviation from rigid order must therefore receive the approval of everyone affected. This means it is not always possible to determine whether people are better off at each step when they move in that direction. This, writes Epstein, "is why the restoration of even modest elements of a market system seem to pose such radical problems for Eastern European and Third World nations."[15]

The point becomes clearer when we think about an individual: a free person can choose to become less free – he can sign contracts that limit his future choices, can voluntarily give up certain rights, or can surrender property he once could have used – but an unfree person cannot choose to become more free. Precisely because he starts out with no freedom, his capacity to choose alternatives for himself has vanished. He must ask his master for permission instead. This is why the road between freedom and unfreedom usually moves in only one direction. As Jefferson said, the "natural progress of things is for liberty to yield, and government to gain ground."[16]

There is a deeper procedural reason why it is better to presume in favor of freedom than against it. The liberty presumption rests on a basic rule of logic: anyone who makes a claim must prove it – or, as a classic legal textbook puts it, "the issue must be proved by the party who states an affirmative, not by the party who states a negative."[17] In Latin, this is sometimes called the rule of *onus probandi*. Since proving a negative is technically impossible, the rule of *onus probandi* applies across the board to all claims: a person who asserts that the moon is made of green cheese, or that Herman Melville wrote *Moby Dick*, or one who claims that he may justly stop another from publishing his opinions or praying to the god of his choice, bears the burden of proving those claims.

The opposite rule – "throwing the burden of proof on the wrong side"[18] – is a logical fallacy, and it too has a Latin name: *probatio diabolica*, or "the Devil's proof." Requiring someone to prove a negative is devilish because it perverts thought and leads to absurd results. It is also sometimes called "Russell's teapot," after an example given by the philosopher Bertrand Russell: nobody can prove that there is *not* a tiny teapot orbiting the sun, so small as to elude the world's best telescopes.[19] If you cannot see it, why, that just proves how tiny the teapot is! If you cannot detect it with the finest instruments, that only shows that you are not looking hard enough – and so forth. It is not possible to *disprove* even an absurd claim. Just as a person who says there is a teapot in space has the duty to prove it, so a person who claims the right to govern another person bears the burden of justifying that assertion. It is not possible to prove that one should *not* be ruled by another.

These procedural differences between the presumption of freedom and the presumption against freedom are a consequence of two substantive differences. First is the asymmetry between the past and the future. The past cannot be changed, but the future is what we make of it. That is why, offered the choice between a prize in cash or frozen assets of equal worth, a rational person chooses cash. Liquidity itself has value: cash can easily be converted into whatever the holder wants, while frozen assets may not serve one's present needs, and selling or trading them takes time and effort. Freedom of choice is the liquidity of human action, just as property is human action in frozen form.

The second asymmetry is the asymmetry of personal consequences: someone deprived of freedom suffers a personal injury that is *qualitatively* different from the cost that a person suffers when he is stopped from taking away another person's freedom. If Tom beats Joe or takes his property, Joe suffers a direct, personal injury different in kind from the harm Tom suffers when someone intervenes to stop him from robbing Joe. Our right to control our own lives and our rights (if any) to control the lives of others are simply not equivalent.

When thinking about government, therefore, it is better to presume in favor of freedom than to presume against it, not only because of the basic procedural rule of *onus probandi*, but also because of the substantive difference between freedom and its opposite. Simply put, the cost of having too much freedom is far smaller than the cost of having too little. At the very least, if we start with a presumption of freedom and later decide that less freedom would be preferable, we can move in that direction – whereas the reverse is not always true. And if we begin with the presumption of freedom and later conclude that that was an error, we are less likely to have hurt somebody as a result of that mistake than if we began the process by assuming away everybody's liberty.

As mentioned earlier, one real-life example of these abstractions at work is the presumption of innocence in criminal law. If a judge put the burden of proof on the defendant to show that he did *not* commit the crime, the judge would be loading the dice against him. Even if the defendant proved he did not own the gun used to commit the murder, well, perhaps he borrowed it! To disprove that, he must now prove that he did not know the gun's owner. But perhaps he paid that person to lie! – and so forth, infinitely. Every disproof only creates a new speculation, which must again be disproved. These speculations might seem silly, but they are not *logically impossible*, and requiring the defendant to prove his innocence – imposing the Devil's proof on him – would require him to disprove even such bizarre conjectures. Every accused person would find himself in a hall of mirrors, forced to prove himself innocent of an endless series of baseless accusations, without regard for the rules of logic.

As a procedural matter, presuming innocence is preferable, because an erroneous conviction is harder to fix than an erroneous finding of innocence.[20] And as a substantive matter, the presumption of innocence is better because a wrongfully convicted person suffers a different, more personal harm than the public experiences if a guilty person goes free.

Likewise, there are an indefinite number of speculative reasons that might defeat anyone trying to prove that he should *not* be deprived of freedom, just as there are an infinite number of "what ifs" that the "Devil" could use against a defendant who tries to prove he did not commit a crime, or a person who tries to disprove the existence of an invisible teapot: What if a person abuses his liberty? What if he doesn't know how to use it wisely? What if he turns out to be a psychopath – or perhaps his children or grandchildren turn out to be psychopaths? What if there are top-secret reasons of state that warrant imprisoning him – reasons no judge may be allowed to see? Wary of the Devil's proof, logicians place the burden on the person who asserts a claim, because that is the only logically coherent way to think. Likewise, the presumption of freedom requires those who would take away our liberty to justify doing so, because that is the only logically workable way to think about politics and law.

The Eleventh Circuit Court of Appeals made this point well in a 2013 case, when it required government officials to justify a policy of random drug testing that was challenged as an unconstitutional search. It would be "impossible," the court said, to force the people who complained about the tests "to speculate as to all possible reasons justifying the policy they are challenging and then to prove a negative – that is, prove that the government had no special needs when it enacted its drug testing policy."[21] For the same reasons, we presume people are free and require those who would limit our freedom to justify doing so.

When the founders spoke of all people being created free and equal, they were not merely uttering slogans. They were making important statements about logic and human nature. Their starting point was equality: every person possesses himself or herself, and no person is singled out to rule another person by automatic right. There are exceptions to this rule – adults are the natural rulers of children, for example – but even this is only a temporary and limited condition; parents do not *own* their children. Normal, mature adults who communicate with one another and use reason have no fundamental entitlement to control one another. As Jefferson put it, nobody is born with a saddle on his back, and nobody is born wearing spurs.[22] Or, as the Continental Congress declared in 1775, "If it [were] possible for men who exercise their reason, to believe that the divine Author of our existence intended a part of the human race to hold an absolute property in, and an unbounded power over others ... the inhabitants of these Colonies might at least require from the Parliament of Great Britain some evidence, that this dreadful authority over them has been granted to that body."[23] Anyone who purports to govern another must justify his right to do so. Merely making the assertion is not enough.

This was the idea James Madison considered the "most triumphant" achievement of the American Revolution. Under the British constitution, where "charters of liberty" were "granted by power," the subject was not free unless he could persuade the government to allow him some freedom. Even then, his freedom might be taken away if the government saw fit to do so. But the American Revolution ushered in a new society, one which recognized that people are basically free, and the government exists at *their* mercy. The new Constitution was a charter of power granted by liberty. Freedom would be the general rule and government power the exception. This principle marked the revolutionary core of the Declaration of Independence.

Nonsense on Stilts?

When the Declaration was published, critics promptly saw it as a dangerous first step toward ending monarchy and proclaiming liberty to all mankind. Many royals prohibited newspapers from printing translations of it.[24] In England, conservatives such as Jeremy Bentham and former royal governor of Massachusetts Thomas Hutchinson published rebuttals of it. Hutchinson dismissed the proposition that all people are equally entitled to freedom as "absurd," because "if these rights are so absolutely unalienable," it would be impossible to "justify depriving more than an hundred thousand Africans of their rights to liberty."[25] That accusation of hypocrisy certainly struck home, but it hardly proved that the patriots were wrong to pronounce the right of all human beings to be free. On the contrary, slavery is unjust only because the Declaration's principles are true. Freedom is not a privilege that white people could justly withhold from black people – it is a right. Freeing the slave is not doing him a courtesy but undoing a wrong.

Bentham was more specific. Ridiculing the idea of equality, he proclaimed that the Declaration's self-evident truths about inalienable human rights were absurd: "nothing which can be called Government ever was, or ever could be, in any instance, exercised, but at the expense of one or other of those rights."[26]

That reaction is unsurprising, given Bentham's well-known view that natural rights are "nonsense upon stilts."[27] Rights, in his opinion, were only privileges created by the government – the "sweet fruits" of government,[28] which are essentially "fictitious,"[29] while law is "real."[30] Law is fundamentally a "command [which] supposes eventual punishment."[31] So when we speak of rights, we only mean that the government will punish anyone who interferes with whatever thing is labeled someone's right. And because "[t]he law cannot confer a benefit, without at the same time, imposing a burthen somewhere," the government can only give one person a right by taking away the rights of someone else.[32]

To this day, many follow Bentham in dismissing the idea of natural rights and arguing that freedom is really given to us by the government, when it restricts the freedoms of others – that, for example, our right to private property is really nothing more than the government barring others from taking away our things. This "positivist" theory found its most influential supporter in the twentieth century in Supreme Court Justice Oliver Wendell Holmes Jr. Holmes, who proudly "sneered at the natural rights of man,"[33] followed Bentham in arguing that what we call rights are really only "preferences," supported by "the fighting will of the subject to maintain them." They are essentially "arbitrary," just as "you cannot argue a man into liking a glass of beer."[34] Rights are only subjective, personal desires, which the government chooses to protect on pain of punishment. They are manufactured at the state's pleasure and for the state's own purposes.

Positivism's adherents have always claimed that this is a more "realistic" way of looking at things and have lauded themselves for waving away the Declaration's abstractions about natural rights, which Holmes likened to "churning the void in the hope of making cheese."[35] But this alleged realism is far weaker than positivists maintain.

For one thing, the idea that rights are created by government fiat depends on the presumption that laws are only commands issued by the ruler. But this is not the case. Laws are not commands, as the influential legal philosopher H. L. A. Hart (himself a positivist) explained in his classic book, *The Concept of Law*. Laws are general rules that remain in place indefinitely, whereas commands are directed to specific people for particular reasons and are usually temporary. Also, laws are not always backed up by punishments: there is no punishment if a person fails to sign a will, for instance, even though a will must be signed to be legally valid. Marriage laws require a person to get a license, but there is no *punishment* for those who fail to get one, and some laws even recognize unlicensed "common-law marriages." The rules for entering into a marriage or for writing a will cannot plausibly be called "commands." Hart called them instead "power-enabling" rules – laws that enable people to act, rather than limiting what they can do – and these are laws even though they are not commands and are not backed up by punishment.[36]

Another way in which laws are not commands involves what the legal philosopher Lon Fuller called "the force which ideas have without reference to their human sponsorship."[37] Most legal questions, or disputes about ownership, are resolved outside a courtroom, by people who extrapolate from the existing rules to determine what they can do and what they own. The government is rarely even involved in this process, and it usually issues no commands. Instead, people consult the law – which has an internal logic from which they can decide whether something is legal, even if the government has never spoken on the question. Judges themselves use this technique to decide what the law is. If asked to determine whether some past event was legal, a judge will not issue a *command*. Instead, he determines that the thing that was done – the contract signed or the will drafted – was legal *at the time it was done*. Even when the Supreme Court issues controversial constitutional rulings, it pronounces that the Constitution *has always* meant such-and-such, that its natural logic *has always* provided this answer, even if nobody realized it at the time. For instance, when the court ruled in 2003 that state laws criminalizing private sex between two men or two women violated the Constitution, it explained that a previous decision holding otherwise "was not correct *when it was decided*."[38] Law has a quality of permanence that commands lack. That is why we speak of a "legal system." Commands do not hold together as a "system" in this way.

Most importantly, *commands* represent a form of organization that Fuller called "managerial direction"; they are intended primarily to ensure that people accomplish tasks that their superiors set for them. But *law* is meant to enable people to accomplish their *own* purposes. It is essentially reciprocal – more like a promise than a command. Whereas managerial direction is a matter of expediently and efficiently achieving the *manager's* purposes, the law is concerned with providing a framework of principles for people to pursue their *own* goals.

If laws are not commands, then the rights secured by laws cannot be privileges manufactured by the government. Rights can be created between people on their own, in accordance with a legal system, without the ruler even being aware of it. This happens whenever people buy or trade things. This is not true of privileges. A person can give or sell a car or a house to another person without first getting approval from some superior, because he owns the house or car by right. But a soldier who is given a special privilege to leave the base for the weekend cannot sell that pass to another soldier without his officer's permission. The soldier has only a *privilege* manufactured by a *command* – not a *right* that the *law* must respect.

Characterizing rights as privileges granted by the command of a ruler deprives rights of the moral weight that is essential to their character as rights.[39] According to the Declaration, rights are rooted in profound principles of justice and human flourishing. They connect government policy to moral rules about how we treat other people. The most essential right – the right to one's own self – is "inalienable" in the sense that no matter how much we try, we cannot give it up. We cannot abandon our own minds, our own responsibility, our own hopes and fears. Self-possession, or what philosopher Tom G. Palmer calls a person's "ownness," is an inescapable fact of nature, not a gift from the government, and it is not possible to abolish it (although people can certainly be killed or imprisoned). "Each person is an individual and the owner of his or her acts," writes Palmer. "[O]ne's personhood is achieved by the acts that one owns, and the responsibility for those acts is the foundation for one's rights, for the reason that hindering another from fulfilling his or her obligations is precisely to hinder that person from doing what is right, and therefore to act contrary to right."[40] That is why it is *wrong* to violate someone's *rights*.

Privileges, by contrast, are parceled out on the basis of policy considerations, not moral considerations, and they may be altered for whatever reason the person who grants them considers sufficient. It is not wrong to decline to give someone a privilege or to revoke a privilege once granted. If freedom were only a privilege – a space the government draws around the individual and gives to him as a favor – then the distinctive character of rights would be lost, and they would lie on the same moral plane as, say, permission to go on land owned by the government, which it can revoke when it pleases. In such a world, we would not own our lives but would only have the permission to use ourselves as long as the government allows us.

This may seem like an extreme conclusion, but Bentham openly embraced it. In his view, the obvious conclusion of "reason and plain sense" was that "there is no right which, when the abolition of it is advantageous to society, should not be abolished."[41]

Even if it were possible to imagine that the government gives each of us our rights, the next question to ask would be, Where did the government get them? Just as the government cannot give away money that it did not either obtain through taxes or print by fiat, so, if rights are the gift of the state, either it must have acquired them from us to start with or it must have simply manufactured those rights itself. The first option is ruled out, because that would imply that we have rights to begin with – something Bentham and his followers rejected. But the latter option only makes sense if the government is qualitatively different from us common folk, in that *it* can create rights when *we* cannot. In this theory, government is somehow fundamentally superior, deriving its powers by mere say-so.

Bentham endorsed this conclusion. Having ridiculed the idea that all men are created equal, he wrote that a law is simply the "wish of a certain person, who, supposing his power independent of that of any other person, and to a certain extent sufficiently ample … is a legislator."[42] In other words, law is whatever the person with the biggest gun declares it to be. The king may parcel out to the people whatever privileges he sees fit and may take from them whatever he considers it necessary to take. In this theory, the government essentially owns us and chooses when to allow any of us to get a job, to marry, to own a house, to publish a book – or even when to *not* be robbed, raped, or murdered – and it may choose to "abolish" these rights whenever it likes. This is just what James Wilson meant when he said that people like Bentham think "man is not only made *for*, but made *by* the government."[43]

One reason for Bentham's rejection of natural rights, shared by many thinkers today, is that these rights can be violated.[44] How can rights be "natural," it is often asked, if they cannot prevent violations of freedom? But the advocates of natural rights never claimed they were inviolable. Indeed, the point of the Declaration was that these rights often had been violated. The natural rights theory only holds that violating a right *is an injustice* and that *this* is inescapable. Unlike a privilege, which can be justly abrogated, a person cannot *justly* be deprived of a natural right, and although the injustice of violating a person's rights may go unpunished, it still remains an injustice. As rights are not created by the ruler's mere will, so an unjust act cannot become just simply because the government does it.

This inescapable quality of justice was given eloquent expression in W. H. Auden's poem "The Hidden Law": although the hidden law "answers nothing when we lie" and "will not try / To stop us if we want to die," it is precisely when we try to "escape it" or "forget it," that we are "punished by / The Hidden Law."[45] As Auden's language suggests, the argument that rights are "nonsense" because they can be violated is akin to arguing that law itself is nonsense because laws can be violated. That actually is what Bentham and his followers believed, which is why they strove to substitute *command* for *law*. Because they could not imagine that law could have any meaning unless backed up by punishment, they confused laws with commands and thus confused rights with permissions.

This leads to the most profound objection to the idea that rights are privileges "granted by power." The Declaration asserts a presumption of equal rights – that everyone has the right to use himself, his skills, and his belongings as he wishes, as long as he respects the equal right of others to do the same. The Declaration therefore regards each person as an individual possessing dignity that the state must respect. Bentham's permission model, on the other hand, depends on a fundamental *inequality*. A permission is something granted by someone above to someone beneath. One must ask one's superior for a privilege and when one receives it, say "thank you." But we do not normally ask our equals to respect our rights or thank those who do. We take it for granted that they should.

In a democratic society, laws are more like promises between equal partners than like commands from superiors to subordinates. Laws contain an element of reciprocity, in which the citizen and the state in some sense agree to act in certain ways.[46] But the Permission Society, in which rights are only privileges conferred by the government, regards people as subjects to be alternately commanded and rewarded. The citizens of the Permission Society must treat their superiors with subservient meekness, begging and praising their rulers in hopes of being given favors. A free society, by contrast, encourages and depends upon a proud sense of self-reliance in the people. Thomas Jefferson emphasized this in his 1774 pamphlet, *A Summary View of the Rights of British America*, when he refused to apologize for the candid words he used when addressing King George III. The "freedom of language and sentiment" in which he expressed himself, said Jefferson, "becomes a free people claiming their rights, as derived from the laws of nature, and not as the gift of their chief magistrate." To "flatter" the king would "ill beseem those who are asserting the rights of human nature.... [K]ings are the servants, not the proprietors of the people."[47]

Is There a Right to Liberty?

Bentham claimed, and his positivist admirers still believe, that the rejection of natural rights represents a modern, scientific attitude. Those who believe in the theory of natural law, said Oliver Wendell Holmes, "seem to me to be in [a] naïve state of mind,"[48] and his contemporary, law professor John Chipman Gray, called the idea of natural law an "exploded superstition."[49] But in fact, it was they who represented a regression to the ancient idea of the divine right of kings.[50] By embracing the fallacy of the Devil's proof – assuming that people are not free unless the all-powerful government says they are – they and their modern followers actually embraced a form of ultraconservatism, harkening back to the ancient mystique of royal absolutism. To them, laws are arbitrary pronouncements by the powerful – essentially a form of magic that citizens must believe in, on pain of punishment – instead of rational principles based on human nature. They were saboteurs, not iconoclasts.

A more curious example of contemporary rejection of the presumption of liberty is the influential philosopher Ronald Dworkin. Although he was no admirer of Bentham, Dworkin advanced a more sophisticated argument against the proposition that people are naturally entitled to liberty, and the problems with that argument reveals some of the essential flaws in the Permission Society generally.

Dworkin set out in his 1977 book, *Taking Rights Seriously*, to defend the idea of individual rights against positivist criticisms. But although he believed that people have rights the government must respect, he nevertheless argued that there is no right to *liberty* – there are only specific rights to particular liberties that are parceled out by the government. People have a right to try to persuade the government to give them these freedoms but no general right to lead their own lives as they choose. Later, apparently recognizing that this was not much improvement over positivism's scorn for rights, Dworkin bizarrely reversed course and embraced the proposition that people *do* have a basic right to freedom.

Dworkin began by arguing that the crucial political question is not how to protect individual autonomy but "what inequalities in goods, opportunities and liberties are to be permitted" in society.[51] This starting point immediately biased his argument, because it implicitly assumes that inequality is something that is or is not "permitted" – that is, that inequality only exists because the government allows it and that government should instead find ways to eliminate inequality by redistributing "goods, opportunities, and liberties."

But inequality is not unjust if it is not the consequence of any wrongful act. To borrow an old example, imagine a world in which everyone has equal wealth. If some people freely choose to pay for tickets to see a famous basketball player demonstrate his superior skills, the ball player will amass millions of dollars, and the fans who paid for tickets will each have less money than they had before. But the resulting inequality is not *unjust*, because nobody has been injured.[52] For the government to seize the basketball player's earnings and redistribute them because inequality is not "permitted" really *would* be unjust. It would mean confiscating his fairly acquired wealth – essentially taking away his unique basketball skills without payment. As James Madison put it, people have "different and unequal faculties," which enable them to earn "different degrees and kinds of property," but although this will result in inequalities, "[t]he protection of these faculties" is the "first object of government."[53]

Dworkin rejected this. He believed that "differences in talent" are "morally irrelevant."[54] In his view, justice did not consist of protecting people's rights to the things they earn by employing their different talents and skills, or the things they inherit, such as their bodies. Instead, it consists of finding a proper "distribution" of the "goods, opportunities, and liberties" that are found in society. Where did these goods, opportunities, and liberties come from? Dworkin ignored this question and focused solely on questions of distribution – on slicing up the cake equally, so to speak, while disregarding the rights of the baker.[55]

Dworkin was wrong to equate justice with distribution.[56] Actual justice occurs when people are allowed to keep what belongs to them or are compensated for having their things wrongfully taken away. Courts do justice by "making people whole" – by remedying injuries people have suffered – not by shaping society through the redistribution of goods, opportunities, or liberties. That is why judges normally do not ask how things *should* be divided up but instead look for evidence about who stole what, or who broke what, or whether the accused had some excuse for doing what he did. Society is not *distributing* goods or liberties to the victim of a robbery when she has her stolen property returned, or to an injured worker who receives compensation for a job-related injury, or to a slave who is liberated. Rather, justice has been done in these cases because the people whose property or rights were wrongly taken away are now having them restored.

Of course, what Dworkin had in mind was not *that* sort of justice but a different *kind* of justice – "social justice" – by which the government allocates property and freedom according to some preconceived formula. Yet calling this "justice" perverts the concept and corrupts the idea of rights. Because it holds that people's talents and inheritances are "morally irrelevant," the only way this theory can justify the ownership of "goods, opportunities, and liberties" is to hold that society has distributed these things in accordance with some recipe. But this takes an enormous stride toward authoritarian government. As philosopher Wallace Matson observed, the essential difference between free and unfree societies "is that in the latter, a person's rank, etc., are assigned by bureaucrats, whereas in the former nobody makes such assignments – the individual decides what sort of life he wants to lead, and then pursues it." Instead of "showing that it is a good idea to *have* a system of assignments *at all*," writes Matson, Dworkin simply assumed this and devoted his energy to figuring out the formula bureaucrats should use when making distributions. But the real question is not between this or that method of distributing things, but between a controlled society, in which people have privileges distributed to them, and a free society, in which people's inherent freedom is respected – or, in Matson's words, "between that condition in which the economic decisions of individuals have their natural effect, on the one hand, and an artificially structured economy on the other."[27] The assumption that society must be artificially structured quietly transforms the free society into the Permission Society.

Dworkin seemed not to have recognized this. He wrote in *Taking Rights Seriously* that the principle of equality in a democracy lets government "constrain liberty only on certain very limited types of justification."[58] But if rights are something the state distributes, there can be no basis for this assertion, and Dworkin's other writings contradicted it. He believed the citizen's "fundamental" right is not a right to be left alone, but a right to "equal concern and respect *in the political decision*" about how "goods and opportunities are to be distributed."[59] This is only a right to take part in a collective, political choice about how to distribute resources, including freedom – essentially, a right to vote, not a right of private enjoyment.

Because his theory was based on distributing things in society, Dworkin had trouble justifying simple, personal freedoms – the right to go on a picnic, the right to compose a poem, or the right to marry a person of one's choice – that have little political valence. True, he referred to a right of "moral independence"[60] – the right to pursue the good life one sees fit – and argued that people should not be allowed to interfere with each other's independence by imposing their notion of the good life on other people. But laws that interfere with "moral independence" do not interfere with a person's right to participate in *political* decisions about distribution, which is the right he labels "fundamental." It's unclear, therefore, how moral independence could fit into his argument.

Dworkin insisted his theory would prohibit deprivations of personal freedoms because the people affected by such deprivations "suffer … because their conception of a proper or desirable form of life is despised by others,"[61] which he considered unacceptable. But this only begged the question, because he gave no reason to nullify decisions motivated by such disapproval, as long as those decisions do not interfere with a person's more "fundamental" right to participate in political choices about the distribution of property or freedom.

When, in one essay, he focused in the question of "external preferences" – efforts by some people to tell others how to live – Dworkin was at last forced to turn to the libertarian theory of rights that he had rejected when arguing that there is no general right to freedom. His argument proceeded this way: a basic principle of democracy is that everyone gets an equal vote. But that principle would be undermined by a rule that, for example, allowed some people to vote twice as often as others. This proves that some kinds of political desires are automatically ruled invalid by the deeper principles of democracy.[62] So, too, with moral beliefs about how others should live. Because such beliefs also have distorting consequences, they should be considered an invalid basis for a person's vote.

To say that a deeper value – equal freedom, moral independence,

or a right to guide one's own life – takes precedence over democratic decision-making is to say that our natural right to freedom
trumps any effort by government to dictate how we should live.
Dworkin was embedding rules that protect liberty into his view of
democracy – even though he had started by denying that there was
any such general right to liberty. Asked why he thought democracy
should remain "neutral" about people's moral choices, Dworkin
answered that he "assumed" the goal of politics is to create a society in which people can "make the best and most informed choice
about how to lead their lives."[63] But that is exactly the basic right
to freedom he had set out to disprove.

The Right to Lead Our Own Lives – Always

This was not the only way Dworkin contradicted himself. The
"assumption" that politics should enable us to lead our own lives is
ultimately incompatible with the idea that justice is accomplished
by "distributing" rights. To take a talented basketball player's earnings away does not enable *him* to lead *his* own life, for one thing. For
another, Dworkin's "assumption" suggests that there are some rights
that may never be justly redistributed by the state. But that means
that distribution *cannot* be the foundation of justice, as he claimed.
Instead, some rights must be too important to be "distributed."

This objection came to the surface when Dworkin argued that
government should not limit someone's freedom "in virtue of an
argument that the [person] could not accept without abandoning
his sense of equal worth."[64] Presumably, "that sense of equal worth"
is not itself one of the "goods, opportunities, and liberties" that the
state may redistribute. But what about the self-worth of people
who resent being forced by the welfare state to support idle people
out of their paychecks? What about the basketball player's sense of
self-worth in a society that considers his talent to be "morally irrelevant"[65] and seizes his justly acquired earnings to give to others?

We see a hint of an answer when Dworkin writes that laws persecuting atheists or other religious minorities would fail his "equal concern and respect" test because "[n]o self-respecting atheist can agree that a community in which religion is mandatory is for that reason finer."⁶⁶ But many self-respecting property and business owners are just as offended by laws that seize their belongings in order to "distribute" them to others. If "self-worth" or "equal dignity" are so important, then the same principles would also protect the rights of property owners. In casting about for a strong foundation for individual rights, therefore, Dworkin ended up finding a principle that really *is* fundamental – a substantive limit on what the state may "distribute." But it was the general right to liberty he rejected: the right to pursue one's own life and keep the fruits of one's labor. Whether called "a sense of equal worth," or "moral independence," or an "assumption" that politics should enable people to "lead their lives," this was just the old-fashioned presumption of freedom.

Why did Dworkin take this bizarre detour? Because as a political liberal, he hoped to fashion an answer to critics who accused him of hypocrisy for endorsing strong protections for "personal" and "political" rights such as sexual privacy and free speech while simultaneously denigrating "economic" rights such as private property and the freedom to make contracts. If, as Dworkin argued, "there is no such thing as any general right to liberty,"⁶⁷ and the justification of "any specific liberty" can differ from the justification for any other, then it would be perfectly consistent for him to support some kinds of freedom while ignoring other freedoms: he could argue that atheists should not have their rights infringed, while also holding that the government could override "the right to liberty of contract sustained in the famous *Lochner* case." "I cannot think of any argument," said Dworkin, "that a political decision to limit such a right" as freedom of contract would "offend the right of those whose liberty is curtailed to equal consideration and respect."⁶⁸

The self-contradiction here is obvious. The *Lochner* case involved a New York law that banned bakers from working more than ten hours a day in bakeries. A product of lobbying by organized labor, Progressive activists, and owners of machine-run bakeries who saw restrictions on working hours as a way to restrict their competition,[69] the New York Bakeshop Act was rooted in just the sort of "external preferences" that Dworkin otherwise considered inadmissible. It was not a decision expressed by bakers themselves but a law imposed on them and on bakery shop owners by the state legislature. The act was plainly designed to dictate the choices bakery workers might make about how to lead their lives – it gave force to government's disapproval about certain types of economic decisions, and it violated the right of moral independence on the part of baker Aman Schmitter and his employer, Joseph Lochner. This was precisely why the Supreme Court ruled in their favor and struck the law down. Bakers, the court declared, were "equal in intelligence and capacity to men in other trades or manual occupations" and were "able to assert their rights and care for themselves" without needing the government's "protecting arm." Laws "interfering with their independence of judgment and of action" were "meddlesome"[70] and demeaning. As mature adults, Lochner and Schmitter were "in no sense wards of the state."[71] The Bakeshop Act was unconstitutional because it offended their right to have their own economic choices accorded equal consideration and respect.

Dworkin's effort to distance himself from *Lochner* was simply a failure. He was right about one thing: political decisions that dictate how others should live their lives ought not to be given the same respect as the choices people make about their own lives. But that argument only makes sense from the perspective of the libertarian position endorsed in the *Lochner* decision. Dworkin's commitment to individual freedom clashed with his effort to justify modern liberalism's hostility toward economic liberty, as symbolized by *Lochner*. To the degree that his argument supported personal freedom, it did so only by giving force – though often in different terminology – to the classical liberal principles of equality and liberty that he tried to refute.

The libertarianism of the Declaration of Independence locks the ideas of freedom and equality together for good reason. Under the monarchical system and its modern variants, government stands in a position of inherent superiority – above the law, dispensing the laws to inferior citizens below. Perhaps, if it thinks fit, it might also issue "charters of liberty," but these are revocable, whenever the ruler thinks abolishing them would be "advantageous to society," or whenever voters think a new "distribution" of our belongings is in order. But on the Declaration's premise of equality, government does not stand in a position of superiority and does not distribute rights to citizens. Each of us is born free, with the right to act as we choose unless we interfere with the rights of others. It is the government that must ask permission of us, not the other way around.

CHAPTER TWO

THE FREE SOCIETY VERSUS

THE PERMISSION SOCIETY

THERE ARE essentially two ways for the government to regulate the things people do: the nuisance system or the permit system. These two approaches are based on the two different conceptions of freedom: right versus permission. The nuisance model rests on the premise that people have a right to act freely unless they harm someone else, while the permit system – as the word implies – assumes that people may not act unless the government allows them.

Nuisance law embodies an old legal principle, typically phrased in Latin: *sic utere tuo ut alienum non laedas*, or "do what you will with your property, so long as you do not harm another." This ancient slogan, well over 1,000 years old,[1] allows a person to use his property as he wishes, but if he harms his neighbor – say, causes too much noise or invites traffic that blocks the roads – his neighbor can sue for damages or for an injunction that will stop such abuses.

The permit system works in the opposite direction. It holds that a person may not do anything with his property that has not been approved by the authorities. This system – sometimes called "prior restraint" – bars the person from acting until he meets whatever criteria are set down as the requirements for obtaining permission to use his property as he wishes.

Each model has costs and benefits. One major drawback to the nuisance system is that it is essentially *reactive*: the neighbor typically cannot seek damages or an injunction until after he has suffered harm from some noxious act (or immediately before he does). This means that if the behavior in question is especially dangerous, the nuisance system might be ill-suited to preventing the neighbor's injury. A property owner, for instance, who discovers that a dynamite factory is being built next door would probably not be reassured by being told that he can sue if the factory blows up. A nuisance system also seems poorly designed for regulating activities that inflict small but cumulative harms – as with some kinds of environmental contamination. If a factory emits tiny amounts of pollution over long periods of time, and problems only become obvious much later, neighbors might not be in a position to seek damages or an injunction afterward. The factory may have gone out of business by that time, or the harm may turn out so much greater than expected that the factory owners cannot afford to pay.

The permit system, by contrast, is *proactive*. It forbids the owner from opening the factory at all unless he first takes steps to prevent pollution or other harms. Neighboring property owners can, in theory, rest assured that the new factory has met certain safety standards before it is allowed to operate. Yet the permit system has severe drawbacks as well.

First, when a permit is valuable – for example, a business permit in a market where the government otherwise blocks people from doing business – those seeking permits will invest valuable time and energy trying to obtain one. This gives rise to the phenomenon economists call "rent-seeking." When the government can redistribute wealth or opportunities – either by transferring money from some people to others or by granting licenses to do profitable things that are otherwise illegal – lobbyists will expend a proportional amount of effort to gain control of those opportunities. So if the government declares that only 13,000 taxicabs may operate in New York City – essentially the law today[2] – then the value of a taxi medallion will be quite high, and businesses will invest heavily in their efforts to obtain a medallion and prevent others from getting one. That's why New York City taxi medallions now sell for about $1 million.

Alongside this rent-seeking problem is the "knowledge problem" identified by Nobel Prize–winning economist Friedrich Hayek. Economic behavior is extremely complex, involving innumerable factors and information dispersed all over the globe. It is simply not possible for any individual or group to gather that information and organize it in ways that will enable them to plan an economy from the top down.

Another economist, Leonard Read, illustrated this point with a simple example.[3] Nobody in the world, Read pointed out, can actually make a pencil. Although a pencil is a simple device, made of wood, graphite, and a few other materials, actually building a pencil from scratch involves too many factors for any central intelligence to actually manage. The wood comes from trees, which must be felled by lumberjacks. But the lumberjacks must be fed, which requires a restaurant to serve them lunch. The restaurant, in turn, needs bread and beef to serve, and that comes from wheat and cattle, which means the economic planner must also arrange for farms and ranches, as well as threshing machines, slaughterhouses, and trains. A few simple steps along this sort of "old lady who swallowed the fly" reasoning, and it is easy to see that all of the planet's economic factors are somehow involved in making even a simple pencil. And if the manufacture of a pencil is too complicated for any person or group to organize, then there can be no hope that government can properly organize the taxicab business in New York City. There are simply too many details involved.

Permit systems run into the knowledge problem because they are based on the assumption that the officials charged with granting permits have the information necessary to make the "right" choices about what things should or should not be permitted. But bureaucrats rarely have that information, and they are often unable to consult the one factor – prices on a free market – that might help them decide. Even if such information were available, it would generally be drowned out by private interests, who (as we will see in chapter 5) often try to influence officials for their own benefit, or activist groups who exercise political influence but do not reflect the actual desires of consumers.

Meanwhile, bureaucrats' own incentives cause further confusion. They face few consequences if they make the wrong choice because they are government employees, paid with tax dollars, and will probably not be penalized if they deny a permit to a much-needed business or give one to a business that does not satisfy consumers. Ordinarily, the forces of supply and demand on the free market would gauge public needs in an objectively measurable way, enabling business owners to determine what consumers want. If the demand for taxi services goes up, prices will increase, creating an incentive for companies to add more taxis to meet the new demand. The relative costs of wood, graphite, and rubber will help pencil manufacturers judge how many pencils to produce and when. But the permit system short-circuits this process, so that prices, the only reliable indicator of public preferences, are ignored. Officials instead base decisions on political considerations – popularity, influence, sound bites, personal favors – rather than the forces of supply and demand that reveal what consumers actually want.

This knowledge problem gets worse when laws that impose permit requirements try to specify the conditions people must meet in order to qualify for permits. Such conditions are often set forth in ambiguous and confusing terms. Vague laws are essentially a way of delegating power to administrators or judges to do as they see fit, with little oversight and virtually no accountability to voters.

Consider the New Jersey law that regulates when and where banks can open new branches. One section of that law, now repealed, blocked any national bank from opening a new office in a city with a population of less than 10,000 if there was already another bank headquartered in that city.[4] State bureaucrats were allowed to waive that prohibition, but because the law did not specify the standards for when or why they should do so, a bank could not know whether it would qualify for a waiver or not. When one bank challenged the law, the Third Circuit Court of Appeals was reluctant to admit that the law provided no standards at all, so it turned to a report drafted years before for members of the legislature when they originally voted on the law. That report told lawmakers that the law would "permit the Commissioner to override the statutory prohibitions against [branches in towns with populations below 10,000] *if he decides that the establishment of such banks is in the public interest.*"[5] Seizing on this extraordinarily broad language – which was not actually in the law itself but appeared in a report written by an unknown, unelected legislative staff member – the court announced that it had found a rule for officials to follow: they could grant a waiver if it was "in the public interest." What does "public interest" mean? Whatever the officials said it meant. This is about as unclear as a law can get, but the court claimed it was not too vague, because after all, "a more precise formula cannot be devised without hurtful inflexibility."[6]

Enforcement by Unelected Bureaucrats

Any law that requires citizens to get a permit before they can do something, and then provides only mushy and obscure criteria for getting a permit, gives officials power to enforce their will arbitrarily and unpredictably. After all, nearly anything can be plausibly described as "in the public interest." That is why philosopher Hannah Arendt wrote that bureaucracy substitutes the "rule of cleverness" for the rule of law.[7]

Yet judges are usually reluctant to interfere with bureaucratic agencies. Agencies are staffed by experts in environmental science, or whatever the bureaucracy regulates, and therefore presumably know best. Judges have adopted a theory of deference, which allows bureaucrats to stretch their authority as broadly as they want so long as their acts are "reasonable,"[8] an expansive grant of power that deprives citizens of the judicial protection promised by the Constitution, emboldens agencies to stretch their prerogative to the limit, and encourages lawmakers to write ever more vague laws to evade their responsibilities to the voters.

The result is something like this: A politician runs for office on a platform promising, say, to stop pollution. Once in office, he writes a bill that forbids anyone from emitting pollutants without a permit – and also establishes a new bureaucratic agency charged with determining what qualifies as a "pollutant" and how one goes about getting a permit. Once the bill is passed, the politician can tell his constituents that he has taken bold action to solve the problem and move on to the next issue. While voters are applauding his achievement, the new agency begins writing regulations, often with little public attention. These regulations are intricately complex, are backed up by severe penalties, and sometimes have nasty unintended consequences. The unelected officials employed by the agency have every incentive to interpret their mandate as broadly as possible because, after all, they act "in the public interest." Within a few years, the agency has implemented thousands of petty and complicated rules, which are in effect a code of laws that no elected official ever approved and which neither they nor the voters can realistically control. If the agency ever takes a step that causes a controversy in the media – for instance, declaring a July 4 fireworks display to be illegal "pollution"[9] – the politician who wrote the law can shake his head, claim that was not his intention, and chide bureaucrats for going too far – again winning the applause of voters. But since nothing short of a new law is likely to rein the bureaucracy in, he can probably do nothing meaningful about it, even if he wants to.

Agencies combine legislative, judicial, and executive powers. They write regulations, prosecute alleged infractions, and punish those they find guilty. This is particularly disturbing because although people can sometimes go to court to challenge an agency decision, judges are generally not allowed to consider evidence that was not first presented to the agency at one of its own hearings. Yet the legal rules of evidence typically do not apply to those agency hearings, which means that agencies can base their decisions on types of evidence that courts are not usually allowed to consider – hearsay, for example. Later, when the agency's decision based on hearsay is appealed to an actual court, the judge is typically forced to rely *exclusively* on the evidence the agency used, including hearsay or other evidence courts normally cannot use. In some cases, courts are not allowed to review agency decisions *at all*.

The agencies that oversee permit requirements form a branch of government not contemplated by the Constitution, run by officials who do not answer to voters. The result is a powerful, invisible branch of government that the people cannot control. After the 2013 rollout of healthcare.gov became a fiasco, many critics demanded that Secretary of Health and Human Services Kathleen Sebelius resign. She refused, saying, "The majority of people calling for me to resign are people who I don't work for."[10] That was true: as the head of an enforcement agency, she worked for the President, not voters. Americans spend much time and energy arguing over who should be elected to Congress or sent to the White House, but most of the laws that govern citizens' lives are written not by elected officials but by bureaucrats whose decisions are shielded against the democratic process.

A fourth problem with permit systems is that whenever officials have the power to make decisions from which citizens will profit, those officials are in a position to demand something in return. At times this can take the form of outright corruption. More often, people seeking permits are forced to provide concessions to the government to serve some general social need. Property owners seeking to develop their land are often subjected to "exactions" that force them to give up property or cash to the government in exchange for development permits – or to surrender some of their property in exchange for permission to sell the rest. As we will see in chapter 6, one California city even forced a couple to *give up their right to vote* on certain property taxes in exchange for a permit to renovate their home.

Still another problem with permit requirements is that any violation of the requirement is itself against the law, even if the requirement is illegal. This two-layer effect often blocks people from challenging these laws in court. In 1963, city officials in Birmingham, Alabama, persuaded a state judge to order Martin Luther King Jr. and his supporters not to march in protest against segregation. City ordinances required protesters to obtain a permit, and King and his allies had not been issued one. King chose to ignore the court order and march anyway. He and over 1,000 protesters were arrested and sent to jail, where he wrote his famous "Letter from Birmingham Jail" on paper smuggled in by friends. His attorneys appealed, arguing that the permit requirement and the court order violated the First Amendment, but even sympathetic justices of the U.S. Supreme Court were unconvinced. Had King patiently appealed the order, they wrote, they might have ruled in his favor – in fact, the court later did declare the Birmingham permit requirement unconstitutional.[11] But King's outright defiance could not be tolerated, the court said, "however righteous his motives." People may not "ignore all the procedures of the law and carry their battle to the streets," because "respect for judicial process is a small price to pay for the civilizing hand of law, which alone can give abiding meaning to constitutional freedom."[12] That is true, but as King explained, such litigation can often take years and can become a "pseudo-legal way of breaking the back of legitimate moral protest."[13]

Faced with endless permitting delays and burdensome demands from bureaucrats, property owners often find themselves in a similar position. A person who is told that he may only have a building permit on certain conditions, and believes those conditions are illegal, may not simply ignore them and build anyway. Laws in California and some other states bar him from accepting the permit under protest, starting construction, and later asking a court to rule on the question. Instead, he must postpone work, file a lawsuit, and wait – often for years, sometimes for decades – for courts to rule. However "civilizing" this might be, it is also a "pseudo-legal way of breaking the back" of property owners, with the effect of insulating permit requirements from judicial review. Few citizens can afford such tedious, expensive delays, and those who lose patience and violate the law can then find it impossible to challenge the validity of that law.

But the most troubling aspect of the permit system is that it stifles innovation. As we will see in chapter 5, some permit rules force people who want to start new businesses to prove to the satisfaction of government regulators that there is a "public need" for the business before the person may set up shop. But it is hardly ever possible to prove such a thing or to justify some new idea or new way of doing business beforehand. It would not have been possible in the late 1980s to prove that the United States "needed" a new chain of coffee shops: the country had plenty. Yet within a decade, Starbucks's brilliant success proved that the public did, in fact, want a new chain of coffee shops. It is never possible to prove – it's often impossible even to guess – whether a new idea will take off. The only way to tell is to try. But the permit system often makes it impossible to experiment, thus hampering the most important quality of free markets: the possibility of innovation.

Innovation is an elusive quality. It cannot be held in the hand or shown to the eye. It is potential. It is a chance for the future. Its impalpable and vital quality is captured eloquently in a story sometimes told about Benjamin Franklin: asked what some new invention was good for, he is said to have replied, "What is the use of a newborn baby?"[14] One can never know what promise a new idea holds. Yet licensing laws and permit requirements essentially force one to know and quantify this unknowable value. And the cost and difficulty of obtaining a permit often stifles the fragile first steps toward innovation.

The costs of permits can be severe. To take just one example, the Endangered Species Act makes it illegal to "harass, harm, pursue, hunt, shoot, wound, kill, trap, capture, or collect" an endangered plant or animal without a federal permit.[15] Since construction usually causes some kind of "harassment," property owners who discover, say, the Delhi Sands flower-loving fly (*Rhaphiomidas terminatus abdominalis*) or the western prairie fringed orchid (*Platanthera praeclara*) on their land must get federal permits before beginning construction. It is impossible to say how much these permits will cost because the government treats each applicant differently, often requiring people to pay for extensive "mitigation" projects in exchange for permits. When one Georgia paper company sought a permit in 1999, the federal government forced it to fund a "conservation bank" to protect the red-cockaded woodpecker, at the cost of $50,000 per bird.[16] In a Texas case, the government forced homebuilders to pay $1,500 per house into a fund for habitat preservation.[17] And when Delhi Sands flower-loving flies were found on the future site of the San Bernardino County Medical Center, the government forced the center to pay over $3 million toward fly preservation[18] – an expense and delay that likely cost human lives for the sake of flies. Simply negotiating over the terms of a permit can take years, with additional delays to prepare mandatory scientific reports, allow public comment, and evaluate proposals.[19]

In places where corruption is common or where permits are distributed only to influential insiders, the process is even bleaker. Permit requirements encourage corruption because the costs and delays lead people to seek extralegal alternatives. In an effort to demonstrate this problem, Peruvian economist Hernando de Soto tried to start a small business in his home country. It took 11 permits and 278 days. He was asked for bribes ten times during the process.[20] That was minor compared to other countries he studied. Tanzania, for example, has such complicated and corrupt licensing rules that, according to de Soto's calculations, a business that lasts 50 years will have to pay $91,000 to government officials and spend four years in bureaucrats' offices seeking some form of permit. That doesn't count the nine years of time waiting for the permits to be issued. "Is it any wonder that 98 percent of all businesses in Tanzania choose to be extralegal?" asks de Soto. "How else could a business owner get things done in an efficient manner, but to grease the palms of underpaid functionaries? No matter where you look, where you find more bureaucracy, you'll find greater corruption."[21]

Even without corruption and high fees, the cost of a permitting system can be incalculably high in one respect: potential new ideas can be lost forever if an inventor or entrepreneur decides he just doesn't want to go through the hassle and delay. Innovations often begin as a hunch, as a barely articulable notion that a new way of doing business, or a new recipe, or a small tweak on existing technology might be better, more useful, or more satisfying. But when told that they will have to undergo expensive and time-consuming permit processes before being allowed to pursue a new idea, many simply give up without trying. The cost to society of stifling innovation is literally immeasurable. It takes the form of what economist Frederic Bastiat called "unseen" costs:[22] wealth that might have come into existence but never does. Because it remains uncreated, it cannot be quantified and people don't notice it precisely because it never exists. Yet these "unseen" costs are real – they are the new businesses, new technologies, new opportunities that never come about.

Consider the licensing requirements that the Food and Drug Act imposes on new drugs and medical technologies. The average cost of federal approval of a new drug is $1.3 billion,[23] and the process involves years of tedious bureaucratic delay. Sick and dying patients – or people whose lives could be improved by new medicines to treat their eyesight, their allergies, or their daily pain – need new medicines now. The Food and Drug Administration (FDA), focused on preventing dangerous drugs from reaching the market, has little incentive to streamline its procedures. It gets no reward for quickly approving new drugs for sale, but it would be harshly condemned if it accidentally let a dangerous drug reach the market. The FDA is therefore biased against approving new medicines, to the detriment of patients who have no alternative but to wait. The diabetes drug Byuredon, for instance, was invented in the 1990s, but in 2010, after the developer had proven it safe through several clinical trials involving thousands of patients, the FDA refused to approve it for sale. Only after two more years of still more tests and reports did the agency grant approval. As we will see in chapter 7, states are now taking action to address the problem of federal delay, but for now the immense cost of developing new drugs makes it impossible to measure how many potential innovations are stifled – and how much needless human suffering is caused – by the permit requirement.

Ideas, said the poet John Milton, are actually more precious than life itself: "no age can restore a life, whereof perhaps there is no great losse," he wrote, but "revolutions of ages do not oft recover the losse of a rejected truth."[24] It's impossible to say how many innovations – whether they be as simple as a new kind of restaurant or coffee shop, or something as life-changing as a new medicine – have disappeared into the ether thanks to rules that block innovation.

Religious Liberty: The Victory of Freedom
over Permission

Milton made that comment in the midst of England's bitter seventeenth-century religious wars, and it was in the history of the struggle for religious freedom that America's founding fathers learned the many problems with the permit system: the knowledge problem, the rent-seeking, the stifling of innovation, and the tendency toward corruption. They chose to reject the Permission Society established by British law. One particularly revealing example was their choice to establish a law of religious liberty, instead of the "toleration" that existed under the law of Great Britain.

When the founders were born, the Anglican Church was the

official religious institution of the British empire. All subjects were expected to attend it and support it financially. For centuries, the monarchy had used the permit power to control both the church and the people. In 1549, for instance, representatives of King Edward VI warned England's preachers that while he had "sent unto you the King's Majesty's License to preach," they were "in no wise" to "stir and provoke the People to any alteration or Innovation … but contrariwise, That you do in all your Sermons exhort Men to … obedience to their Heads and Rulers."[25]

Matters improved in the century that followed. The 1689 Toleration Act, signed by William and Mary as one of the conditions of taking the throne, promised to withhold persecution from Christians who believed in the Trinity, rejected the doctrine of transubstantiation, and pledged allegiance to the king as head of state and of the Anglican Church. This act, wrote the English jurist William Blackstone, represented "a very just and christian [sic] indulgence" toward religious minorities. Yet it excluded Unitarians, Catholics, and, of course, Jews, Muslims, and atheists. Even Baptists and Quakers were barred from public office and regularly jailed for unlicensed preaching. Although Blackstone believed "all persecution and oppression" on account of religion was "highly unjustifiable,"[26] he supported the limited scope of the Toleration Act, writing that "care must be taken not to carry this indulgence" of other religions "into such extremes as may endanger the national church." In other words, the Toleration Act, though liberal by the standards of its day, was only a "liberty granted by power" – a privilege, not a right – or, in Blackstone's words, a "spirit of true magnanimity" on Parliament's part, an "indulgence" granted by courteous lawmakers.[27]

Madison, Jefferson, George Washington, Thomas Paine, and others found this idea repugnant. In their view, "magnanimity" was a poor substitute for freedom because it could always be revoked at the ruler's pleasure. "Toleration is not the *opposite* of Intoleration, but is the *counterfeit* of it," wrote Paine. "Both are despotisms. The one assumes to itself the right of withholding liberty of conscience, and the other of granting it."[28] Washington agreed. In a 1790 letter to a Jewish congregation, he wrote, "It is now no more that toleration is spoken of, as if it was by the indulgence of one class of people, that another enjoyed the exercise of their inherent natural rights." In the United States, "[a]ll possess alike liberty of conscience."[29]

In 1776, the Virginia legislature asked the respected 51-year-old statesman George Mason to prepare a Declaration of Rights. His fellow lawmaker James Madison was then half Mason's age and new to elected office, but he was not too shy to object to part of Mason's draft – specifically, as Madison wrote in a memoir, to "the terms in which the freedom of Conscience was expressed." Mason had "inadvertently adopted the word toleration," and the brash young Madison urged the elder statesman to "substitute[] a phraseology which declared the freedom of conscience to be a natural and absolute right."[30] The change was adopted, and the Virginia Declaration of Rights proclaimed that "all men are equally entitled to the free exercise of religion, according to the dictates of conscience."

The difference between toleration and liberty was also made clear in a passage in Jefferson's book *Notes on the State of Virginia*. Jefferson had proposed legislation to proclaim religious liberty in the state and prohibit the government from subsidizing any established church. Defending the proposal in the *Notes*, Jefferson made many of the same arguments that apply to all permit systems. For instance, he argued that government cannot be relied upon to choose the "correct" religion (the knowledge problem) and observed that people tried to use government's power over religion to benefit themselves (the rent-seeking problem): "Fallible men; men governed by bad passions, by private as well as public reasons," he wrote, would use the power of "coercion" to impose their own beliefs on others.[31] Even worse, using government to control religious belief stifled innovation and discovery: "Had not the Roman government permitted free enquiry, Christianity could never have been introduced. Had not free enquiry been indulged, at the era of the reformation, the corruptions of Christianity could not have been purged away."[32]

But the most essential problem with established religion was that it regarded religious freedom as a privilege bestowed by the state, rather than a freedom that people are born possessing. "Our rulers can have authority over such natural rights only as we have submitted to them," Jefferson wrote. "The rights of conscience we never submitted, we could not submit. We are answerable for them to our God."[33] It took ten years of lobbying by Jefferson and Madison to get the Virginia legislature to pass the Statute for Religious Freedom, which proclaimed that "Almighty God hath created the mind free" and that government-established churches represented a "sinful and tyrannical" effort by rulers to "assume[] dominion" over our freedom.[34]

The Propiska

The most extreme form of Permission Society – in which all rights were considered gifts bestowed by the state – has been communism. Under totalitarian rule in the Soviet Union, property was collectively owned, with its management and disposition overseen by government authorities. Consequently, some form of government approval was required for even the most mundane activities. Anyone wanting to live in Moscow, to get a job, or to reside in an apartment building was required to obtain a permit called a *propiska*.

First used by the czars, then reintroduced under Stalin, *propiski* gave the government absolute power to enforce conformity, punish undesirables, exclude unwanted foreigners, and restrict people's travel. At first, writes anthropologist Rano Turaeva-Hoene, the Soviet government portrayed the system as "a positive initiative, granting access to all kinds of benefits, which the Soviet government offered its citizens." This gave the *propiska* "a *razreshitelniy kharakter* (from Russian 'allowing character') which cast it in the more positive light of allowing or granting rights."[35] But soon the government began restricting the availability of *propiski*. Some people resorted to political influence, family connections, or outright bribery to obtain the stamps on their passports that would let them reside in Moscow, live in a state-owned apartment, or get a job – a necessity in a nation where joblessness was a crime punishable by deportation to the gulag.

In his epic novel *Life and Fate*, which was confiscated in manuscript by the KGB and banned in Russia until the Gorbachev era, Vasili Grossman depicted with chilling reality the effect the *propiska* system had on Russians. Early in the novel, Yevgenia, whose lover is away fighting the Nazis at Stalingrad, gets a job in a factory. But because she does not yet have a residence permit, she must visit the local police station with a letter confirming her employment. "There a police officer took Yevgenia's passport and documents and told her to come back in three days' time." When she goes back, she is told that her permit has been denied.

She stands in line for hours to speak to the bureaucrat in charge. "While she waited in the queue, Yevgenia heard her fill of stories about people who had been refused residence permits: daughters who had wanted to live with their mothers, a paralyzed woman who had wanted to live with her brother." At last allowed to speak to the officer, she finds him sympathetic but unyielding. "'You need an official request on your behalf,' he said. 'Without that I can do nothing.'"

Yevgenia returns to her boss and asks him to write another letter certifying that her job is part of the war effort. He hesitates: "The police must first send a request," he tells her. "Without that I can't write such a document." She goes again to the police station and stands in line once more to ask the officer to send her boss the request. He refuses. He first needs a request from the officer in charge of residence permits. Hungry and desperate, she returns to that office and waits in line yet again to see the residence permit officer. "I have no intention of making any requests," he tells her at last. "It is not my responsibility."

"It was his absolute calm that was so bewildering," writes Grossman. "If he had got angry, if he had shown irritation at her muddle-headedness, Yevgenia felt it would have been easier. But he just sat there in half-profile, unhurried, not batting an eyelid." At night she returns to the building where she is living illegally, terrified of being reported, certain her neighbor Glafira Dmitrievna is spying on her. At last, her boss writes the needed request, and with a rush of relief, she hurries back to the passport office, only to be told that she must wait three more days for a decision. When the answer arrives, it is crushing: "Residence permit refused on grounds of having no connection to the living space in question." Yevgenia begins shouting and is escorted out by police. "This life without rights, without a residence permit, without a ration-card, this continual fear of the janitor, the house-manager, Glafira Dmitrievna, had become quite unbearable."

Yevgenia writes a resignation letter, hoping to return to her hometown before she is punished for violating the permit requirement – and then the telephone rings. It is Limonov, a prominent official who has been making advances at her. She tells him her story, and he offers to put in a good word for her at an official meeting he's attending that day. "Then he asked, 'Are you free this evening?' 'No,' answered Yevgenia angrily." Nevertheless, the next morning, the phone rings at work. "An obliging voice asked her to call at the passport bureau in order to collect her residence permit." The next time she sees Limonov, she invites him in for tea. "Well yes, thank you," he says as he enters her room. "I suppose really you owe me some vodka for your residence permit."[36]

A half century after the end of the war, the *propiska* system remained in place, its social consequences no less perverse. Eager to obtain government permission to live in Moscow, some Russians arranged sham marriages with those allowed to reside in the city.

Others simply broke the rule, which was sometimes only loosely enforced. But violators risked arrest and deportation at any time – illegal immigrants in their own country.[37] Sadly, the *propiska* system survived the fall of the Soviet Union, in modified form. Today, people must still be registered at a local address to get jobs, open bank accounts, enroll in school, or obtain medical benefits.[38]

The *propiska* was only one of the many forms of permit required of Soviet citizens. Publishing anything required a *viza* from Glavlit, the government ministry of literature.[39] Music concerts required a license from Muzo, the ministry of music.[40] Owning a typewriter or a Xerox machine required permission.[41] Soviets had to carry with them not only their *propiska* but also their birth certificate, their "labor book" (which listed their education and work history), and other documents. So essential were these papers that Russians were fond of a saying attributed to Dostoyevsky: "A human being is composed of three things, a body, a soul, and a passport."[42] When the Berlin Wall fell in 1989, Communist officials told citizens they could leave, but if they did, the government would confiscate their homes. In defiance, thousands hung their house keys on fences or around the necks of statues, or nailed them to trees, before fleeing to the west.[43]

Who Must Ask Permission

The difference between rights and privileges becomes clearer when we consider what sorts of people are typically required to ask permission. Slaves, children, and, until recently, women all stand in a position of having to seek approval rather than being free to act as of right. They are, or were, regarded as inferiors, whose freedom existed only at the will of their betters.

Slavery obviously rested on the proposition that blacks were "so far inferior, that they had no rights which the white man was bound to respect," as the Supreme Court put it in *Dred Scott*.[44]

Nineteenth-century southerners denounced the proclamations of equality and freedom in the Declaration of Independence. For John C. Calhoun, the pro-slavery South Carolina senator and vice president, there was "not a word of truth" in the Declaration's "erroneous" opening paragraphs.[45] People were not born "either free or equal." Rather, freedom is a privilege society gives people: "a reward to be earned ... a reward reserved for the intelligent, the patriotic, the virtuous and deserving." The idea that people are born free, and that others must justify any restriction on that freedom, was "a great and dangerous error."[46]

Calhoun's ally George Fitzhugh agreed, denouncing the Declaration as "unphilosophical," "presumptuous," and "infidel philosophy."[47] Slaves were not entitled to any abstract conception of equality, because they were essentially like children, who "cannot be governed by mere law; first, because they do not understand it, and secondly, because they are so much under the influence of impulse, passion and appetite, that they want sufficient self control." A "government of mere law" could not "suffice for the individual negro. He is but a grown up child, and must be governed as a child. . . . The master occupies towards him the place of parent or guardian."[48]

For generations, women, too, were deprived of their freedom under rules that treated them like children who needed permission from men. Until the passage of the Married Women's Property Acts in the nineteenth century, married women had few legal rights to own or use private property or to sign contracts without approval from their husbands. In 1871, the Connecticut Woman Suffrage Association complained that "[t]he legal rights of the husband to the custody of the person, to the strict obedience, and to the services, of the wife, are almost precisely the same that the father has to the custody, obedience and services of his minor child."[49]

Such infantilizing treatment was eloquently exposed eight years later, in Henrik Ibsen's classic play, *A Doll's House*. The action centers around the realization by Nora Helmer that her marriage has only been a part of a system of debilitating rules and attitudes. She illegally borrowed money while her husband was recovering from an illness, by signing a loan agreement without his permission. Now he is well, and she is paying it back with money earned by working on the sly. The work, she confesses to a friend, has actually been "a tremendous pleasure." To earn her own money "was like being a man."[50] But when her creditor tries to blackmail her, Nora learns that her husband does not admire her independent spirit. Instead, he regards her as a child – he finds her "womanly helplessness" attractive.[51] Nora is shocked by the realization that he sees her only as a plaything, not a person. "When I was at home with papa," she tells him in the play's climax, "[h]e called me his doll-child, and he played with me just as I used to play with my dolls. And when I came to live with you ... I was simply transferred from papa's hands into yours." As a "doll-wife," she has been comfortable – but crippled. "It is your fault that I have made nothing of my life."[52]

For nearly another century after these words were written, American women were generally barred from economic and social spheres unless they got permission from men. Texas did not allow a married woman to sign contracts or own property without her husband's permission until 1967.[53]

In the 1908 case of *Muller v. Oregon*,[54] the United States Supreme Court upheld the constitutionality of a law that decreed how long a woman was allowed to work. Assuming that women were incapable of making wise choices about what jobs to take, the legislature prohibited employers from offering them jobs that required more than ten hours per day. Businesses challenged the law as a violation of the constitutional right to make contracts, the same right the Supreme Court had protected against the government's "meddlesome interference" in the *Lochner* case only three years before.[55] But the justices rejected the argument that women are "as competent to contract with reference to their labor as are men."[56] It was "obvious," they wrote, that women's "physical structure and the performance of maternal functions place her at a disadvantage in the struggle for subsistence."[57] A woman's "disposition and habits of life" made her inherently incapable of making such choices for herself, and justified "limitations ... upon her right to agree with her employer as to the time she shall labor." These limits were "not imposed solely for her benefit," but would also "preserve the strength and vigor of the race" by keeping women fit for childbearing. The male bakers in the *Lochner* case may have had the "intelligence and capacity" to make their own economic decisions, but the female workers in *Muller* did not.[58]

The natural consequence of limiting women's right to work long hours was to create a disincentive to hire them. Laws barring women from certain jobs or restricting their freedom to negotiate employment contracts encouraged businesses to hire men instead, since men were willing and able to work longer hours for lower wages. Male-dominated labor unions therefore supported these laws, typically using the excuse the court had provided: protecting women from themselves.[59]

Fifteen years later, the court overruled the *Muller* decision in a case called *Adkins*.[60] Congress had adopted a law that decreed a minimum wage for women working in the District of Columbia. Willie Lyons, an elevator operator at a hospital in Washington, lost her job when the law made it too expensive to retain her. She sued, arguing that she had the right to decide for herself what jobs to take, and on what terms, and that any law that deprived her of that freedom without good reason violated her right to liberty without due process of law. Speaking through Justice George Sutherland – an outspoken advocate of women's rights – the court agreed. Even assuming the *Muller* case had been correctly decided, Sutherland wrote, the newly adopted Nineteenth Amendment had ended the era of female subordination. "In view of the great – not to say revolutionary – changes which have taken place," he wrote, the legal differences between the "contractual, political, and civil status" of men and women had "now come almost, if not quite, to the vanishing point." Women had been freed "from the old doctrine that [they] must be given special protection or be subjected to special restraint in [their] contractual and civil relationships."[61]

By freeing women to make their own choices, decisions like *Adkins* helped women escape the infantilizing control of the Victorian era's Permission Society, just as James Madison and his colleagues had helped free religious minorities and dissenters from the control of established churches by replacing the rule of toleration with the principle of religious liberty.

Whatever form it takes, the permit system, which presumes that people may not act unless they get permission from the authorities, clashes with freedom by forcing people to obey the will of those in power. It allows rulers to dictate terms to the people, often in vague, incomprehensible language that maximizes bureaucratic authority. It conflicts with the principle of equality, the basis of our Constitution, by regarding people not as equals to be respected but as subjects to be punished or rewarded – as children, not as mature citizens ultimately responsible for their own actions. And it treats government officials as parents, who rule by command, rather than as fellow citizens bound by the same laws that govern everybody else.

CHAPTER THREE

PRIOR RESTRAINT OF SPEECH

WHEN WILLIAM BLACKSTONE boasted in his *Commentaries on the Laws of England* that the British enjoyed more freedom than the people of virtually any other nation in history, he was right. Not only did British subjects enjoy religious toleration, but they were also not required to obtain government permission before publishing a book, pamphlet, or newspaper. Writing in the 1760s, Blackstone viewed this rule against "previous restraints on speech" – what lawyers today call "prior restraint" – as one of the common law's many noble protections for individual freedom.

But it was only in 1695, less than a century before Blackstone wrote, that British law prohibited prior restraints. Before then, the law required anyone wishing to print a book or pamphlet to first get permission from officials at the royal Stationer's Company.[1] That requirement provoked one of the most famous episodes in the history of free speech when, in 1643, the poet John Milton published his scandalous pamphlet, *The Doctrine and Discipline of Divorce*, without a government license.

The 34-year-old Milton, already beginning to lose his sight, had married 16-year-old Mary Powell a year before. Chafing at life with her puritanical husband, Mary soon moved back in with her parents, prompting her husband to write the pamphlet arguing that divorce should be legalized – a shocking proposition in seventeenth-century

England.[2] But the radical Milton believed that God had created marriage to cure man's loneliness, not merely to breed children. Being married to an uncongenial person, a person with whom one had nothing in common and could not share life's joys, only made loneliness worse. It was therefore more sinful, he maintained, to stay in an unhappy marriage than to separate. As for biblical passages proscribing divorce, they had just been misinterpreted.

These arguments scandalized the Puritan clergy. When the pamphlet was published, a member of the House of Commons denounced it and demanded that it be censored and burned. Milton had not even tried to obtain the required license before publishing, he noted. A disgusted Milton shot back with a new pamphlet, again unauthorized, called *Areopagitica*. To this day, it remains the most eloquent defense of free expression ever written.

Censorship was worse than murder, Milton wrote, for "who kills a Man kills a reasonable creature, Gods Image; but hee who destroyes a good Booke, kills reason it selfe, kills the Image of God." The idea that government should impose permit requirements on publishing to protect readers from bad or dangerous ideas was an insult to truth itself, which would always defeat falsehood "in a free and open encounter."[3]

The idea of requiring approval from a government licenser before a book could be published struck Milton as not merely wrong, but un-English and anti-Protestant. The whole point of the Reformation, he thought, was to vindicate the right of believers to understand Christianity without the intercession of religious or political authorities. And the state of the Catholic countries he had toured as a student seemed to him evidence enough of the dangers of persecution. He recalled visiting the elderly Galileo in Italy, "a prisner to the Inquisition, for thinking in Astronomy otherwise then the Franciscan and Dominican licencers thought," and he remembered how Europeans who learned he was from England had congratulated him on living in a country free of censorship. Milton had known at the time that this was untrue, but "neverthelesse I took it as a pledge of future happines, that other Nations were so perswaded of [England's] liberty." He was distressed now to discover "that what words of complaint I heard among lerned men of other [nations] utter'd against the Inquisition, the same I should hear by as lerned men at home utterd in time of Parlament against an order of licencing."[4]

Milton's arguments for abolishing the licensing requirement raise many of the same concerns about other types of permit requirements discussed in the previous chapter. The bureaucrats who enforced the licensing laws were a "mercenary crew of false pretenders to learning," who often struck out important or inoffensive passages from manuscripts or demanded changes that only confused readers. Books emerged from censorship boring and full of mistakes. Banning books was counterproductive, in any event, because it only piqued people's curiosity about what the forbidden writings contained. "[I]nstead of suppressing sects and schisms," the prior restraint of the press "raises them and invests them with reputation."[5] In fact, if the government hoped to abolish improper or sinful writing, it would have to do much more than simply require licenses – it would also have to burn the many sinful books already in existence. And why stop there? Why not censor all personal behavior?

Prior restraints were unnecessary, Milton continued, because truth could defend itself.[6] Books full of error and evil were still valuable as models of what to avoid. A people whose government did not let them see bad ideas would be intellectually disarmed if they ever encountered real sin. Such a government could at best cultivate only "a fugitive and cloister'd vertue, unexercis'd & unbreath'd," that would "slink out of the race" if it ever crossed paths with a truly heretical idea. What good would that do? "Assuredly we bring not innocence into the world" when we try to shield people from the rough facts of life. Instead, "we bring impurity," because "that which purifies us is triall, and triall is by what is contrary."[7] Worse, to put the government in charge of personal

52

virtue encouraged people to be lazy about their own morals. "What need they torture their heads with that which others have tak'n so strictly[?]"[8] A person who "is not trusted with his own actions" when it comes to reading would have no reason take his duties as a citizen seriously, since he could hardly "think himself reputed in the Commonwealth."[9]

Eloquent as Milton's arguments were, they failed to persuade. England kept its licensing requirement in place for another half century, and when at last it was abolished, it was not a bold vindication of individual freedom but an almost silent acquiescence on Parliament's part. In 1695, the Licensing Act came up for renewal and was quietly allowed to lapse.[10] Amazingly, this moment – the birth of free speech in the Anglo-American world, which the historian Thomas Macaulay said "has done more for liberty and for civilisation than the Great Charter or the Bill of Rights" – came without any eloquent appeal to the glorious cause of intellectual liberty. When the House of Commons explained its reasons for withholding renewal, it cited only the difficulty, expense, and embarrassment caused by trying to enforce the act. "Such were the arguments," Macaulay wrote, "which did what Milton's *Areopagitica* had failed to do."[11]

The First Amendment and Prior Restraints

The fact that Parliament's abolition of prior restraint was no vindication of the principles of free expression is made still clearer by the limits that remained in place. British law still harshly punished blasphemy and sedition. Blackstone and other British lawyers argued that these rules did not contradict the freedom of press because they did not require government permission prior to publication – they only punished a person *after* publication.[12] Yet given how brutal these punishments could be, that seemed a dubious technicality. In 1792, Thomas Paine was tried *in absentia* for the crime of seditious libel for publishing his antimonarchical pamphlet *Rights of Man* and was sentenced to death. By that time, he had fled to France, never to return to the country of his birth. It seems silly to say that this was not a form of censorship.

Yet that was just the argument that President John Adams and his allies advanced in 1798 in support of the Sedition Act, a federal law that prohibited any "false, scandalous and malicious writing ... against the government of the United States, or either House of the Congress ... or the President."[13] The act was meant to target those whom Adams's Federalist allies suspected of sympathy with French Revolutionaries, foremost among whom were Vice President Thomas Jefferson and his close ally, Congressman James Madison.

The two Virginians watched indignantly as the Adams administration jailed its critics, including a grandson of Benjamin Franklin and a Congressman from Vermont. When the Jeffersonians protested that the act violated the First Amendment, Adams's supporters answered that the amendment only constitutionalized Blackstone's rule against prior restraints. Since the Sedition Act only punished speech *after* the fact and did not require a permit *before* speaking, they claimed it was constitutional.

In a lengthy response known as the "Report of 1800," Madison explained that punishing speech after it was uttered made a "mockery" of the First Amendment because it ignored "the difference between the nature of the British government, and the nature of the American governments." That difference, once again, lay in the fact that under the British government, subjects only enjoyed freedom as a permission from the Crown, whereas the American Constitution presumed that all people are fundamentally free. "The state of the press ... under the [English] common law, cannot ... be the standard of its freedom in the United States."[14] While American law did include the rule against prior restraints, it also went further.

The British, wrote Madison, had always considered the king the most dangerous part of their government. Magna Carta, the

English Bill of Rights, and other "ramparts for protecting the rights of the people" were therefore aimed only at the Crown, not Parliament, which was considered sovereign and "unlimited in its power; or, in their own language … omnipotent." The British people therefore had no rights valid against Parliament. The American Constitution was "altogether different." Here, sovereignty was held by "the people, not the government," and Congress did not have absolute or omnipotent power. The Constitution therefore protected the people against the legislative as well as executive branch. Individual rights were "secured, not by laws paramount to [royal] prerogative, but by constitutions paramount to laws." This meant that not only were prior restraints forbidden, but so were "legislative restraint[s]," including punishments for the expression of opinion. It should come as no surprise, wrote Madison, that the First Amendment protected speech more than British law did: after all, the same amendment protected religious liberty far beyond the more limited "toleration" principle of British law. It was thus reasonable that the Constitution's guarantees for speech would also be broader than the British tradition.

A friend of Madison, the prominent Virginia lawyer St. George Tucker, reiterated this point when he published an edition of Blackstone's *Commentaries* in 1803. Tucker's corrections and clarifications of Blackstone's text were so extensive, they take up an entire extra volume. He explained that the "genuine freedom of the press" was to be found in the right of every person "to speak, or publish, his sentiments on the measures of the government … without restraint, control, or fear of punishment."[15] Laws against libel or fraud were constitutional because they protected the rights of other citizens, but government officials could not use such laws to prosecute their critics.[16] For the government to claim that *it* had been slandered, by punishing sedition, would mean destroying the essence of free discussion. The U.S. Constitution's protections for freedom, therefore, went further than the old common-law system Blackstone was describing.

Today, American lawyers continue to argue over exactly how much protection the First Amendment provides. But the one thing they have always agreed upon is that, at a minimum, the Constitution forbids government from imposing prior restraints on speech, just as British law did in Madison's time. That principle was tested most notably in two twentieth-century Supreme Court decisions, *Near v. Minnesota* in 1931[17] and *New York Times v. United States*, also known as the Pentagon Papers case, in 1971.[18]

Near involved an anti-Semitic Minneapolis tabloid called *The Saturday Press*, which published sensational accusations of graft, corruption, and Jewish conspiracies. After a few issues appeared, featuring scurrilous claims of official wrongdoing, one of those accused, Floyd Olson, sued the publisher, arguing that the paper was a "public nuisance." Olson, a crusading socialist lawyer who later became the state's governor, argued that the allegations were false and that the paper's attacks on Jews were likely to stir up violence and hatred – what would today be called "hate speech."

The judge issued a temporary restraining order barring the *Press* from publishing any more issues until he decided whether it qualified as a nuisance. On appeal, the state supreme court allowed the case to proceed, declaring that a newspaper that encouraged hatred and violence could be as much a nuisance as a brothel or a liquor store. The case then went to trial, where the paper was declared a nuisance and prohibited from publishing. The case was appealed again, and this time the U.S. Supreme Court held the nuisance law unconstitutional because it allowed trial judges to issue injunctions that ran afoul of the rule against prior restraints. That rule was "generally, if not universally, considered ... the chief purpose" of the First Amendment.[19]

In the context of the case, this statement was odd because the lawsuit did not actually involve a prior restraint: Olson prosecuted the *Press* only *after* the paper was published, and the trial judge, after reviewing several issues, found that it had violated the law in the past. His order did not shut down the paper or require it to

obtain permission before publishing future issues; it only prohibited any future illegal acts. Whatever else one might think of such
a ruling, it simply was not a *prior* restraint. The *Near* decision is
therefore an anomaly. Yet the facts of the case are today largely
forgotten, and it has come to stand for the proposition that prior
restraints on expression are virtually never allowed.[20]

In 1971, that question arose again when the *New York Times*
and the *Washington Post* began publishing a series of secret documents about the Pentagon's plans regarding the Vietnam War that
had been leaked by military analyst Daniel Ellsberg. After the
Times and the *Post* printed some of the papers, the Nixon White
House sued for an injunction to bar any more publications. This
was a tactical mistake because it put the government in the position of asking the court to stop the printing – thus placing the
burden of proof on the President's lawyers. Had Nixon instead
ordered the FBI to arrest the editors and impound the documents,
the publishers would have had to ask a court for protection instead,
placing the burden of proof on them.[21] That was not the only tactical disadvantage Nixon faced. Because they based the lawsuit on
the Espionage Act of 1917, federal lawyers were required to prove
that the leaking and publication of the papers qualified as spying,
which was a stretch. And unlike in the *Near* case, there was no
question that the case involved a classic prior restraint. Nixon was
seeking outright censorship of newsworthy documents.

The case rapidly reached the Supreme Court, which issued its
ruling only five days after hearing arguments. It was a three-para-
graph, unsigned decision, holding simply that "[a]ny system of
prior restraints of expression comes to this Court bearing a heavy
presumption against its constitutional validity" and that "the Government ha[d] not met that burden."[22] This was followed by separate opinions in which each justice explained the basis for his ruling.
Although the case produced no single landmark opinion, it was
nevertheless a stunning moment in the history of the First Amendment.[23] The President of the United States could not stop the

publication of sensitive military documents during wartime – a real testament to the law's protections of free press. Unfortunately, as we will see in chapter 4, what the court described as a nearly air-tight prohibition on prior restraints is actually nothing of the sort.

Is Free Speech an Individual or Collective Right?

James Madison viewed freedom of speech as more than merely a social institution. As important as open discussion may be in a democracy, Madison saw free speech as a personal right of all individuals. In a short 1792 essay about property rights, he noted that the word "property" refers not just to tangible objects but also to "every thing to which a man may attach a value and have a right; and which leaves to every one else the like advantage." This included a person's ideas. Just as "a man's land, or merchandize, or money is called his property," so too "a man has a property in his opinions and the free communication of them" and "a property of peculiar value in his religious opinions."[24]

Freedom of speech or religion were therefore kinds of property. Both prior restraint and punishment after expressing unpopular views violated freedom of speech because they contradicted this basic element of personal liberty. Freedom was violated not only when a person was barred from speaking but also when he was forced to speak against his will – to pledge allegiance to a doctrine he detested or to spread a message with which he disagreed. As Jefferson wrote in the Virginia Statute for Religious Freedom, it is "sinful and tyrannical" for the government "to compel a man to furnish contributions of money for the propagation of opinions which he disbelieves."[25]

During the early twentieth century, however, political philosophers and judges came to reconsider the nature of free speech. Turning away from Madison's individualistic views, such Progressive Era thinkers as John Dewey, Louis Brandeis, and Oliver Wendell Holmes saw the freedoms of speech or press not as property rights but as tools for ensuring that the public could reach wiser collective decisions. Thus, while some Progressives took important strides toward greater protections for free expression,[26] they also compromised it in a fundamental way, making it into an essentially public rather than private value. Speech, in their eyes, was a privilege the government gives citizens for society's purposes, rather than an individual right the government must respect.

A key actor in this transition was Holmes, author of the renowned dissenting opinion in the 1919 free speech case *Abrams v. United States*.[27] That case involved the same 1917 Espionage Act that later formed the basis of the Pentagon Papers case. A group of communists who opposed American involvement in World War I had printed up antiwar flyers and thrown them from a fourth-floor window in Manhattan to passersby on the sidewalk. They were arrested and charged with trying to hinder the war effort, which the act prohibited. When the case reached the Supreme Court, the justices upheld the convictions 7–2.

Holmes had already written several opinions allowing the imprisonment of antiwar activists under the Sedition Act, including the Socialist Party's presidential candidate, Eugene V. Debs. Yet he dissented in the *Abrams* case, and that dissent became a landmark of free speech law. In 2014, law professor Thomas Healy published *The Great Dissent: How Oliver Wendell Holmes Changed His Mind and Changed the History of Free Speech in America*, arguing that modern freedom of speech began with Holmes's dissent – a view shared by most judges and law professors today. Andrew Cohen of *The Atlantic* was more effusive. Reviewing Healy's book, he called Holmes's opinion "the most powerful dissent in American history."[28]

That was surely an exaggeration – Justice John Marshall Harlan's dissent in *Plessy v. Ferguson*,[29] Justice Harry Blackmun's in *Bowers v. Hardwick*,[30] or Justice Stephen Field's in the *Slaughter-House Cases*[31] are all more eloquent and persuasive, and Holmes's own wrongheaded but historic dissent in *Lochner*[32] has proven more influential. But Holmes's *Abrams* dissent is also far from the resounding declaration of individual liberty that one might imagine given this extravagant praise.

"Persecution for the expression of opinions," Holmes declared in *Abrams*, "seems to me perfectly logical."[33] This sentence could never have been written by Madison, Jefferson, or any of the classical liberals who gave birth to the First Amendment. Such words are actually a throwback to the pre-Constitution days of Puritan censorship, which regarded the expression of ideas as inherently dangerous. Yet they were typical of Holmes, who, like Jeremy Bentham, considered the founders' principles of natural law and natural rights superstitious nonsense. In Holmes's eyes, all law, all justice, all principles of right and wrong were nothing more than emotionalistic impulses, with no stronger foundation than one's taste for a brand of beer. Democracy, he believed, uses the process of voting to aggregate people's subjective preferences, and those desires for which people are willing to fight the hardest prevail – and become law. At bottom, law is not a process of reasoning but an arbitrary command from the majority.

Still, Holmes thought, the majority chooses not to persecute people for expressing their opinions – not because every person has a right to state his views, but because the majority benefits from a "free trade in ideas." The Constitution protects the "effort to change the mind of the country" because "men have realized that time has upset many fighting faiths," and open debate is a better way to avoid error. But this freedom of debate is only a privilege society gives to citizens to achieve collective goals, and Holmes emphasized how narrow that protection was when he declared that he "never ha[d] seen any reason to doubt" that his previous rulings allowing the imprisonment of dissenters – including Eugene Debs – "were rightly decided."[34]

This was exactly the opposite of the views of James Madison. The First Amendment's author believed that persecution of opinion could never be logical or moral, because individual rights are not created at society's pleasure but are like private property that government must respect. The "Sovereignty of the Society as vested in & exerciseable by the majority," Madison wrote, may only do things "that could be *rightfully* done, by the unanimous concurrence of the members." That meant the majority cannot legitimately violate natural rights – "Conscience for example" – which are always "beyond the legitimate reach of Sovereignty."[35]

For Madison, justice and injustice, right and wrong, were prior to – and therefore imposed limits on – the authority of the ruler, whether that ruler be a single dictator or a majority of voters. Himself a wartime president, Madison never sought to jail the many voluble critics of his administration's efforts during the War of 1812, even when some went so far as to propose seceding from the union.[36] Holmes had no such scruples. According to his *Abrams* dissent, the majority comes first, and the individual has no rights beyond government's reach. The majority determines what is right and wrong, and although it gives people a limited opportunity to speak their minds so that it can make more informed decisions, that opportunity is not a morally obligatory right. It is only a permission based on policy considerations that may be revoked when society thinks it necessary – for example, if it chooses to jail antiwar activists like Debs.

Holmes's *Abrams* dissent also compares unfavorably to Jefferson's Statute for Religious Freedom. Jefferson believed "God hath created the mind free" and that "attempts to influence it by temporal punishments or burthens" represented an "impious presumption of legislators and rulers," who "have assumed dominion" of something that does not belong to them.[37] But for Holmes, the reverse was true. Like Bentham, Holmes believed that the individual does not own his own mind; it is only his because society has not chosen to take it away. Like any other resource, society may confiscate and distribute the individual's freedom of conscience at will. It is the individual who "assumes dominion" – an unwarranted dominion –

over his own mind, if and when he claims a right to his own self.[38]

This is no overstatement. Holmes – who likened the notion of rights valid against government to "shaking one's fist at the sky, when the sky furnishes the energy that enables one to raise the fist"[39] – scoffed at the idea that people have a right to their own lives. "I don't believe," he wrote a friend, "that man always is an end in himself – that his dignity must be respected, etc."[40] On the contrary, people belong presumptively to the state and may be conscripted into military service, deprived of their property[41] or economic freedom,[42] taxed,[43] censored,[44] or even forced to undergo sterilization[45] whenever society considers such acts necessary. "[T]he word liberty," he wrote in his *Lochner* dissent, "is perverted when it is held to prevent the natural outcome of a dominant opinion."[46] He viewed people as insignificant "ganglion[s]" or "grain[s] of sand" in the universe, who should "accept the vision of [them]selves as parts inseverable from the rest" – a vision that "justifies the sacrifice even of our lives for ends outside of ourselves."[47]

In short, Holmes supported the freedom of speech not to protect individual liberty but because he saw it as a useful tool for collective decision-making. The well-known metaphor of the "marketplace of ideas," which originated in Holmes's *Abrams* dissent, is revealing: speech is protected only when it is public. Speech that does not occur in the marketplace – or a person's desire not to appear in the marketplace at all – could not claim protection. His *Abrams* opinion was therefore entirely consistent with his pro-censorship views in Eugene Debs's case: together, they recast speech as a permission government grants and can revoke to serve politicians' notion of the public good.

Holmes was certainly the most extreme and outspoken of the intellectuals who assailed the natural rights theories of the American founders, but he was far from the only one. His fellow justice Louis Brandeis also viewed individual rights as privileges the government may give or take away to serve political goals. "[I]n the interest of the public and in order to preserve the liberty and the property of the great majority of the citizens of a state," he wrote, "rights of property and the liberty of the individual must be remolded, from time to time, to meet the changing needs of society."[48]

Although today he is admired as an eloquent champion of free speech, Brandeis's devotion to that right was based on the idea that freedom is a privilege subject to collective "remolding." Open discussion was essential for society to decide which rights to remold and how. Thus in *Whitney v. California*, probably his best-known discussion of free speech, Brandeis argued that the First Amendment was written to protect "free and fearless reasoning applied through the process of popular government" and "public discussion" – rather than the freedom of individuals to make their own choices in peace. Where the founders saw free speech as only one part of the individual's right to self-ownership, Brandeis saw it as a component of "political change" and "stable government." He acknowledged that the founders "valued liberty both as an end and a means," but he understood this to mean that the individual's personality is molded and improved by participating in public debate. Free speech encouraged collective deliberation, which made individuals "courageous" and "self-reliant" rather than "inert." Liberty was a tool for fostering a healthy society and "remolding" citizens' characters, not a means of protecting individual autonomy. In other words, Brandeis held what law professor Cass Sunstein has called a "civic conception" of free speech.[49]

The Right Not to Speak

Because it is primarily devoted to fostering collective decision-making, this Progressive version of free speech leaves little room for a person's or a group's right *not* to speak, particularly when silence only serves the individual's own conscience and when being forced to speak might serve community interests. For that reason, the right *not* to speak has often given rise to more interesting problems in First Amendment law than has the freedom to speak.

The most dramatic such episode involved laws that compelled high school students to pledge allegiance to the flag. Originally written in 1892, the Pledge of Allegiance was quickly adopted by schools across the country as a patriotic exercise to instill reverence for American institutions at a time when heavy immigration was raising fears about the future of American culture. The Pledge and similar practices were expected to ensure cultural unity. In retrospect, this emphasis on unity has a foreboding quality: until 1942, the salute was said not with the hand over the heart but with the hand outstretched toward the flag. Only when that gesture became associated with Hitler and Mussolini did Congress change it.

Beginning in the 1930s, members of the Jehovah's Witness church refused to participate in the flag salute on the grounds that it contravened the biblical commandment against worshipping images. In 1937, eight-year-old Carleton Nicholls of Lynn, Massachusetts, was expelled from school for refusing to salute the flag. His family sued, but the state's highest court ruled in favor of the school, declaring that there was "nothing in the salute or the pledge of allegiance which constitutes an act of idolatry."[50] Three years later, 11-year-old Lillian Gobitas and her 10-year-old brother Billy were teased, abused, and finally expelled from their Pennsylvania school for refusing to join in the Pledge. They too sued, arguing that the expulsion violated their First Amendment rights, but the U.S. Supreme Court ruled against them.

That 1940 decision, called *Minersville School District v. Gobitis* (the court misspelled the family's name in the official decision), was written by the Progressive Justice Felix Frankfurter, a fervent admirer of Holmes, who declared that the goal of public education is not merely to teach children but to create a "binding tie of cohesive sentiment"[51] – that is, to indoctrinate children with "patriotic impulses" during their "formative period."[52] Frankfurter claimed he was not *approving* of such indoctrination – although he could not resist demeaning the Jehovah's Witnesses' "crochety beliefs."[53] Instead, he was simply saying that the question of whether a compulsory flag salute served those ends was a matter for the legislature to decide. To hold that the First Amendment barred states from forcing children to salute the flag would "stigmatize legislative judgment."[54]

Just three years later, the court reversed itself. By that time, the nation was at war against fascist powers that had indoctrinated their own children very well indeed.[55] The court reviewed a case in which two more Jehovah's Witness schoolchildren, eight-year-old Marie Barnett and nine-year-old Gathie Barnett, were expelled for silently declining to salute the flag. The decision in *West Virginia Board of Education v. Barnette*[56] – once again, the court misspelled the children's names – was written by the newly appointed Justice Robert Jackson, who would later serve as lead prosecutor at the Nuremberg tribunal.

Jackson rejected Frankfurter's collectivist approach. "The very purpose of a Bill of Rights was to withdraw certain subjects from the vicissitudes of political controversy," he wrote, "to place them beyond the reach of majorities and officials and to establish them as legal principles to be applied by the courts. One's right to life, liberty, and property, to free speech, a free press, freedom of worship and assembly, and other fundamental rights may not be submitted to vote; they depend on the outcome of no elections."[57] Frankfurter, in dissent, remained resolute, accusing the majority of "writing [its] private notions of policy into the Constitution."[58]

Barnette indicated a turn back toward the founders' individualistic view of the First Amendment and a partial renunciation of the collectivist attitudes that Progressives like Holmes, Brandeis, and Frankfurter had proclaimed so recently before. In the years that followed, liberal justices became increasingly divided as some, particularly Justice William Douglas, built on this resurgent individualism to protect rights of sexual privacy. In the eyes of Justice

Frankfurter and others of the old guard, those decisions were a misguided effort to restore the libertarian understanding of the Constitution that Progressives had labored to abolish.

While *Barnette* is generally celebrated today, some prominent lawyers, judges, and law professors, viewing freedom of speech as more of a collective than an individual right, remain doubtful. Among these is Professor Cass Sunstein, who for decades has argued in favor of what he calls a "New Deal for speech."[59] According to him, the First Amendment is part of a "system of free expression" designed more to serve "the central constitutional goal of creating a deliberative democracy"[60] than to protect individual freedom. The Constitution, he writes, is "emphatically not designed solely to protect private interests and private rights."[61] Instead, individual freedom is manufactured by society to accomplish social purposes, meaning that "respect for private rights" must be "justified by publicly articulable reasons." Only where individual rights are either "preconditions or the appropriate outcomes" of a "well-functioning deliberative process" should the government grant those rights protection.[62]

If free speech can be analogized to a "marketplace of ideas," then Sunstein suggests that the government should control that "marketplace" just as dozens of regulatory agencies now control the economic market. "What if a marketplace of ideas," he asks, "yields little attention to public issues and diversity of view …? What if government tries to regulate the marketplace in the interest of promoting attention to public issues and diversity of view?"[63] In such cases, politicians should redistribute free speech rights to achieve a more "democratic" outcome: taking away the expressive rights of some speakers to give others more influence. Sunstein suggests forcing broadcasters to provide free airtime for political candidates,[64] giving taxpayer money to candidates whose opponents have raised hefty contributions, limiting how much people can donate to campaigns, and restricting what candidates are allowed to spend to convey their messages. He also recommends outlawing children's programming that is excessively commercial,[65] imposing a new version of the fairness doctrine,[66] and taxing advertisers in order to subsidize "shows that advertisers will not support."[67] He acknowledges that these restrictions on speech would be "intrusive"[68] but contends that they should not be "foreclosed by the Constitution" because such approaches might better serve "our self-definition as a democratic system."[69]

The problems with these proposals are as obvious now as they were when the First Amendment was written. Giving government the powers Sunstein suggests is a recipe for censorship, exploitation, and the power politics typically associated with banana republics and premodern theocracies. After all, established religions and censorship have usually been defended on exactly the same grounds: government should limit what people can say and read so as to ensure that they are morally upright, not materialistic, more devoted to "higher" things. When Sunstein argues that government should "maintain a civilized society"[70] by controlling what television programs people watch, it is impossible not to hear the echoes of Puritan censorship.

Perhaps more telling, Sunstein rarely mentions the right *not* to be forced to speak or *not* to be forced to subsidize the expression of views one despises. In fact, he appears to have almost never discussed that subject in his four decades of scholarship on freedom of speech. When he does address the rights of dissenters, he does so almost exclusively in terms of collectivist values rather than individual freedom. Thus, in his 2003 book, *Why Societies Need Dissent*, he argued that nonconformists should be protected, not because they have the right not to be forced to join a multitude against their will, but because dissenters "perform valuable social functions."[71] Democratic governments should "take steps to discourage conformity and to promote dissent, partly to protect the rights of dissenters, but mostly to protect interests of their own."[72]

Even more strikingly, Sunstein suggested in a 1990 article on the legal and moral consequences of forcing people to take oaths that the *Barnette* decision striking down the compulsory flag salute was "too cavalier" because it was based on a "belief[] in individual immunity from communal ties."[73] The earlier *Gobitis* case, he wrote, was more supportive of "the virtues of ensuring national attachments."[74] Although he stopped short of explicitly endorsing the *Gobitis* decision, one can easily see how his collectivist "emphasis on political virtue, on public spiritedness, [and] on public deliberation"[75] instead of individual rights would easily support rules forcing people to pledge allegiance to the flag against their will.

The right not to express opinions one finds repugnant – not to join a church, not to salute the flag if one thinks it sinful, not to subsidize the promulgation of messages one considers wrong – is fundamentally personal. As a form of dissent, it can play an important role in democratic debate, but that is not the primary reason people value the right not to speak. Rather, that right is an essential form of self-expression and personal autonomy. When Jehovah's Witnesses choose not to salute the flag, they are focused not on making a political statement or on converting the public, but on fulfilling what they consider to be their duty to God: to quote eight-year-old Carleton Nicholls, they refuse to "adore the flag and to bow down to the flag" when they can "only adore and bow down to Jehovah."[76]

Dissenters sometimes refuse to join with the majority as a way of making a political statement. But they often do it only to honor and preserve their integrity: "not because the world would then be changed for the better," as Hannah Arendt puts it, "but simply because only on this condition could they go on living with themselves at all."[77] This is an inescapably individualistic value, one for which the collectivist theory of speech has little room.

Forcing People to Speak

One area in which the rights of dissenters are often violated is in the workplace. Thanks to laws premised on the Progressive view that speech is about political participation rather than individual freedom, employees are often forced to subsidize the activities of labor unions, even if they oppose those activities and refuse to join the union.[78] Courts have ruled that the First Amendment forbids unions from forcing workers to support union *political* activities, but it's not always easy to differentiate political activities from the other things unions do. Worse, the law places the burden not on unions to justify taking money from workers' paychecks, but on the worker who wishes to exercise his First Amendment rights. This is the same Devil's proof that forces people to justify their freedom. Like a prior restraint, which bars a person from speaking unless the government gives him permission, laws like these are biased against individual rights. They force a person to speak unless he proves that he should be allowed to remain silent.

The theory behind compulsory union fees is that because unions advocate on behalf of all workers, including nonmembers, the nonmembers could get a "free ride" by enjoying the benefits the union obtains without paying for them. Under this "free rider" theory, states have adopted laws that deduct "agency fees" from the paychecks of nonmembers, even against their will. But this free rider theory is problematic. Indeed, it is the same argument that in generations past was used to justify established churches: society, it was said, benefits from a morally upright populace, and if people are not forced to contribute to the church that encourages morality, they might "free ride" by enjoying those social benefits without paying for them. In opposing established religion, Jefferson and others argued that these benefits, while real, could not justify forcing people to subsidize religious views they found repugnant. Even if churches do benefit society, seizing money from working people to support them was wrong and dangerous. In short, the fact that someone enjoys a benefit provided by someone else is not always good reason to force him to pay for that benefit.

The "agency fee" privilege that unions enjoy gives them tremendous and unwarranted influence. Organized labor is among the most powerful political forces in the country today. Exact figures are unreliable, as unions typically refuse to divulge their financial data, but some experts estimate that unions now contribute $800 million annually to political campaigns, including "in-kind contributions," such as dispatching people to hand out flyers or man phone banks.[79] In the 2008 presidential election, one union, the Service Employees International Union (SEIU), spent more than $33 million in independent political expenditures.[80] Like most union money, this went almost entirely to the Democratic Party, even though many union members are politically conservative.

Since people have a First Amendment right not to subsidize political expression of which they disapprove, the Supreme Court has struggled to navigate a narrow channel between enforcing mandatory agency fees and protecting the rights of those who choose not to join unions. In the 1977 case of *Abood v. Detroit Board of Education*,[81] Justice Potter Stewart quoted Jefferson's Statute for Religious Freedom to the effect that forcing people to subsidize the propagation of opinions they do not believe is "sinful and tyrannical," and ruled that the government could not force an employee "to contribute to the support of an ideological cause he may oppose as a condition of holding a job."[82]

Neither *Abood* nor later cases, however, employed the court's strongest tool for protecting free speech: the "strict scrutiny" test. That test, which applies in typical First Amendment cases, requires judges to presume against any limit on free expression unless the government can provide a strong justification for that limit. And although courts normally assume that people do not intend to give up important constitutional rights unless they clearly say they are, the *Abood* case took the opposition position. "Dissent is not to be presumed," Stewart wrote.[83] Instead, workers must "affirmatively [make] known to the union their opposition to political uses of their funds," and unions can satisfy the First Amendment by establishing a way for dissenters to get refunds. In short, unions can take the money first and ask permission later. Workers are not given the choice of "opting in" to subsidizing the union. Instead, they must "opt out."

In practice, this presumption against dissent operates like a prior restraint. It places the burden on workers who want to express themselves – or, rather, who want to remain silent – instead of on the union that would curtail that right. Naturally, this presumption against dissent has encouraged unions to fashion slow and cumbersome refund procedures to deter dissent. For example, in *Chicago Teachers' Union v. Hudson*,[84] the court reviewed a complicated three-step refund procedure, which required dissenters – who had no opportunity to object before fees were taken from their paychecks – to write to the union's president within 30 days of the first withholding. Their objections would then be considered by a union committee, which had another 30 days to issue a decision. The workers then had 30 more days to appeal that decision to another union committee. If that committee rejected the appeal, the worker had to go through arbitration. Unsurprisingly, the union's committees rarely found in favor of nonmembers.

Worse, because agency fees are typically only slightly less than the full cost of union membership, the more complicated the objection procedure gets, the more likely it is that nonmembers will not bother to complain. In the Chicago case, union members were charged $17.35 per month for dues and nonmembers were charged $16.48. Objecting nonmembers would have to go through the refund process to obtain less than a dollar extra per month. The court ruled against the union in that case, holding that the procedure was so complicated that it essentially deprived dissenters of their right to a refund. But unions continued their obstruction tactics. In a 2000 case, the Office and Professional Employees International Union adopted rules that forced dissenters to specify the exact amount of fees they thought were wrongly withheld and what they thought the money had been spent on. Any imprecision was treated as a waiver of rights.[85] In still another case, the International Association of Machinists and Aerospace Workers forced workers to object in writing within a 30-day window each year. At one point, the union moved its headquarters and refused to honor objections sent to its old address. In ruling against the union, a federal court found that this "unduly cumbersome annual objection requirement" was "designed to prevent employees from exercising their constitutionally-based right of objection."[86]

Aside from the cost and hassle of complying with refund procedures, nonmembers also face peer pressure at the hands of unionized coworkers. A rule that forces objectors to attract attention, and possibly retaliation, if they want to defend their rights can effectively silence dissent. In 1958, similar concerns weighed heavily when the Supreme Court invalidated Alabama's effort to force the NAACP to publish its supporters' names. "Compelled disclosure of affiliation with groups engaged in advocacy may constitute as effective a restraint on freedom of association" as actual censorship, said the court, "particularly where a group espouses dissident beliefs."[87] But judges have often shown less sensitivity to these concerns when cases involve unions.

Even where intimidation is not a factor, simple inertia unfairly aids unions in cases where workers just don't have time to fill out paperwork and engage in a complex hearing and appeal process. The power of that inertia became clear in 1992, when Washington state voters approved a "paycheck protection" initiative that precluded unions from funding political campaigns with money taken from nonmembers unless workers affirmatively authorized them to do so. Unsurprisingly, replacement of the "opt-out" rule with an "opt-in" rule caused a dramatic fall in the amount of money workers were "willing" to devote to political expenditures. About 85 percent of the contributions that the Washington Education Association (WEA) had claimed as "voluntary" under the prior rule disappeared.[88] Evidently, many nonmembers had simply been stifling their objections under the rule, saw little point in seeking refunds, or never got around to filling out the paperwork.

The WEA challenged the constitutionality of that law, arguing that "opt-in" added to its "administrative expenses," thus infringing on *the union's* free speech rights.[89] The Supreme Court disagreed. Unions, it held, have no constitutional right to dock nonmembers' paychecks. But while the justices allowed the state to replace the opt-out rule with an opt-in rule, they refused to declare that the First Amendment itself *requires* opt-out in order to protect the rights of dissenters. Sadly, shortly after the court upheld the Washington law, the state legislature effectively repealed it by redefining "expenditures" in a technical way that once again allowed unions to spend money obtained from nonmembers on political campaigns.

In July 2005, the SEIU announced a "temporary assessment," under which it garnished the wages of both members and nonmembers to campaign against two California ballot initiatives – one of which, like the Washington initiative, would have imposed an opt-in rule. The union did not notify nonmembers of their right to object, however, because it decided that it had done enough when it issued such notices at the beginning of each year. A group of workers filed suit, arguing that the union's failure to remind people of their objection rights violated the First Amendment. The Ninth Circuit Court of Appeals ruled for the union. Courts must balance "the right of a union ... to require nonunion employees to pay a fair share of the union's costs" with "the First Amendment limitation on collection of fees from dissenting employees for the support of ideological causes," wrote Judge Sidney R. Thomas.[90] In dissent, Judge Clifford Wallace objected to the notion of "balancing" a worker's constitutional right to free speech and the union's special privilege to tax nonmembers. "The Union's interest in this case is not a 'right' to nonmembers' funds," he wrote. "The Union has no legitimate interest ... in collecting agency fees from nonmembers to fill its political war-chest."[91]

When the Supreme Court agreed to review the case, it at first seemed unlikely that the justices would reconsider the question of "opt-in," since the case only directly involved the narrower question of the SEIU's failure to issue a second notice. But in a 5–4 decision, it ruled that the opt-out procedure was unconstitutional.[92] Forcing dissenting workers to bear the burden of objecting was an "anomaly," wrote Justice Samuel Alito.[93] In every other realm of First Amendment law, courts presume in favor of individual rights and require anyone wishing to limit those rights to justify doing so. Employing the opposite rule in cases involving unions made no sense. "[W]hat is the justification for putting the burden on the nonmember to opt out of making such a payment? Shouldn't the default rule comport with the probable preferences of most non-members?"[94] By presuming against dissent, *Abood*'s opt-out rule created "a risk that the fees paid by nonmembers will be used to further political and ideological ends with which they do not agree,"[95] and likely silenced many people who would refuse to contribute to union activism if given a fair choice.

Rejecting the Ninth Circuit's "balancing" approach, Alito concluded that the Constitution is about protecting individual rights, not "a balancing of rights or interests." Thus "any procedure for exacting fees from unwilling contributors must be carefully tailored to minimize the infringement of free speech."[96]

Yet the justices stopped short of overruling *Abood* directly, and that decision remains on the books.[97] Organized labor – and the politicians who benefit from it – continues to benefit from agency fee laws that treat speech like a privilege a person must ask for rather than a right the state must respect. Thanks to Progressive Era theories that prioritize "democratic" goals over individual rights, citizens are often forced to seek some form of permission before they may express themselves – or remain silent.

Restricting Democracy in the Name of Democracy

The collectivist theory of free speech devised by Progressives doesn't just curtail the rights of individuals. It also hinders the very democratic process that Progressives claim to support. This is most obvious in the realm of campaign finance regulations, where an ever-growing network of rules and restrictions blocks candidates and citizens from expressing their views on political issues or contributing money to help spread political messages.

One of the foremost defenders of these rules is Supreme Court Justice Stephen Breyer, whose books *Active Liberty* and *Making Our Democracy Work* endorse government control over political campaigns as a means toward the "promotion of a democratic conversation."[98] Like Holmes, Brandeis, and Sunstein, Breyer thinks the First Amendment's primary purpose is to further "basic democratic objectives" rather than to protect the rights of individuals. This means that "a restriction on speech, even when political speech is at issue, will sometimes prove reasonable, hence lawful."[99] In Breyer's view, a law forbidding campaign contributions or limiting what a person may spend on political advertisements may still have a "*positive* impact upon the public's confidence in, and ability to communicate through, the electoral process," and should therefore be allowed to stand, notwithstanding the Constitution's unequivocal prohibition on all laws abridging freedom of speech.[100]

Breyer made his opinion clear in a 2000 case involving a state law that prohibited anyone from donating more than $1,075 to a gubernatorial candidate.[101] A political action committee sued, arguing that this rule interfered with people's First Amendment right to support candidates of their choice. But the Supreme Court upheld the restriction, declaring that "a contribution limit involving 'significant interference' with associational rights" would still pass muster if it is "'closely drawn' to match a 'sufficiently important interest,'" such as increasing public confidence in the electoral process.[102] The court admitted that its ruling would enable the government to deprive some people of the right to support their preferred candidates, but it considered this an acceptable tradeoff, as long as contribution limits are not "so radical in effect as to render political association ineffective."[103]

Justices Anthony Kennedy, Clarence Thomas, and Antonin

Scalia disagreed. The government had never been allowed to censor individuals to accomplish some allegedly greater good, they pointed out, even where the censorship was comparatively minor. The court had refused to uphold restrictions on speech in earlier cases involving "a single protester with a hand-scrawled sign, a few demonstrators on a public sidewalk, or a driver who taped over the motto on his license plate because he disagreed with its message." So how could it justify "suppress[ing] one of our most essential and prevalent forms of political speech"?[104] Confidence in the democratic system may be important, but "it hardly inspires confidence for the Court to abandon the rigors of our traditional First Amendment structure."[105] Justice Thomas was especially succinct: the court's vague approach, he wrote, "balance[s] away First Amendment freedoms."[106]

Replying to these criticisms, Breyer explained that he saw "constitutionally protected interests ... on both sides."[107] On one hand was the individual's First Amendment right to express political opinions and support candidates. On the other hand was the "integrity of the electoral process – the means through which a free society democratically translates political speech into concrete governmental action."[108] Legislatures and courts should try to reach a compromise between these two. "The Constitution," he wrote, "often permits restrictions on the speech of some in order to prevent a few from drowning out the many."[109]

But the Constitution does no such thing. It never refers to "balancing" freedom of speech against other values, and it does not allow lawmakers to restrict the expressive rights of some so as to amplify the impact of others. Notably, the only example Breyer cited of the Constitution supposedly "permitting" such restrictions was the Speech and Debate Clause, a provision which applies only to members of Congress and gives them immunity from prosecution for any words they utter during debates. That provision has nothing to do with speech by citizens, and it is hardly evidence that the Constitution "often permits restrictions" on free expression – especially given the First Amendment's unequivocal promise that "Congress shall make no law … abridging the freedom of speech or of the press." Yet Breyer's version of the Constitution allows legislators to limit the right of some people to support political candidates in order to "seek[] a fairer electoral debate."[110]

The Constitution guarantees freedom, not "fairness." It secures to each person the right to speak, not the right to be heard by the same size audience as other people. As Breyer's opinion suggests, efforts to achieve such "fairness" for some people typically involve limiting the freedom of others – taking away their money, restricting the number of ads they can run, or curtailing what they may say. Thanks to the Progressive collective-rights understanding of the First Amendment, the field of political expression is now riddled with legal barriers that censor individual expression in the service of supposedly "fairer," more "democratic" objectives.

Campaign finance laws are so complicated that the nation's best lawyers have difficulty understanding them, with the result that people who wish to advocate for or against candidates or ballot initiatives are often forced to ask the government's permission before they may speak. Federal law requires a political action committee to register with the Federal Election Commission (FEC) and provide details about the committee's members and bank accounts.[111] Committees must submit to intricate reporting requirements and are limited in how much they can spend on political campaigns, when, and for what purpose. After the Bipartisan Campaign Reform Act, also known as "McCain-Feingold," added still stricter limits, the FEC fashioned a network of regulations that divided campaigning into 33 different kinds of speech, each subject to different rules and restrictions. The resulting limits were so complex that candidates were usually forced to ask the FEC for advice before they began campaigning, to enable them to comply with the law.

This punishment of unauthorized politicking, combined with an option for pre-approval, formed a modern-day version of licensing speech. "As a practical matter," declared the Supreme Court in

2010, "a speaker who wants to avoid threats of criminal liability and the heavy costs of defending against FEC enforcement must ask a governmental agency for prior permission to speak." The law's "onerous restrictions" were therefore "the equivalent of prior restraint" and gave the FEC "power analogous to licensing laws implemented in 16th- and 17th-century England."[112]

A law that punishes people who speak without a permit is an archetypical prior restraint. In 1945, the Supreme Court struck down a Texas law that forced union organizers to register before they could solicit workers to join unions. "If the exercise of the rights of free speech and free assembly cannot be made a crime," wrote Justice Wiley Rutledge, "we do not think this can be accomplished by the device of requiring previous registration as a condition for exercising them." If the state could force unions to comply with a restriction like this, it could also force people to register before advocating any political, religious, or social proposition, which would be "quite incompatible with the requirements of the First Amendment."[113] Yet campaign finance regulations today routinely require people to register with the government before they run for office or support those who do.

Registration requirements may seem minor, but they can serve as effective prior restraints on political speech. In 2008, a University of Colorado graduate student named Diana Hsieh founded a group she called the Coalition for Secular Government to oppose efforts to restrict abortion rights in the state.[114] It was a small group – consisting of herself and a friend – and its entire budget was about $200, all from Hsieh's own pocket. She and her friend built a website and published a position paper expressing their opinions on the legality and morality of abortion. The paper received some attention, and the Coalition received about $3,000 in contributions in its second year. But the paper also included one sentence that urged voters to reject a proposal to amend the state constitution. For anyone agreeing with her arguments, she wrote, "the only moral choice is to vote against Amendment 62."

Whatever one's opinion on abortion, Hsieh's paper was a perfect example of pure political speech, protected – in theory – by the full force of the First Amendment. But because it contained a single sentence that urged readers to oppose a pending ballot initiative, Hsieh and her friend automatically qualified as an "Issue Committee" under a Colorado law that requires groups of two or more people who come together with "a major purpose of supporting or opposing any ballot issue" – or who give or receive "contributions or expenditures" of more than $200 to "support or oppose any ballot issue" – to register with the Secretary of State. The law is so broadly worded that if an organization spends only a third of its time on a political issue, that qualifies as "a major purpose." "Expenditure" might mean any cost associated with writing or printing Hsieh's 34-page paper. Had she omitted that one sentence, none of this would have mattered, but as it was, the law required her to register with the government.

Hsieh's failure to register marked only the beginning of her trouble. A group that fails to register is subject to investigation by the state's attorney general or by competing political groups, who can demand an administrative hearing to review suspected violations. Rival groups can demand detailed financial information and question a group's members – all of which causes anxiety and delay and requires expensive legal representation. Such rules can be a powerful weapon for censoring the opposition. In 2005, when the Independence Institute in Denver published a report about the potential costs of two referenda then pending before the voters, the bills' supporters filed a complaint with the Secretary of State, triggering a costly administrative hearing.[115]

Fearing similar prosecution, Hsieh filed a lawsuit to challenge the constitutionality of the Colorado laws. More than seven years later, the Tenth Circuit Court of Appeals finally ruled in her favor. Whatever "informational interest" the public might have in knowing who supports or opposes a ballot measure, the state's "onerous reporting requirements" were "too burdensome" for "small-scale" operations like Hsieh's.[116] Unfortunately, the Third Circuit Court of Appeals upheld a similar law in Delaware, and the Supreme Court has not yet resolved that disagreement.[117]

The basic assumption behind such restrictions is the Progressive premise that free speech is a privilege designed to serve collective goals rather than a right that each individual possesses. If government can "redistribute" speech rights to equalize the expression of opinion or ensure that public debate is "fair" rather than free, individual freedom will inevitably be sacrificed. Law professor Owen Fiss, an advocate of campaign finance rules, frankly admits that "we may sometimes find it necessary to restrict the speech of some elements of our society in order to enhance the relative voices of others."[118] He and other Progressives believe such restrictions are necessary to prevent those with more money or greater popularity – especially corporations – from using their advantages to gain a soapbox to express their ideas. They view corporate speech, or speech supported by wealthy advocates, as inherently corrupt because they envision the democratic process as one that aims at the vaguely defined goal of "social justice." Democracy should allocate resources in a "fair" manner, they believe, which typically involves taking from the wealthy and giving to the poor. As a result, they view political campaigns in which business owners oppose redistribution programs as essentially undemocratic – as distorting the "true" will of the people.[119]

Disturbingly, even the Supreme Court has used the term "corruption" to refer to the "distorting effects" that "immense aggregations of wealth" have on political debate, since that wealth has "little or no correlation to the public's support for [a] corporation's political ideals."[120] But there is nothing "corrupt" or "distorting" about famous people or wealthy corporations using their money or fame to promote a political position. Some people are better known, more knowledgeable, or more persuasive than others and therefore wield influence out of proportion to the public's support for their beliefs. But that is hardly a form of corruption.[121] People seeking to change their neighbors' minds will *often* have an influence out of proportion to the public's support for their ideals – that's just why they try to change what the public supports. Martin Luther King Jr.'s influence was certainly "out of proportion" to the public's support for his ideas, and segregationists regarded his fame and eloquence as having a "distorting" effect on politics, but that hardly justified censoring him. In fact, when King was jailed in Birmingham, it was for disobeying a law that required him to register with the government before expressing his political opinions.

A century ago, Progressives believed their reforms would "restore popular government as they imagined it to have existed in an earlier and purer age" and "make government accessible to the superior disinterestedness and honesty of the average citizen."[122] Today, they still hope that another round of regulations, and then another and yet another, will prevent "moneyed interests" from gaming the system. That is a foolish hope. Laws against free electioneering reinforce the security of incumbents and, ironically, close the door to anyone but the wealthy. This is because incumbents can obtain valuable news coverage for free by appearing on talk shows. *Face the Nation* or *Meet the Press* will always give airtime to a John McCain or a Russell Feingold – while a little-known challenger or outsider must buy airtime to compete. Campaign contribution limits make that prohibitively difficult. Incumbents thus get all the broadcast exposure they need, while idealistic newcomers are locked out. Meanwhile, because the Supreme Court has rightly declared that candidates cannot be barred from spending their own money to run for office, campaigning is increasingly a luxury that only wealthy candidates like Bushes or Clintons can afford.

Most alarmingly, campaign finance rules give powerful politicians an unjust power to threaten their critics. In the summer of 2004, Los Angeles radio talk show hosts John Kobylt and Ken Chiampou began a series of broadcasts complaining about what they saw as the Republican Party's failure to take the issue of illegal immigration seriously.[123] One of their targets was Orange County Congressman David Dreier, whom they accused of hypocrisy for speaking strongly about the problem but in practice doing nothing. In an effort to send the GOP a message about discontent among Republican voters, Kobylt and Chiampou encouraged listeners to vote against Dreier – their own candidate – in the coming election. They called their idea "fire Dreier" and "political human sacrifice," and in the end, it was moderately successful: Dreier won reelection, but by a much slimmer margin than anticipated.

Only weeks before the election, on October 14, 2006, the National Republican Congressional Committee sent the FEC a complaint, arguing that the "fire Dreier" broadcasts violated campaign finance regulations because they were a kind of unauthorized "contribution" to the campaign of Dreier's opponent. Because Kobylt and Chiampou broadcast on Los Angeles's powerful radio station KFI AM-640, which is owned by a corporation, the complaint asserted that the broadcasts were "illegal in-kind corporate contributions." Their broadcasts urging voters to vote against Dreier constituted "knowing and willful ... criminal" activity – indeed, "felonies," which "should be prosecuted to the fullest extent of the law."[124]

Fortunately, KFI's managers refused to cower before such threats, and the complaint went nowhere. But many station managers receiving such a letter would have been intimidated and no doubt would have ordered the troublemaking talk show hosts to shut up rather than pay the cost of legal defense. There is no other word for what the Republican Party attempted in that case than censorship – all made possible by campaign finance laws that supposedly advance "fair" and "democratic" outcomes.

Those who lose a political argument will often complain that the other side's success was somehow "unfair" or "disproportionate," but to restrict speech on that basis is a recipe for truly undemocratic results. Political incumbents could then use their power to restrict speech by their opposition. The only workable option is to let everyone who has something to say in the public debate, including individuals, unions, and corporations, do so – with their own money and without government enforcing "fair" or "proportionate" outcomes.

CHAPTER FOUR

Prior Restraint

and Businesses

IN THE EARLY YEARS of the twentieth century, while Supreme Court Justices Oliver Wendell Holmes and Louis Brandeis were fashioning their new collectivist theory of free speech, a cutting-edge communications technology was appearing on the scene: the motion picture. Many states adopted laws that prohibited the display of movies without pre-approval by the government – the classic prior restraint of speech. But when filmmakers challenged these restrictions in court, the resulting decisions changed forever how judges applied the protections promised by the First Amendment.

Thanks largely to those film censorship precedents, courts today allow government distressingly broad power to limit speech that involves some economic element. While judges typically give the strongest possible protection to "pure" speech, any communication associated with business – including advertising, the use of official titles like "accountant" or "attorney at law," and speech uttered by professionals in the course of their work – can be restricted with little interference from the courts.

* * *

The First Amendment Goes to Hollywood

Now that films have been around for a century and have become the nation's foremost medium of artistic expression, it is shocking to reflect that for the first 50 years of their existence, the Supreme Court did not regard movies as a form of speech *at all*, and accorded them minimal constitutional protection.

In 1915, D. W. Griffith's film *The Birth of a Nation* was shown at the White House to President Woodrow Wilson, whose racist writings on southern history the film repeatedly quoted. *The Birth of a Nation* proved to the world that movies were no fad: it told a gripping epic story, complete with chase scenes and special effects that astonished audiences of the day. Yet that same year, the court upheld an Ohio law that required pre-approval from a Board of Censors – the state was unashamed to use that term – before any motion picture could be shown in the state.[1] The Mutual Film Corporation, which a year later would sign the contract that made Charlie Chaplin rich, challenged the law as a prior restraint. But the Supreme Court unanimously ruled that "the exhibition of moving pictures is a business, pure and simple, originated and conducted for profit," and was therefore "not to be regarded ... as part of the press."[2] Both the law and the "common sense of the country," it said, were "against the contention" that "motion pictures and other spectacle" were shielded by the First Amendment.[3] Movies may entertain and instruct, but the idea of "extend[ing] the guaranties of free opinion and speech to the multitudinous shows which are advertised on the billboards of our cities and towns" was "wrong or strained." "Besides," the court added, "there are some things which should not have pictorial representation in public places and to all audiences."[4]

Some found the decision wrongheaded at the time. An unsigned article in the *Columbia Law Review* commented that it could only be "regarded as exhibiting the tendency of the court to construe constitutional provisions [loosely] rather than invalidate legislation which is directly connected with the interests of public safety and morals."[5] Yet for the same reason, the *Michigan Law Review* praised the ruling for taking a "modern progressive view of the subject."[6]

In 1922, a New York court upheld a law requiring makers of *newsreels* to get pre-approved by a government censorship board. Admitting that motion pictures were "a medium of thought,"[7] the court nevertheless found that they were also "something more" – films "reproduce[d] the life of the world" so vividly that their "value as an educator for good is only equaled by [their] danger as an instructor in evil." Children in particular needed to be shielded from the sight of real news until they learned enough from the "school of experience" that "current events may be revealed in all their nakedness."[8]

In another case, a New York judge struck down the censorship of a film that editorialized against the state's anti-contraception laws – bravely insisting that it was "needless to speak of the importance of freedom of speech in a republic like ours"[8] – but was promptly overruled. That film, made by birth control crusader Margaret Sanger, depicted nothing obscene or lewd, but simply made the case for legalizing contraception. It was, wrote Judge Nathaniel Bijur, "a pictured argument against an existing law."[10] Relying on the *Lochner* decision for the idea that government regulations must be "fair, reasonable, and appropriate" rather than "unreasonable, unnecessary, and arbitrary interference[s] with the right of the individual to his personal liberty," Bijur ruled the ban invalid.[11] But a higher court reversed his decision. "The Legislature has declared it to be against the public interests to have contraceptive information disseminated," it declared.[12] Therefore "the matter must be left to the official to whom the Legislature has delegated authority."[13]

As Hollywood became increasingly sophisticated, laws requiring government approval before films could be displayed caused more and more problems for the industry. Censorship boards in different places imposed different, often subjective standards, meaning that a film might be approved in New York City but banned in Kansas or Minnesota. Delays also made it impossible for studios to release the same movie across the country on the same day. Filmmakers tried to resolve the arbitrariness and delays caused by local censorship boards by creating the Motion Picture Association of America (MPAA), a private group that would implement a form of "voluntary" censorship. But not until 1930 was the MPAA able to take the lead within the industry.

By then, films had become a respected medium of artistic expression, political argument, and social commentary. Yet it was still another two decades before the Supreme Court overruled the *Mutual Film* case and acknowledged that movies were entitled to full constitutional protection. In 1948, in the midst of an antitrust lawsuit against movie studios, Justice William Douglas commented that there was "no doubt that moving pictures, like newspapers and radio, are included in the press whose freedom is guaranteed by the First Amendment,"[14] but because that was not directly at issue, his words technically had no legal force. Only in 1952 did the justices make it official, declaring that "motion pictures are a significant medium for the communication of ideas" and were protected by the Constitution.[15]

That case, however, made no mention of the nation's many existing film censorship boards. The court simply declared that it was "not necessary for us to decide" whether it was constitutional for states to prohibit the display of movies without permission.[16] Such rules were obviously prior restraints that, as the court said in *Near v. Minnesota*, were "generally, if not universally, considered" unconstitutional.[17] Yet the court left them in place. In 1961, it rejected the argument that such pre-approval requirements were always invalid, holding that states could impose them in "exceptional cases."[18] But film censorship rules were not "exceptions." They were systematically applied to all movies in many states.

Five years later, the court again watered down the once-absolute rule that the First Amendment forbids prior restraints on speech. That case involved a Baltimore theater manager named Ronald Freedman, who was arrested and convicted when he refused on principle to apply for a permit before showing a movie called *Revenge at Daybreak*.[19] State officials admitted that the film was unobjectionable and that Freedman would have been given a license if he had applied, but showing the movie without a permit was still a crime. Before the Supreme Court, Freedman argued again that prior restraints on speech were intolerable, but instead of enforcing that long-standing rule, the justices transformed it into a set of flexible procedural standards instead: "a noncriminal process which requires the prior submission of a film to a censor" could "avoid[] constitutional infirmity," they wrote, if there were "procedural safeguards" in place "to obviate the dangers of a censorship system."[20]

Three such "safeguards" were essential: First, the censors must bear the burden of justifying censorship, rather than requiring the theater to justify showing the film. Second, the ultimate decision about the licensing rule must be made by a judge, not the government itself. Third, state laws forcing people to get permits before displaying movies must include specific time limits within which bureaucrats would decide whether to grant or deny permits. This would protect filmmakers and theater managers from being left in limbo.[21]

These safeguards were certainly better than nothing. But the rule against prior restraints had never before been described in these merely procedural terms. Instead, that rule had been categorical: the government simply could not require an author a speaker to obtain approval before speaking. This was *partly* because the delay and uncertainty of licensing requirements are problematic, but it was also because enabling the government to choose what communications would be allowed inevitably deters the expression of controversial messages or the display of innovative, potentially offensive artworks. Most of all, such restrictions on speech violate the fundamental human right to freely express one's opinions. Yet the *Freed-*

man decision proclaimed that the once-absolute protection against prior restraints was actually not absolute. It and similar cases expanded the First Amendment, by recognizing that it covered films, but did so at the cost of diluting the amendment's strength.[22]

This dilution of the rule against prior restraints was foreshadowed by Justice Felix Frankfurter, the Progressive author of the *Gobitis* flag-salute decision. In 1957, he had ruled in favor of New York City officials who sought an injunction forbidding the sale of a book depicting sadomasochistic sex, under a state law that banned "printed matter of an indecent character."[23] Relying on the *Near* precedent, the publisher argued that an injunction would be an unconstitutional prior restraint. But Frankfurter rejected that contention. "The phrase 'prior restraint,'" he wrote, cannot be regarded as "talismanic." Rather than enforcing a consistent, principled rule against prior restraints, courts should employ a "pragmatic assessment" and weigh the "particular circumstances" involved in any case of censorship. "The generalization that prior restraint is particularly obnoxious ... must yield to more particularistic analysis."[24] The *Freedman* decision now made Frankfurter's flexible approach the law of the land.

The Fairness Doctrine As a Prior Restraint

Frankfurter's "pragmatic" attitude proved convenient to federal regulators with the advent of radio and television. The power of the Federal Communications Commission (FCC) to grant or withhold broadcasting licenses put officials in the position of choosing which broadcasts the American public would be allowed to hear and see.

One rule FCC regulators devised proved especially potent: the "fairness doctrine," adopted in 1949, which forced station owners to present political disputes in a way that "fairly" presented opposing views. Any station that aired a political opinion was required to provide time for people who disagreed, on pain of losing its license. The effect was to impose a type of prior restraint: owners, knowing that speaking their minds would require them to donate costly broadcast time to air contrary opinions, often chose to avoid expressing any opinion at all.

When, in 1964, a Pennsylvania radio station aired a discussion of a book critical of Republican presidential candidate Barry Goldwater, the book's author demanded airtime to respond. The station refused, and the author sued. The case reached the Supreme Court, which unanimously upheld the equal time requirement. "It is the right of the viewers and listeners, not the right of the broadcasters, which is paramount," it declared,[25] citing Progressive Era precedents that characterized speech as a means of collective decision-making rather than an element of individual freedom. "It is the purpose of the First Amendment to preserve an uninhibited marketplace of ideas in which truth will ultimately prevail," wrote Justice Byron White. "It is the right of the public to receive suitable access to social, political, esthetic, moral, and other ideas and experiences which is crucial here."[26] Thus the station's owners could be forced to express ideas they found repugnant, because the Constitution was concerned not with protecting individual rights but with advancing an abstract, collective interest in thorough public debate.

A year later, the FCC revoked the license of another Pennsylvania station on the grounds that it had broadcast a show by a controversial clergyman named Rev. Carl McIntire without allowing rebuttal time for McIntire's critics. Upholding the FCC's decision, a federal appeals court declared once again that the First Amendment's primary purpose was to ensure "that the public be given access to varied information,"[27] not to protect the rights of individuals. McIntire argued that he had paid the station for the broadcast time, and when an angry listener demanded that he be given an opportunity to respond on the air, McIntire replied that the station's broadcast time "is ours and not yours; nor does it belong to both of us with an obligation upon me to share it equally with you."[28] The court rejected this idea as "more brazen bravado than brains."[29] Broadcasters had no right to present "one sided" discussions of "issues of controversial importance" or to go "on an independent frolic broadcasting what [they] chose, in any terms [they] chose."[30]

Courts sometimes denied that the fairness rule was a prior restraint, since it did not force broadcasters to submit material for approval before broadcast.[31] But it still had the effect of "chilling" expression, particularly by bold and outspoken voices, who were essentially taxed whenever they expressed their views. This chilling effect was only eased in the late 1980s, when the FCC abandoned the fairness doctrine – leading to a flourishing of new, interesting, politically oriented radio and TV shows by such successful and controversial hosts as Rush Limbaugh and Al Franken.

Behind the explicit prior restraint of movies and the implicit restraint of the fairness doctrine was the Progressive conception of free speech as a collective enterprise instead of an individual right. This "democratic impetus" as one scholar calls it – the view that the First Amendment is primarily concerned with ensuring "that the political community [will] hear a wide range of opinions"[32] – led to a series of rules that allowed government to veto the expression of unpopular, controversial, or offensive ideas and to force people to subsidize the expression of opinions they despised.

Titling and Occupational Licensing

Even outside the realm of politics, government frequently imposes prior restraints on speech when money is involved. And thanks to legal precedents that transformed the long-standing rule against prior restraints into a weak, "pragmatic" set of procedural requirements, courts usually allow such restraints to stand. Today, many professionals are prohibited from using certain words to describe their services or are subjected to rules that restrict what they can say to their clients. Some occupations consist of nothing but speech itself – tour guides, for example – yet the government bars people from practicing these "talking professions" without a license or imposes laws that define speech as a kind of business for which a license is required. The consequences are the same: barring people from speaking unless they are licensed first. But courts typically refuse to call these laws what they are: unconstitutional prior restraints on speech.

In 1991, Texas passed a law forbidding people from describing themselves as "interior designers" without satisfying certain standards. Technically speaking, such a "titling law" is not an occupational licensing law because a person may still actually *do* interior designing without government approval. But it was illegal to use the term "interior designer" on business cards, websites, or advertisements without two years of post–high school education and six years of education and experience in interior design. Designers also had to pass a state test.[33] In essence, the state confiscated the words "interior designer" and only allowed people to use them if they got government permission – a classic prior restraint on speech.

Proponents of titling laws often say that they protect consumers by forbidding businesses from claiming expertise they lack. But consumer protection laws already bar them from defrauding or injuring customers. And laws that make it illegal to truthfully describe one's business, as the Texas interior designer law did, cannot ensure that consumers are fully informed. On the contrary, they deprive consumers of information they need. This is unsurprising, since titling laws are actually meant not to protect consumers but to restrict economic competition against the existing industry. Established firms can satisfy the sometimes stringent requirements for titling, while a person who wants to start a new business, or who has little experience, or who finds college too expensive, cannot. Titling laws therefore allow existing companies to limit consumer choice and charge customers more.

The First Amendment, however, forbids the government from requiring people to get official permission before uttering certain words. A person who designs interiors *is* an interior designer and should be free to say so. Restricting him from using the term unless he gets a certificate from the American Society of Interior Designers (ASID) – the trade group that lobbies for titling laws – does not protect the public. It only protects the ASID's turf against newcomers who might change the industry.

That was the argument a group of would-be designers made in 2009 when they challenged the Texas law in court. They argued that it violated their right to freedom of expression. In reply, the state's lawyers argued that it would be "misleading" for people to use the title "interior designer" without state approval because the state had declared those words off-limits to anyone without a license. The Fifth Circuit Court of Appeals rejected that argument as "circular."[34] A law that bars people who practice interior design from truthfully calling themselves by that term, the judges ruled, violates the First Amendment.[35]

More intrusive than titling laws are licensing laws that forbid people from engaging in professions that consist entirely of speech – "talking professions" such as teachers, psychologists, and tour guides – unless they get the government's permission. Strangely enough, judges have never managed to explain why the government may require people to get approval before practicing professions that consist entirely of communication. Such licensing laws are often indistinguishable from the sorts of prior restraints on speech that the Constitution supposedly forbids.

Consider psychology. Unlike psychiatrists, psychologists do not prescribe medicines. They use only communicative and mental therapies: talking, thinking, feeling, remembering, and coaching. Psychologists receive extensive training in theories of the mind and learn about mental illness, phobias, eating disorders, stress, and the like, as well as techniques that aim to remedy these problems. But as sophisticated as the practice of psychology has become, it still remains *talk* – the communication of ideas. A psychologist might counsel a patient with a phobia to confront her fear, or to try a mental trick to deal with it, or to talk out her past experiences to make the fear go away. Trained psychologists may be better at what they do and have more knowledge and training than laymen, but the therapies they administer are still *speech* – no different in constitutional terms from the advice offered by friends, pastors, rabbis, teachers, coaches, grandparents, or radio talk show hosts.

Nevertheless, every state requires psychologists to get government licenses. These laws purport to regulate the "practice" of psychology – actions – but those actions are made up entirely of communication. California, for example, makes it a crime to professionally "render ... any psychological service involving the application of psychological principles, methods, and procedures of understanding, predicting, and influencing behavior, such as the principles pertaining to learning, perception, motivation, emotions, and interpersonal relationships," without a license. The law goes on to prohibit any unlicensed person from using "psychological methods" to help someone "acquire greater human effectiveness or to modify feelings, conditions, attitudes and behavior which are emotionally, intellectually, or socially ineffectual or maladjustive."[36]

These are all acts of communication. Suggesting that someone meditate to relieve stress or envision his goals to better achieve them, or encouraging him to get right with God, or just letting a person talk through his problems – these are all efforts to assist that person in modifying maladjustive attitudes and behavior. Friends, relatives, and office mates use psychological principles all the time to advise people and change their motivation or fix their interpersonal problems. Psychologists are better trained at it than others, but such training cannot justify forbidding non-psychologists from engaging in communication without government approval. It was because they recognized that fact that California lawmakers added a long list of exemptions for religious leaders, medical doctors, clinical social workers, marriage therapists, nurses, lawyers, and even dentists and optometrists – who receive absolutely no training in psychology.[37] If unlicensed psychology is so dangerous, it would make no sense to allow these people to practice without a license. Yet the law does just that.

The licensing of physicians or pharmacists is typically justified on the grounds that they prescribe medicines, touch patients, or conduct surgery. Other professionals also enjoy special state privileges – lawyers, for instance, can issue subpoenas to force people to testify or to hand over documents. Licensing these professions is supposed to protect the public by limiting who may distribute pills or exercise subpoena powers. But psychologists engage only in communication, and licensing laws for them only restrict free speech. Nor is there a long tradition of such licensing requirements. Doctor and lawyer licensing has been around since ancient Roman times, but psychologist licensing was unknown until 1945.[38] When the First Amendment was written in the 1780s, the idea that someone could be forced to get government permission before giving people advice about their troubles would have been regarded as absurd and unconstitutional.

A group of psychoanalysts challenged California's licensing requirement in a lawsuit in 2000, but the Ninth Circuit Court of Appeals ruled against them, concluding that the state's purpose in regulating the profession was to protect the safety of patients who, if treated by an incompetent analyst, might be at risk of deteriorating mental health, job and family stress, "and even suicide."[39] There was no actual evidence of such risks; the court accepted without question the state's claim that such risks "might" follow – a degree of credulity courts are not supposed to employ in free speech cases. Nevertheless, the court declared that the licensing requirement was not a prior restraint but instead "a valid licensing scheme designed to protect the mental health of Californians."[40]

This, however, was always the rationale used to justify prior restraints: seventeenth-century laws requiring pre-approval before the publishing a book were also designed to "protect" people from the harms that "might" follow from unrestricted speech. If the risk that bad advice might cause depression or suicide is good reason to prohibit certain kinds of speech, why not impose the same rule on pastors, neighbors, coworkers, and friends? The court's answer was that psychologists charge for their services, while friends and neighbors do not. But the Supreme Court has repeatedly declared that speech still receives full First Amendment protection even if the speaker charges a fee.[41] Newspapers, after all, are also published for profit.

Government officials charged with regulating psychology have even tried to censor newspaper advice columnists. In 2013, a writer named John Rosemond received a threatening letter from the Kentucky Board of Examiners of Psychology, warning him that his syndicated parenting-advice column constituted the unlicensed practice of psychology.[42] Rosemond, a licensed family counselor in his home state of North Carolina, had been writing his column for nearly 40 years before the board decided that, because it appeared in Kentucky newspapers, Rosemond also needed to get a license in that state. They sent him a cease-and-desist order, threatening him with fines and even criminal prosecution.

Rosemond went to court, arguing that his articles qualified as pure, old-fashioned First Amendment speech, no different from the Dear Abby columns newspapers have published for decades. In fact, America's first advice columnist was probably Benjamin Franklin, who, under the pseudonym Silence Dogood, published answers to reader letters (many of which he wrote himself) decades before he helped write the Constitution. Neither he nor Dear Abby went to college or held licenses. It's hard to imagine that he and his colleagues thought the Constitution allowed the government to impose a licensing requirement on the publication of a newspaper column. Fortunately, in September 2015, a federal judge ruled in Rosemond's favor and ordered Kentucky bureaucrats to stop pursuing him.[43]

Perhaps no profession is more innocuous than that of a tour guide. Skilled guides can teach fun and interesting facts about museums or cities, and tours are often designed around special or obscure interests. Some guides on Boston's Freedom Trail dress up in period costume and pretend to be people from Revolutionary times. Some Los Angeles tour guides take people on "Haunted Hollywood" tours, telling them ghost stories that center on movie industry landmarks. There are certainly dull or incompetent tour guides in the world, but bad tour guides do not hurt people. They might be boring or get their facts wrong, but they are unlikely to cause anyone an injury. Laws against robbery or fraud already prevent rogue tour guides, if there are such things, from stealing people's money. Nevertheless, several cities, including New Orleans and Washington, D.C., make it a crime to take people on tours without a government license.

A group of guides sued New Orleans in 2013, arguing that the city's licensing requirement violated the First Amendment, but federal judges disagreed. Because the city was not restricting what the guides could say, only requiring them to take a class on city history and pass a test, the trial judge declared that the rule "applies to conduct, not speech."[44] The court of appeals agreed. "Those who have the license can speak as they please," wrote Judge Thomas Reavley. "Tour guides may talk but what they say is not regulated or affected by New Orleans."[45] That was true, but it was beside the point. Any rule requiring him to get permission before he can speak is still an infringement on his First Amendment rights, even if the government allows people to speak freely after they get licenses. The law is a prior restraint because it forbids anyone who has not taken the required class and passed the test to lead people around the city and talk to them.

Judges in Washington, D.C., took a different view. Judge Janice Rodgers Brown scornfully struck down that city's tour guide licensing law, noting that there was no reason to think uneducated tour guides were a real danger to the public. "The only record 'evidence' supporting the District's beliefs regarding the perils of unlicensed tour guides," she wrote, consisted of "deposition testimony that guides with criminal convictions might pose a danger, though no evidence exists they actually have." The government argued that, like New Orleans, the District of Columbia left guides free to speak as they pleased, but Judge Brown pointed out that this very fact undercut the rationale for licensing in the first place. If consumers really needed protection against incompetent tour guides, there was no sense in *not* restricting what guides could say: "Exactly how does a tour guide with carte blanche to – Heaven forfend – call the White House the Washington Monument further the District's interest in ensuring a quality consumer experience?"[46]

The Professional Speech Doctrine

Government often imposes prior restraints on speech by categorizing it as a "profession" that requires a license. Nevada law, for example, requires private investigators to get licenses, but until it was amended in 2015, the law defined a "private investigator" as anyone who is paid to "obtain" or "furnish ... information" about the "identity, habits, conduct, business, occupation, honesty, integrity, credibility, knowledge, trustworthiness, efficiency, loyalty, activity, movement, whereabouts, affiliations, associations, transactions, acts, reputation or character of any person," or the "location, disposition or recovery of lost or stolen property," or the "cause or responsibility for ... accidents or damage or injury to persons or to property," or about any "crime or tort that has been committed ... or suspected."[47] To provide such information without first getting government approval was deemed a crime. Certain categories of people – including lawyers, insurance adjustors, and people working at banks[48] – were exempt, but the prohibition plainly applied to reporters, historians, genealogists, and tour guides. To teach a class about the murder of Abraham Lincoln, or to write a biography of him, or to publish an article about his "reputation" and "character" was therefore forbidden.

In 2013, the state's Private Investigator Licensing Board prosecuted a man who testified as an expert witness in two civil trials,[49] despite the fact that testifying in court is quintessential First Amendment speech. After that happened, the legislature promptly changed the statute to exempt expert witnesses – but others remained at risk. After California-based investigator Troy Castillo filed suit arguing that the requirement violated the Constitution, state officials argued that there was nothing wrong with forbidding people from furnishing information unless they are "thoroughly vetted" by the government.[50] Castillo's lawsuit ultimately helped persuade the legislature to change the law so that it no longer applies to people who only access or provide "public information."[51]

The Supreme Court has occasionally warned that the government may not classify speech as an "activity" and require a license for that activity. "It is well settled that a speaker's rights are not lost merely because compensation is received," wrote Justice William Brennan in one case. "[A] speaker is no less a speaker because he or she is paid to speak." Yet under a legal theory called the "professional speech doctrine," some courts have held that the First Amendment imposes no restriction *at all* on laws that forbid licensed professionals such as doctors, psychologists, and stockbrokers from communicating information. This has the strange consequence that while government cannot censor speech *outside* a profession, it can block certain types of speech *within* a profession: if a layman recommends that a friend take an aspirin to relieve a headache, that speech receives the strongest constitutional protection available – but if a trained and licensed doctor gives the same advice to the same person, his speech is entirely unprotected by the Constitution, and the government may censor him at will. Still more confusingly, some courts have declared that the speech of licensed professionals should receive *more* protection than other kinds of speech. And, most astonishingly of all, the professional speech doctrine has never been endorsed, *or even discussed*, by the United States Supreme Court. Lower courts have patched it together in response to two non-binding, concurring opinions from cases in 1945 and 1985.

The first case struck down a law that required any person acting as a union recruiter to get a government license. This, the court declared, was an unconstitutional prior restraint.[52] The government might call union recruiting an "activity," but the activity consisted only of communication, so the licensing requirement really prohibited free speech.[53] In a concurring opinion, Justice Robert Jackson observed that it is sometimes hard to draw a line between regulating businesses and regulating speech, because "the one may shade into the other."[54] But he offered no solution to the problem except to say that lawmakers should not be free to restrict speech by labeling it a business.

The second case, *Lowe v. SEC*,[55] involved a professional investment advisor named Christopher Lowe who had been stripped of his license after being convicted of fraud charges. A year later, Lowe began publishing a newsletter about the stock market. The Securities and Exchange Commission (SEC) charged him with illegally offering investment advice without a license. But Lowe argued that he was only publishing his ideas and requiring him to get a license before printing his opinions was an unconstitutional prior restraint. The Supreme Court issued a narrow ruling that did not address the First Amendment question but held that Lowe had not actually violated the law. But three justices, led by Justice Byron White, disagreed. In a separate opinion, they argued that Lowe had broken the law when he published his opinions but that the law was unconstitutional.

"[T]he principle that the government may restrict entry into professions and vocations through licensing schemes has never been extended to encompass the licensing of speech," White declared. "At some point, a measure is no longer a regulation of a profession but a regulation of speech or of the press; beyond that point, the statute must survive the level of scrutiny demanded by the First Amendment."[56] In White's view, the difference between the two was that a professional "takes the affairs of a client personally in hand and purports to exercise judgment on behalf of the client in the light of the client's individual needs and circumstances" – and such a person is engaged not in constitutionally protected speech but in activities the government may regulate. The government could also regulate any speech "incidental to the conduct of the profession."[57] Because Lowe was only speaking and not engaging in professional activities, he should not have been prosecuted.

In the three decades since *Lowe* was decided, lower courts have relied upon these opinions by Justices White and Jackson to declare that states may limit the speech rights of professionals without violating the First Amendment – despite the fact that the two opinions actually disagree in an important way: Jackson believed that when professional activity combines with speech, the courts should provide *more* First Amendment protection, whereas White thought such a combination should *reduce* the protections for speech. Be that as it may, neither opinion is binding law, and because White's discussion of professional speech was not necessary to his conclusion, it would not be binding even if all the other justices had agreed with him. Given such meager guidance from the Supreme Court, the nation's judges have fashioned a set of confusing, sometimes self-contradictory rules, which allow state lawmakers to substitute their own preferences for the educated judgment of the doctors, psychologists, and other professionals they regulate.[58]

One controversial example involves efforts by psychologists and counselors to change the sexual orientation of their patients. The validity of such therapy is hotly contested, yet when lawmakers in California and New Jersey passed laws banning the therapy, psychologists sued, arguing that since their practice consists solely of communication, such restrictions violate the First Amendment. Both courts rejected that argument. The professional speech doctrine, they held, allows the government to dictate what kinds of advice professionals may offer their patients.[59] But as one dissenting judge observed in the California case, giving government so much power to classify speech as an "activity" and to control it by law is a dangerous step toward censorship. "If a state may freely regulate speech uttered by professionals in the course of their practice without implicating the First Amendment, then targeting disfavored moral and political expression may only be a matter of creative legislative draftsmanship."[60]

Worsening the confusion,[61] some courts have said that the Constitution should give professional speech *more* protection than ordinary speech, considering the greater education and training professionals receive. In one recent case, the Fourth Circuit struck down a North Carolina law that forced doctors to discourage patients from having abortions. The doctors were required to show each patient a sonogram of the fetus, explain its location and dimensions, and say whether it had visible fingers or internal organs. The doctor also had to offer the woman a chance to listen to its heartbeat.[62] Although the patient was allowed to cover her ears or close her eyes, the physician was required to recite the litany no matter what – even if he thought it caused the patient to suffer.

A group of doctors sued, arguing that forcing them to express opinions with which they disagreed – and to manipulate their patients through guilt and shame into a course of conduct doctors themselves might consider harmful – offended the Constitution. Relying on the precedents that upheld bans on sexual-orientation therapy, state officials replied that the law only regulated professional speech and therefore was not subject to the First Amendment review. They admitted that the law was designed "to support the state's pro-life position," but the professional speech doctrine meant the state could force doctors to comply, just as California and New Jersey lawmakers could enforce their views about what psychological therapies are appropriate.[63]

The court found the law unconstitutional. Doctors, it said, "do not leave their speech rights at the office door."[64] However broad the state's power to regulate medicine, it may not force doctors to express opinions they do not hold.[65] In fact, the North Carolina statute went further than that, requiring doctors to "use the visual imagery of the fetus to dissuade the patient from continuing with the planned procedure."[66] And this interfered with doctors' professional judgment. Being forced to express the state's message "regardless of whether the patient is listening" and while the patient was stressed and impaired – "half-naked or disrobed on her back on an examination table, with an ultrasound probe either on her belly or inserted into her vagina" – was "in direct contravention of medical ethics and the principle of patient autonomy."[67] This "virtually unprecedented burden on the right of professional speech" offended the First Amendment.[68] But other federal courts have upheld similar laws that force physicians to show patients sonograms, to play the audio of fetal heartbeats,[69] and to tell patients that a fetus is "a whole, separate, unique, living human being" – a proposition with which many doctors disagree.[70]

Although the freedom of speech is generally considered foremost among constitutional rights, courts give it less protection in cases that involve business and economic affairs. Government is free to censor what entrepreneurs can call themselves, to compel businesses to speak against their will, and to force professionals to get government permission before they may communicate messages to others. The Constitution promises that all people will be free to express themselves without government interference. But when it comes to businesspeople, the idea that free speech is not a right, only a privilege the government may give or take away, has dangerously undermined the protections of the First Amendment.

CHAPTER FIVE

THE COMPETITOR'S VETO

STARTING A NEW business is risky and exhausting. Accumulating capital, doing market research, hiring talent – all these tasks and more make opening a small business among the hardest things a person can ever attempt. But people surmount these obstacles because the rewards of working for themselves can be enormous, whatever the risks. Economic independence and opportunity are a crucial part of the liberty protected by the Constitution. We are all indebted to the entrepreneurs who developed some new idea into a business and thus improved our lives.

Sadly, government often imposes a kind of prior restraint on economic opportunity: licensing laws, which block people who want to go into a business from doing so without the government's permission. In fact, nearly a third of all Americans now need some form of permit to practice their trades,[1] and getting one can be hard. Some licensing laws require a person to have a college degree or to take years of classes and pass a difficult examination, all of which takes time and money that many entrepreneurs don't have. But while licensing is supposed to ensure that doctors, lawyers, massage therapists, or taxi drivers are trained, competent, and honest, many licensing laws do nothing to protect the public. They exist simply to prevent competition against existing businesses that already have licenses.

The Supreme Court has made clear that everyone has a constitutional right to earn a living at a job of his or her choice and that while government may require a person to get a license before taking a job, any such licensing laws must relate to the person's "fitness and capacity to practice" that business.[2] Unfortunately, state and local governments often ignore this rule and impose licensing requirements that have little to do with whether a person is honest or qualified.[3] In fact, one kind of licensing law, called a "Certificate of Public Convenience and Necessity" or "Certificate of Need" (CON) requirement, is intended solely to prohibit competition, regardless of whether a business owner is honest and competent. CON laws do not require that people be qualified. They prohibit people from starting a new business, *regardless* of their qualifications, unless they first get permission *from all the existing businesses in the industry*. Hence their nickname: "the Competitor's Veto."

Raleigh Bruner and Michael Munie

Devised in the late nineteenth century to regulate railroads and other public utilities,[4] CON laws exist in many varieties and apply to many different industries – taxi companies, limousine drivers, moving companies, liquor stores, car lots, even hospitals.[5] Unsurprisingly, existing firms use these laws to block potential competition, drive up the cost of living for consumers, and deprive entrepreneurs of their constitutionally guaranteed right to economic liberty.

In 2010, shortly after earning an MBA from the University of Kentucky, Raleigh Bruner decided to start a moving business. He hired 31 people and put together a fleet of five moving trucks, which he painted with the name of his company: Wildcat Moving, in honor of the university's beloved basketball team. But on May 21, 2011, he got a letter from state officials warning him that his business was operating illegally. Bruner was shocked. He and his employees were fully qualified, with clean safety records. Customers were happy and had rated the company highly on Yelp! and Angie's List. But the state was trying to shut him down because he had not received a CON, and the requirements to get one seemed absurd.[6] First, he had to fill out a lengthy application, providing details about his financing and insurance. Then, before filing the application, he had to notify every licensed moving company in the state and invite them to file objections, called "protests," against his application.[7] (A person or company filing a protest was referred to as a "protestant.") State officials would then hold a hearing to decide whether to grant Bruner a CON,[8] and the protestants could participate in the hearing to oppose him.

That hearing would not be about whether Bruner was qualified. Instead, state transportation officials would focus on whether the state's existing moving companies were "adequate" and whether Wildcat Moving "is or will be required by the present or future public convenience and necessity." These legal terms had no clear legal meaning. Vague words like "need," "inadequate," and "present or future public convenience and necessity" were not defined in any statute, regulation, or court decision in Kentucky.[9] It's hard to guess how bureaucrats could determine what *future* public needs might be, let alone how they were to predict future *convenience*,[10] particularly given the fact that, as one official later testified, they used "no independent standard[s] or document[s] or list of factors or statistics" when making such determinations.[11]

Even if Bruner could be sure that he would get a license, the hearing procedure was an expensive and time-consuming process. Like many states, Kentucky law requires that businesses like Wildcat Moving hire a lawyer to represent them at the hearing – Bruner was not allowed to represent the company himself. And from the filing of a protest to an ultimate decision took, on average, ten months.[12] Protestants were not required to submit any evidence before triggering this expensive delay. Protests did not need to be signed, notarized, or accompanied by affidavits.[13] Simply saying that they were opposed to new competition was enough. And even if no protests were filed, Bruner would still need to prove that there was "a need for [his] service" before getting a license to operate.[14]

Bruner was not alone. A year earlier, a St. Louis entrepreneur named Michael Munie was threatened with prosecution under a similar CON law when he sought to expand his moving company beyond the city's limits. Munie had worked in the moving business since he was 16 and started building his own company from scratch in 1990. Over time, that company, ABC Quality Moving, grew to employ 15 people. "I treat my employees like they're family," he said. "When you take good care of your staff, they take good care of your customers, who tell other people about their good experience with your business."[15]

ABC became the top-rated St. Louis–area moving company on Angie's List. Munie did not have a CON, but his business was still legal because Missouri law exempted certain major cities, including St. Louis, from the requirement. That meant Munie could move people's belongings within the city, and because he also had a federal transportation license, he could move them across the river into Illinois or to any other state. But he could not move things anywhere else in Missouri unless he first got a CON.

Missouri's law, like Kentucky's, was riddled with the vague language and anticompetitive rules typical of CON requirements.[16] Munie would first have to prove to the government that he was "fit, willing and able" to run a moving company – a simple assessment of his safety and honesty, which Munie did not object to. But he would also have to prove that ABC Quality Moving would "serve a useful present or future public purpose," and if any existing company filed a protest – called an "intervention" in Missouri – he would have to prove that his business would be consistent with "the public convenience and necessity."[17] Once again, the law did not explain what "useful present or future public purpose" or "public convenience and necessity" meant.[18] In fact, the phrase "useful present or future public purpose" appeared in no other law in the nation. Such opaque language gave bureaucrats unlimited discretion to decide what sorts of purposes were "useful" or not, now or in the "future."

One thing was clear: the law expressly required bureaucrats to evaluate "the diversion of revenue or traffic from existing carriers"[19] – that is, they would have to determine whether Munie would successfully compete against the businesses that opposed his request for a license. If he would, the law suggested (if it did not require) that bureaucrats reject his application for a CON. Even if Munie could persuade them not to, the whole thing could take a long time. Once an intervention was filed, the average wait for a CON application was almost six months and could be as long as three years.[20]

Why CON Laws Make No Sense

The idea of prohibiting businesses from starting unless they first get permission from their own competitors began with nineteenth-century regulations of railroads.[21] The theory was that such restrictions would prevent "wasteful duplication" of services and bar "excessive competition." CON laws would also prevent what economists call "cream-skimming" – which occurs when a business refuses to engage in government-mandated but inefficient business practices, such as providing train service to small, isolated towns. CON laws were also meant to encourage private investments in public utilities and to empower the government to stop businesses from polluting or engaging in other undesirable practices.[22]

But now that they have been on the books for a century, these arguments have been either rendered obsolete or revealed as wrong-headed. For example, while the effort to prevent cream-skimming or to protect private investment in public services might make sense with regard to public utilities like railroads or buses, it doesn't make sense when applied to ordinary competitive businesses like moving companies. Cream-skimming occurs when a business seeks an advantage over its competitors by avoiding the costly practices that the government forces those competitors to engage in. If the government mandates that a railroad serve small, out-of-the-way towns at an economic loss, a competing railroad might "skim the cream" by serving only profitable routes. CON laws were supposed to prevent this by ensuring that all railroads served those isolated towns. Yet this argument contradicts the argument that CON laws reduce waste; the cream-skimming theory holds that the government should *force* companies to engage in wasteful practices. The "cream" is only there for the "skimming" because the government requires inefficient behavior.[23] "Often what is characterized as 'cream skimming,'" write legal scholars Herbert Hovenkamp and John A. Mackerron, "is really a sign that, because of technological change, the market is becoming competitive."[24]

Encouraging private investment in public utilities may also have been an important goal in the past, but in the years since CON laws were invented, it has become less relevant. In the 1880s, public utility services were often provided by private contractors acting under some form of government charter: trolleys and streetcars, for example, were privately owned but operated as government franchises. By forestalling competition against them, CON laws were thought to encourage private investors to build and operate these utilities, just as patents are today seen as incentives for researchers and inventors.

But during the Progressive Era, government replaced many of these private utilities with a civil service system under which government owns and operates utilities directly, rather than outsourcing them to favored corporations.[25] This shift away from the franchise system made CON laws largely unnecessary: fewer private investors needed the promise of a near monopoly because the streetcars they once financed were now built and run with tax dollars instead.

Certainly Bruner's and Munie's moving companies did not

compete with trains or with government-run businesses. They were ordinary private companies in a competitive market, like any car wash or sandwich shop, and should have been governed by the same basic public safety rules as those businesses, instead of being shoehorned into a category fashioned in the days of the iron horse. As for preventing pollution, the deterioration of roads, or other kinds of social harms, these goals are better served through environmental regulations, nuisance lawsuits, inspections, and other ordinary rules than by forcing companies to get permission from their own competition before operating.

In practice, bureaucrats rarely consider these factors in the CON process anyway. Instead, they simply block new companies from competing if they think there are already "enough" companies in business, without asking whether the newcomer might actually run a better, cleaner operation, or damage the roads less than existing companies do.

The justification most often given for CON laws is that they prevent "wasteful duplication" and "excessive competition." These arguments reflect an economic theory fashionable a century ago, which held that free markets were inefficient and destructive.[26] Some writers thought that it was wasteful to allow people to establish multiple railroad lines between the same cities if only one rail line was really needed.[27] Free competition would drive prices down, progressively forcing railroads to cut services and quality in order to stay solvent. Eventually they would go bankrupt, and consumers would be left without a railroad.

This theory was never very plausible, and it has been fully debunked by modern economists, who have explained that competition, far from being "destructive," is actually dynamic and creative. It enables buyers and sellers, manufacturers and consumers, to figure out what people really desire and to find creative new ways to meet those ever-changing demands. Free competition thus *increases* efficiency because nobody can know ahead of time whether one railway line or two are actually "needed" or whether any other product or service will prove "convenient" to the public. The only way to learn what customers actually "need" is to try the experiment and see what succeeds and what fails. If there is only enough demand for one railroad line, the second will be unable to meet its expenses and will either go out of business or find some way to innovate and attract more customers. Free competition is therefore not "wasteful." It is a valuable form of experimentation. It is a "discovery procedure."[28]

The alternative – putting politicians in charge of deciding what products will be sold and what services offered – ensures that crucial economic decisions are transformed into political calculations that turn more on favoritism, prejudice, corruption, or feel-good populism than on what the public genuinely desires.[29] As judge and economist Richard A. Posner wrote in 1969, "the fear of ruinous competition seems largely groundless.... [T]here is now a good deal of evidence that the certificating power has been used to limit greatly the growth of competition in the regulated industries."[30]

This is just one instance of the "knowledge problem": to coordinate the economy from the top down, government officials would need access to a virtually infinite amount of information, which cannot be gathered or understood by any single person or group. Such information is often not even available to consumers or businesses themselves.[31] It would not have been possible in, say, the 1980s for anyone – least of all a government agency – to determine whether Americans "needed" a new chain of coffee shops, or whether gourmet cupcake stores would be "convenient" or "necessary." Yet evidently there *was* such a need – witness the success of companies like Starbucks and Sprinkles. Even major companies with enormous incentives to anticipate consumer demand often fail to predict future needs. Coca-Cola, one of the most successful and sophisticated corporations in the history of capitalism, was humiliated when New Coke proved a flop in 1985. Despite having the world's best market research at its disposal, Coca-Cola came to believe that the public wanted a new recipe for Coke. The product proved so unpopular that only two months later, the company restored its original recipe and "New Coke" became a byword for bad marketing decisions.[32] Many other major corporations have devoted millions of dollars to products that fell flat: the Microsoft Zune, the Apple Newton, and the Ford Edsel, to name a few. If these corporate giants, with so much expertise at their disposal and so much investment on the line, failed to predict what customers wanted, it's simply delusional to imagine that a government agency – which has little incentive to get the answer right – could do a better job.

New Coke, Starbucks, or the Edsel might seem like frivolous examples, but this issue can be a matter of life or death. Societies in which bureaucrats decide what products and services are available to the public are crippled by the knowledge problem. Consider just one dismal example: beginning in 1983, the people of Romania were forced by dictator Nicolae Ceaușescu to pay for the construction of the House of the People in Bucharest. The world's second-largest building, it was to be 696,000 square feet, and today it contains 1,100 rooms, 480 chandeliers, and over 35 million square feet of marble – though it remains unfinished. While bureaucrats devoted enormous resources to its construction, ordinary Romanians were suffering shortages of food and medicine, and sitting on three-year waiting lists for washing machines and televisions. When politicians, rather than consumers, decide what the economy "needs," the results can be tragic indeed.

Government efforts to choose which businesses should be allowed to operate encourage rent-seeking as politically powerful groups try to pressure regulators into blocking new competition. This benefits the existing companies in the form of increased prices, but it hurts the public by increasing the cost of living and reducing innovation.[33] In the context of CON laws, this phenomenon was dramatically demonstrated in recent years with the advent of "ride-sharing" companies like Uber and Lyft, which use smartphone technology as an alternative to traditional taxicabs. Drivers give people rides in their own cars, and passengers pay through their smartphones instead of hailing a taxicab. Customers can use online rating systems to report bad drivers. Any driver whose ratings fall too far below the average – or who is rude to customers or treats them badly – runs the risk that the company will "deactivate" him.[34] Drivers like the flexibility of working only part-time for money on the side, and customers enjoy the lower prices, greater convenience, and faster response times that ride-sharing provides.

But taxi firms, seeking to defend their turf against economic competition, have lobbied hard to ban ride-sharing and have sued the companies for operating without a license.[35] New York City, home of the nation's most powerful taxi monopoly, has tried to ban Uber and cracked down on ride-sharing, even confiscating hundreds of cars in sting operations.[36] In 2015, taxi drivers in London, Madrid, and Paris led protest rallies against the company. Rather than improve their own services or lower their prices, they demanded that their competition be outlawed. Some governments complied. After French taxi drivers rioted, overturning Uber cars and setting fires, police responded by arresting Uber's top executives.[37]

The Real World of CON Laws

Another common argument in favor of CON requirements is that giving existing firms a role in deciding whether to allow a new company enables officials to gather important information about the new company's qualifications or honesty or about the state of the industry in general. Since existing companies know the business best, they are in a good position to know whether an applicant is safe and qualified and whether a new company will benefit society.[38] But this argument ignores the obvious conflict of interest in allowing incumbent businesses to veto their own competition. In fact, most CON laws – including those in Missouri and Kentucky – do not require an existing firm to give the government any information at all when they object to a new competitor.

Instead, these laws allow the government to deny a license to an entrepreneur for the sole purpose of blocking competition – without any consideration of the applicant's character and skills.[39] That, at least, was the case in Kentucky and Missouri.

In 2012, Michael Munie filed suit to challenge the constitutionality of Missouri's Competitor's Veto, and a year later, Raleigh Bruner sued Kentucky officials to challenge that state's CON law. The evidence gathered during the course of their lawsuits confirmed their worst suspicions about the unjust and irrational effects these laws have.

In the five years before Bruner filed his case, 39 applicants had asked for permission to start moving companies in Kentucky. Nineteen were protested by one or more existing firms, for a total of 114 protests during that five-year period. All of those protests were filed by existing moving companies – in fact, all were filed by the same lawyer. And despite the government's claim that the protest procedure helped officials gather information about an applicant's qualifications, those officials later admitted that they never investigated any allegations contained in a protest. Even if they had, they would have learned nothing, because no protest ever suggested that an applicant was incompetent or unqualified or that a new moving company might endanger the public. On the contrary, all 114 protests said the same thing: the reason they opposed the applicants for new moving company licenses was that they would "directly compet[e] with … these protestants and [would] result in a diminution of [their] revenues."[40]

During that five-year period, Kentucky officials rejected *every* protested application, solely on the grounds that existing moving services were "adequate." None was ever denied out of public safety concerns.[41] All were rejected merely to block competition. Little wonder that most of the entrepreneurs whose applications were protested chose simply to abandon their efforts. The cost and delay involved in going through an administrative hearing, and the virtual certainty that they would lose, made that a wise choice.

But an applicant who withdrew his application did have another option: instead of getting a new CON, he could *buy* one from an existing moving company. This required government approval, too, but because buying a license did not result in increased competition, those applications were treated differently: none was ever protested, and none was ever denied.[42] On many occasions, entrepreneurs who applied for new CONs and were protested chose to abandon their applications and file new applications seeking permission to buy an existing CON instead – only to buy one from one of the companies that had protested their initial applications. For example, when Little Guys Movers applied for a license in March 2012, eight existing companies protested, including Affordable Moving, Inc. Little Guys withdrew its application and, five months later, asked for permission to buy a CON. No protests were filed, and officials gave their blessing a month after that. The firm that sold Little Guys a CON was Affordable Moving, Inc.[43]

Still, some applicants *did* try to go through the hearing process and get a new license. Their experiences proved just how apt the name "Competitor's Veto" really is. One applicant, Michael Ball, had worked for his father's moving company for 35 years when he decided to start his own.[44] But when he applied for a license, six existing movers filed protests.[45] None suggested that Ball was unfit or unqualified. In fact, one testified that Ball "would be [a] great [mover]."[46] But the protestants all complained that competition from Ball would "result in a diminution of [their] revenues."[47] At the end of the hearing, the government denied him a license in a written opinion that admitted he was qualified and honest and had the required insurance – but declared that he had "not prove[n] that the existing household goods moving service in Louisville is inadequate and that his proposed service is needed."[48]

Ball's case also shows how vague the "inadequacy" standard really was. Kentucky courts had never defined the word, although they had ruled that the public's desire for better or more convenient service was *not* enough to prove that existing services were inadequate.[49] Nor was "proof of some instances of unsatisfactory service."[50] One Kentucky court rejected the testimony of five witnesses who swore that existing shippers were inadequate.[51] Even if an applicant did prove that existing moving services fell short of public needs, the court declared that the government could still reject an applicant if the established firms could *become* adequate at some point in the future.[52] Such an amorphous rule ensured that the state's moving cartel could block competition at will.

Another applicant's experience was still more revealing. Margaret's Moving & Storage requested a CON in September 2008, only to be protested by eight existing movers.[53] As usual, none suggested that Margaret's Moving was unsafe, unqualified, or dishonest. One protestant declared outright that he "did not complain about [Margaret's] quality of work or ability to do [its] job."[54] Instead, the protests simply said that existing moving services were "adequate" and that more competition was undesirable. Refusing to back down, Margaret's Moving decided to go through a hearing. But by the time Kentucky officials ruled on the case, the company had been illegally operating for months without a CON. The government therefore rejected Margaret's application for two reasons: first, because existing moving services were adequate, and second, because these illegal operations proved the company was not "fit, willing, and able" to follow the law.[55]

Margaret's Moving responded to that denial by filing a racial discrimination lawsuit – the company's black owners pointed out that the state's moving companies were overwhelmingly owned by whites.[56] Transportation officials then moved quickly to settle the case out of court. One condition of settlement was that Margaret's would be allowed to buy a CON from an existing moving firm. This time around, no protests were filed, and the government swiftly approved the purchase, issuing a report that made no reference to the company's previous unlicensed operations but commented favorably on the owners' extensive experience in the moving industry.[57] The company that sold Margaret's a license was J. D. Taylor, which a year earlier had been among those protesting Margaret's original application.[58]

Missouri's Competitor's Veto was even worse. Between 2005 and 2010, there were 76 applications for CONs to operate moving companies in that state.[59] The applications fell into two categories: 17 wanted to operate statewide,[60] and 59 asked to operate either within a "commercial zone," such as St. Louis, where the intervention rule did not apply,[61] or in a small, rural area, where they would pose little competitive threat to existing companies. All of the statewide applicants suffered interventions from existing companies, and once again, every intervention – 106 in all – declared that the only reason for intervening was that a new competitor would cause "diversion of traffic or revenue" from them.[62] None ever alleged that an applicant would endanger the public or provided information about the applicant's qualifications.[63] And the government could not identify a single instance in which it had rejected an applicant for reasons having to do with public safety.[64]

As in Kentucky, most would-be movers in Missouri tried to avoid a hearing whenever possible. Of the 17 contested cases in the previous half decade, 15 applicants withdrew their applications when interventions were filed and either bought CONs from existing companies or amended their applications to request permission to operate only in a small, rural area or an exempt commercial zone. Whenever this happened, existing companies withdrew their interventions and the CON was promptly granted. In 2010, when Billy Holloway Jr. applied to operate within a 75-mile radius of Salem, three existing companies intervened. None said Holloway was unqualified, but knowing that a hearing would be expensive and time-consuming, Holloway's lawyer advised him to amend his request and ask for only a 50-mile radius instead. That satisfied the intervenors, and when they withdrew their objections, Holloway's application was approved.[65]

Only two Missouri companies chose to run the gauntlet of a hearing: a businessman named Daryl Gaines and a corporation called All Metro Movers. After his hearing in 2005, Gaines was denied a CON even though the state acknowledged that he was fully qualified. Existing companies, it declared, "already reliably provide statewide common carrier household goods service throughout the State," and Gaines's company "would merely duplicate service already provided."[66] Three years later, Gaines applied again. Five existing companies intervened, again complaining that his business would "divert revenue" from them. This time, Gaines backed down and amended his request to ask only for permission to operate within the Columbia commercial zone, where the CON requirement did not apply.

That same year, however, state officials approved All Metro's application despite the opposition of nine existing companies, on the grounds that "increased competition" would be "a benefit to the public"![67] In other words, Missouri's CON law was so vague that two virtually identical applications could have the opposite outcome: an experienced, qualified entrepreneur could not predict whether he would be *granted* a license on the grounds that competition benefits the public or whether that same competition might count as reason for *refusing* his application. Only one thing was certain: in five years, *every* application to run a statewide moving company in Missouri had been protested, and only one had succeeded.

The Constitution and the Competitor's Veto

When Raleigh Bruner and Michael Munie took their cases to court, they faced an uphill battle. Thanks to legal precedents dating back to the New Deal, business owners have a much harder time than others do when they ask courts to protect their rights. Judges usually presume that laws restricting speech or religious freedom are unconstitutional and require the government to prove that such laws are carefully designed to accomplish an especially important goal. But laws that restrict the right to earn a living are given much more leeway. In cases challenging economic restrictions, courts apply the lenient "rational basis" test, meaning that judges presume in favor of the law and require the plaintiff to *disprove* every possible justification for it. As with all other prior restraint rules, this rational basis test forces people to make the "Devil's proof" – to prove they should be free – instead of requiring the government to justify restricting their freedom.

The Supreme Court has acknowledged as much. In 1993, it declared that plaintiffs can only win such cases if they "negative every conceivable basis which might support" the laws they challenge. Judges using the rational basis standard must imagine whether there could be *any* justification for the law, even if it is one the legislature never actually considered, and even if the legislature's decision had no factual basis. "In other words," wrote the court, "a legislative choice is not subject to courtroom fact-finding and may be based on rational speculation unsupported by evidence or empirical data."[68] Although the justices later backed away slightly from that extreme position, the rational basis test remains strongly biased toward the government – so much so that attorney Clark Neily calls it a "rubber-stamp style of judging,"[69] which nearly always ends with a law being upheld.

To get a flavor for just how biased toward the government the rational basis test is, consider the exchange that took place in one 2005 case, when a judge on the Ninth Circuit asked a federal lawyer whether courts using that test would have to uphold a law if the reason Congress gave for passing it was that invisible extraterrestrials were invading the planet.

"[I]f ... the person sponsoring the bill said, 'Space aliens are visiting us in invisible and undetectable craft, and that's the basis for my legislation,' we can't touch it?" the judge asked.

"Your Honor," answered the Justice Department attorney, "I think if Congress made a finding of that sort, I think, Your Honor, it would not be appropriate for this Court to second-guess that."[70]

Nevertheless, courts have ruled that certain kinds of laws are unacceptable even under the rational basis test. In particular, several courts have declared that as broad as the government's power over the economy may be, it may not use that power simply to forbid competition against favored businesses. In 2003, the Sixth Circuit struck down a Tennessee law that prohibited people from selling coffins unless they had funeral director licenses.[71] The plaintiffs did not officiate at funerals or handle corpses – they just sold caskets – but the law required that they learn embalming, emotional counseling, and other skills for which they had no use – schooling which took years and cost thousands of dollars. The court found this unreasonable. The only possible purpose of such a law was to "protect[] a discrete interest group from economic competition," which "is not a legitimate governmental purpose."[72]

A decade later, the Fifth Circuit agreed and declared a similar restriction on casket sales in Louisiana unconstitutional. "[M]ere economic protection of a particular industry," the judges declared, is not a legitimate government purpose.[73] And in 2008, the Ninth Circuit struck down a licensing law that was "designed to favor economically certain constituents at the expense of others similarly situated."[74] The government's power to regulate the economy may be broad, but "mere economic protectionism for the sake of economic protectionism is irrational with respect to ... [the] rational basis [test]."[75] The Second and Tenth Circuits have reached the opposite conclusion, however. They have ruled that states *may* use their licensing laws to block people from engaging in a trade solely for the purpose of benefiting established firms.[75]

Although the Supreme Court has not resolved that specific question, it has often struck down anticompetitive licensing laws. Well over a century ago, in its first ruling on the constitutionality of occupational licensing, it declared that states may only impose requirements that are "appropriate to the calling or profession, and attainable by reasonable study or application."[77] It reaffirmed that rule in 1957, when it ruled that New Mexico could not block a person from practicing law simply because he was a member of the Communist Party.[78] Licensing requirements, the justices said, must relate to a person's character, knowledge, and skill. And the court has taken an unfavorable view of Competitor's Veto laws, striking them down in three cases between 1925 and 1935.[79] One case involved a Washington state CON law that unfairly prohibited some bus companies from using the state's highways "while permitting it to others for the same purpose and in the same manner."[80] A year later, it struck down a similar law in Missouri that was designed "to protect the business" of existing companies "by controlling competitive conditions."[81]

The case that most directly addressed the constitutionality of Competitor's Veto laws was 1932's *New State Ice Co. v. Liebmann*,[82] which struck down an Oklahoma CON law for companies that – in the days before refrigerators became commonplace – made and delivered ice to people's homes. When businessman Ernest Liebmann began building an ice plant without their approval, the existing firms sought an injunction to prohibit him from entering the business. The trial judge ruled in his favor, concluding that the manufacture and delivery of ice was not a public utility like a railroad and therefore could not be subjected to a CON requirement.[83] Such a requirement, wrote Judge John C. Pollock, did not protect consumers. It only established a cartel, with "the result in many cities and towns … of absolutely destroying all competition" and "enhancing the price charged by the ice plants."[84] Worse, the law blocked honest entrepreneurs like Liebmann from exercising their constitutionally protected freedom to earn a living.

On appeal, the Tenth Circuit agreed.[85] The Fourteenth Amendment, it declared, protects the liberty to practice a trade or profession, and although the government may restrict that freedom when necessary to protect the public from harm, it may not block competition simply to benefit politically powerful interest groups.[86] To do so would be a "great[] encroachment on the rights of the citizen."[87]

The law fared no better before the Supreme Court, which ruled that the manufacture and delivery of ice was an ordinary business that anyone should be free to practice, and that it made no sense to regulate it like a railroad.[88] Oklahoma's law was simply a tool for excluding newcomers from the marketplace:

> *Stated succinctly, a private corporation here seeks to prevent a competitor from entering the business of making and selling ice.... There is no question now before us of any regulation by the state to protect the consuming public.... The [law's] aim is not to encourage competition, but to prevent it; not to regulate the business, but to preclude persons from engaging in it. There is no difference in principle between this case and the attempt of the dairyman under state authority to prevent another from keeping cows and selling milk on the ground that there are enough dairymen in the business; or to prevent a shoemaker from making or selling shoes because shoemakers already in that occupation can make and sell all the shoes that are needed.*[89]

Two years later, the court began to allow more extensive government control over the economy, with a series of decisions that created the rational basis test and reduced constitutional protections for economic liberty.[90] But it never repudiated *New State Ice*. In 1941, well after the new regime was in place, it invalidated a New York CON law for milk processing facilities, making clear that while states may regulate milk production to protect public safety, a restriction not "supported by health or safety considerations" but "solely" aimed at the "limitation of competition" was unconstitutional.[91] "This distinction between the power of the State to shelter its people from menaces to their health or safety" and efforts to "retard, burden or constrict the flow of such commerce for their economic advantage," said the court, "is one deeply rooted in both our history and our law."[92] The theory of "destructive competition," at which the statute explicitly aimed, could not justify restricting the rights of entrepreneurs.

That decision, however, was based not on the Fourteenth Amendment, as *New State Ice* had been, but on the Commerce Clause, which forbids states from discriminating against businesses located in other states. Ever since the 1930s, courts have become increasingly reluctant to use the Fourteenth Amendment to protect economic freedom, although they have continued to forbid discrimination between states under the Commerce Clause. This means that while courts take care to bar anticompetitive laws that restrict business across state lines, the anything-goes rational basis rule applies whenever states deprive their *own* citizens of economic freedom.

In 2012, a federal judge in Virginia declared that the rational basis test barred him from even considering the evidence in a case challenging a CON law. "The concept of" the law was valid, he ruled, so any actual facts "about the negative effects of [the challenged] laws" were "entirely beside the point."[93] In short, "[e]ven if plaintiffs had evidence that Virginia's [CON] laws do not in fact advance [the government's asserted] interest," such evidence "would be of no moment."[94] The appeals court agreed, and tossed out the plaintiffs' Fourteenth Amendment argument, but noted that the law might violate the Commerce Clause.[95]

Competitor's Veto Laws and Individual Rights

Competitor's Veto laws are not just barriers to economic freedom. They also harm other kinds of individual rights, including even the freedom of expression. Martin Luther King Jr.'s 1955 Montgomery bus boycott, for example, has become a cherished part of American history, but few remember that CON laws almost shut it down before it really began.

In organizing the protest, King and his followers faced a tough logistical problem: how to get thousands of boycotters to work every morning. "In the early stages of the protest the problem of transportation demanded most of our attention," King explained.

"For the first few days we had depended on the Negro taxi companies who had agreed to transport the people for the same ten-cent fare that they paid on the buses." But when the police warned him that a local law required taxis to charge a minimum fare higher than that, he "caught [the] hint."[96]

Knowing that officials in Baton Rouge had used a similar law two years earlier to shut down a boycott of that city's segregated buses, King and his colleagues devised a new plan: they recruited a network of volunteer drivers to supply 20,000 rides – more than 130 rides per car per day – to transport the boycotters to their jobs.[97] Gas, tires, and maintenance were paid for by donations collected at the city's black churches every Sunday.

The system worked for a year before city officials filed suit against King for operating an unlicensed taxi service. Although King and his friends applied for a CON, the application was rejected, and on November 13, 1956, a state judge issued an injunction shutting down King's carpools. But in a minor miracle, the U.S. Supreme Court issued its decision in *Gayle v. Browder* – declaring bus segregation unconstitutional – that same day.[98] Nevertheless, King had pledged not to end the boycott until the city actually dismantled its discriminatory practices, so for the final month of the boycott, the protesters were forced to walk.[99] CON laws had nearly doused the first spark of the civil rights movement.

Michael Munie experienced a small miracle of his own in 2013. His lawsuit against Missouri's CON law went to court that summer, but shortly after all the arguments were presented to the judge, the state legislature backed down and replaced the restriction with a new, pro-competitive rule. Today, Missouri law provides that anyone who is qualified and has the required insurance "shall" be issued a license to run a moving company or a taxi company.[100] Five months after this became law, the state's Department of Transportation reported that the waiting period for a license had dropped from an average of 154 days to 19 days – from nearly half a year to a little over two weeks.[101] Entrepreneurs no longer have to hire lawyers and prove to bureaucrats that a new moving company is "needed" (whatever that means). And hardworking business owners like Munie do not face the possibility that the state may bar them from operating just to serve the interests of favored firms that don't want competition.

Still better was the federal court's decision in favor of Raleigh Bruner in February 2014, declaring Kentucky's CON restriction unconstitutional. The law did not protect the public, the court ruled, but only created "an umbrella of protection for preferred private businesses while blocking others from competing, even if they satisfy all other regulatory requirements."[102] By "effectively requir[ing] competitors to approve a new company," the law functioned "as a 'Competitor's Veto'"[103] that "protect[ed] existing moving companies – regardless of their quality of service – against potential competition."[104] The very fact that many movers successfully operated illegally for years without licenses proved that there was unmet demand for moving services in the state.[105] Broad as the government's power to regulate the economy might be, Kentucky's CON law was just "a measure to privilege certain businessmen over others at the expense of consumers."[106] As for the state's argument that the law prevented "destructive competition," the court noted that the government "never [took] such factors into consideration." Faced with the prospect of similar lawsuits, Montana and Pennsylvania quickly changed their Competitor's Veto laws in 2015. Sadly, they remain on the books in most states and major cities. But the tide at last appears to be turning.

American Values and Competitor's Vetoes

Competitor's Veto laws raise costs to consumers by blocking competition and reducing the incentive for existing companies to improve their services or lower their prices. But worse than these economic consequences are the personal and social consequences of laws that condition the right to economic freedom not on honest hard work but on political favoritism. Such rules foster an us-versus-them mentality, which often magnetizes around racial or class differences, and encourage people to devote their energies to political scheming instead of productive effort. Worse, they send people the message that social mobility is only an illusion. Especially given the fact that they bar qualified people from practicing a trade, CON laws breed resentment and make the promise of opportunity seem a mockery for those who need it most.[107]

Among the values essential to a free society are the principles of equality, public-spiritedness, and individual liberty. Equality means that laws should treat people as equal citizens, without regard to privilege of birth or their race or class background. Public-spiritedness means ruling authorities must govern in the public interest, rather than using their offices to serve their own private interests or those of their family, friends, or cronies. And individual liberty requires that each person enjoy the same autonomy to make his own choices and direct the course of his own life. Americans would be disgusted if the law allowed Catholics to decide how many Protestant churches should be allowed in a town, or gave Republicans the right to decide how many people could register Democrat, or banned publishers from printing new books if bureaucrats thought there were already "enough" books available. Such laws would serve the private interests of the politically powerful at the expense of individual freedom – thus contradicting the basic principles of equality, public-spiritedness, and personal choice.

The equality of economic opportunity is just as important as freedom of religion or the press. Just as the government should have no role in choosing what we read or how we may pray, so it should have no role in choosing what businesses customers may patronize, let alone protecting its favorites from having to compete fairly against new entrepreneurs. That, at least, was what the founding fathers thought.

In *Rights of Man*, Thomas Paine proudly contrasted the corrupt British constitution, under which people were barred from going into business without some form of permission from a guild or government agency, with the system of freedom that revolutionary France was then embracing: "In England," he wrote, "the country is cut up into monopolies.... An Englishman is not free of his own country; every one of those places presents a barrier in his way, and tells him he is not a freeman – that he has no rights." But the new French constitution decreed "that all trades shall be free and every man free to follow any occupation by which he can procure an honest livelihood, and in any place, town, or city throughout the nation."[108] Sadly, as the 2015 Uber riots demonstrated, the French gradually abandoned that liberty. One hopes Americans will not do the same.

If equality, public-spiritedness, and freedom are *social* values, they find their echo in the *private* values of responsible citizenship: mutual respect, civic involvement, and personal industry. These "bourgeois virtues"[109] received their most eloquent early expression in *The Autobiography of Benjamin Franklin*, which became a classic text for entrepreneurs in America's first century.[110] Franklin's descriptions of his young self – arriving penniless in Philadelphia with a loaf of bread under each arm, looking for a job,[111] pushing his wheelbarrow full of paper down the main street to build his reputation as an industrious printer,[112] and devoting himself to good civic works and clever new ideas, like lending libraries and street sweepers – became a model for industrious American citizens. Many of them devoted their honest industry to providing for themselves and their families, thereby building a healthy society and preparing the way for the next generation.

Only a few decades after Franklin's death, Alexis de Tocqueville observed that in America, all honest trades were considered dignified. "Among democratic peoples," he wrote, "every man works for his living, or has worked, or comes from parents who have worked. Everything therefore prompts the assumption that to work is the necessary, natural, and honest condition of all men." Unlike in

Europe, there was not only "no dishonor associated with work, but among [Americans] it is regarded as positively honorable; the prejudice is for, not against it." The "habits born of equality," the Frenchman concluded, "naturally lead men in the direction of trade and industry."[113]

These industrial, bourgeois virtues are democratic because they make a society productive, respectful, and mutually encouraging. Such virtues demand much of people. But they operate within an atmosphere of public attitudes – what Tocqueville called "mores" – and when those mores are twisted to different purposes, they can be counterproductive. When society rewards political favors instead of entrepreneurship, and encourages people to look to the government rather than themselves to solve their problems, the bourgeois virtues can wither into resentment, bitterness, and fear. In a society where industry, responsibility, and mutual respect are punished instead of rewarded, people will follow incentives and transform themselves into antisocial, grasping creatures, who seek advantage at the expense of others without regard for social costs.[114] When institutions like Competitor's Veto laws deny people economic opportunity solely to benefit political insiders, entrepreneurs will be less likely to take risks with new ideas and will seek instead to protect their own "turf." And those who do take risks will suffer for virtues that our society should reward.

Imagine some penniless Ben Franklin, arriving unknown in Philadelphia, being forced to obtain a CON before he can open a new printing business. Existing printers can file objections that bar him from publishing *Poor Richard's Almanac* until he persuades the government that the colony of Pennsylvania "needs" a new printer. Ben must ask his neighbors to take a day off of work and testify at a hearing in support of his application. But even this is not enough to prove that existing printers are "inadequate," because the rules require the bureaucrats to give preference to the existing printers. It is hard to believe that Ben would get his chance in such a world.

It is harder still to imagine a working-class resident of today's inner city, or an immigrant or a member of a minority group, having much chance to obtain permission to compete under modern CON laws. Such laws are often an effective barrier against would-be entrepreneurs, depriving them of the opportunity all Americans should enjoy.

What Happens to a Dream Deferred?

One tragic example of the consequences of anticompetitive licensing laws comes from a 2003 case in Louisiana, the only state that requires florists to get government licenses. Anyone wanting to practice that trade was required to pass a one-hour written examination and a four-hour practice test.[115] The examination fee was $150, not a small sum, and the exam was administered only once every three months in Baton Rouge – meaning applicants from other cities had to pay travel and lodging expenses to take the test. Worse, applicants were graded on such subjective factors as the "scale," "harmony," "accent," and "unity" of their floral designs.[116]

Sandy Meadows, a widow from Monroe, Louisiana, moved to Baton Rouge in 2000, where she found a job in the floral department at an Albertson's supermarket.[117] She was a high school dropout with no training and no degree. She had taken the floral exam three times without success, but she had nine years' experience working with flowers, and her arrangements were good enough that she was put in charge of the store's floral department – that is, until the state Horticulture Commission learned that she was arranging flowers without its permission. The commission fined her $250 and notified Albertson's that she could work only as a "floral clerk" – meaning the store would have to hire a full-time, licensed florist to "oversee" her. Employing two people to run the floral department was not economically feasible, and Meadows lost her job.

She filed a civil rights lawsuit, arguing that the licensing law unreasonably deprived her of her right to earn a living.[118] In defense, the government did remarkably little to conceal its anti-competitive intentions. The state's agriculture commissioner testified that he "committed to the florists when [he] ran [for office] in 1980 that [he] would support their desires,"[119] meaning that he would retain the law not to protect the public but to advance the interests of existing businesses seeking to protect their turf.

There was no evidence that unlicensed florists had ever endangered the public or that floristry was a particularly dangerous occupation. Nevertheless, a federal trial judge upheld the law, on the flimsiest of pretexts: florists, he ruled, often use wires and plastic sticks to hold flower arrangements together, so the licensing restriction ensured that they would know how to do this in a way that would not lead to consumers scratching their fingers.[120]

The case was appealed, but during the ensuing delay, Sandy was left unemployed and could not pay her utility bills. Her health broke down, and then Hurricane Katrina struck. Her attorney, Clark Neily, visited her soon after. "[S]he was lying on a couch in about 100 degree temperature in Baton Rouge, about 98 percent humidity, outside of her apartment in a common area with no air conditioning," he recalled. "She had just had gall bladder surgery, so she was literally stapled with surgical staples ... barely able to breathe. I checked her into a Motel 6 so she could have some air conditioning. I went to the Piggly Wiggly grocery store and paid her utility bill so it could get turned back on." But it was too late – she died only days later.

> [T]hat's the last time I ever saw her. Sandy died because the state of Louisiana [took away] her economic liberty and put it in the hands of a bunch of special interest[s]. The Louisiana state florist association's straight-up cartel had gotten that law passed that said that a woman like Sandy Meadows can't make a living doing the one thing she knows how to do.... And I hold them at fault, in part, for her death.[121]

Sadly, although the Louisiana florist law was later modified to remove the subjective grading scheme, the rest of the law, including the testing requirements, remains on the books.

Sandy Meadows's case is just one tragic example of the deleterious effects that barriers to economic liberty can have on some of America's most vulnerable people: the uneducated poor, who lack the wherewithal to obtain training or to undergo the expensive and time-consuming process of licensing. According to a 2015 White House report,[122] unnecessary licensing laws like Louisiana's cost consumers $1 billion a year. But it is really impossible to assess the *economic* costs of these restrictions because those costs are "unseen": they consist of the countless businesses nobody ever starts, the productivity that is never begun, and the wealth that is never created.[123] It would be even harder to measure the terrible *moral* damage such restrictions inflict. It's hard for someone at the bottom of the economic ladder to believe she can climb it – or that our nation's claim to being the land of opportunity means something – when such a harmless business as floristry is ruled off-limits to anyone who lacks the wherewithal to get the government's permission.

The Natural Aristocracy and the Aristocracy of Influence

CON laws betray the values of entrepreneurship even more. Louisiana's florist licensing requirement at least *pretended* to protect the public, but CON restrictions exist for the express purpose of blocking competition against existing firms and allowing them to keep their prices high. They stifle creativity and industry and reward not what Thomas Jefferson called the "natural aristocracy" of "virtue and talents,"[124] but an artificial aristocracy of political influence and insider connections.

Limits on economic freedom perpetuate old patterns of wealth and poverty and foster the perception, if not the reality, of a caste system. An entrepreneur who cannot get a license is driven into the underground marketplace, illegally operating without a license and risking search, arrest, and even jail time,[125] or he obeys the law and abandons his dream of running a business. This encourages what sociologists call "learned helplessness": the acquired passivity of people who see no point in trying to improve their situation.[126] Starting a job and working one's own way up comes to seem like an illusion – something one reads about but never actually sees happen.[127] Social mobility becomes unimaginable, and society is divided into one class of those for whom economic opportunity is a reality, and another, isolated class of those who lack the necessary connections and are left on the outside.

Obviously there are many different overlapping causes of poverty. But a society that distributes opportunity to politically entrenched interests is going to become increasingly stratified and resistant to change.[128] That, in turn, foments a sense of despair that can lead to social disruption and even violence.[129] This is what Supreme Court Justice Stephen Field meant when he warned that if the freedom to earn a living without government favoritism were not protected, the United States would become "a republic only in name."[130]

A young entrepreneur named Evan Baehr has eloquently described the risk that licensing laws pose to the American dream. In 2011, he and a friend came up with a business idea they called Outbox. Customers would pay the company to scan their mail into a computer and allow them to read it in email format. This would enable people to categorize their bills and other important documents, and it would eliminate junk mail, which customers could delete by pushing a button.

Wealthy investors expressed interest, but when Baehr met with bureaucrats at the U.S. Postal Service, he ran into a dead end. Postal officials explained that they would not allow Outbox to touch the mail because the Postal Service's primary customers are senders, not receivers of mail. Cutting out the clutter would hurt their bottom line. Although Baehr and his partner tried to find another way to run the company, they were eventually forced to close down. Baehr has since started a new business, but the experience left him worried.

"I believe there are dozens, hundreds, probably thousands of young entrepreneurs who are thinking about dropping out of college, or starting a company instead of going into law or ... whatever," he told an audience in 2015. "They're on the edge and they're thinking about starting some kind of company – and in conversation with their friends, they're like, 'Oh, you're going to run into the government on that one.' It's going to dissuade young people from going out and building extraordinarily valuable companies ... that dramatically improve services and goods for Americans and the entire world."[131]

The stifling of entrepreneurship is a cost that can never be measured, but we are all worse off for it. The point was put more even more succinctly by the poet John Greenleaf Whittier. "Of all sad words of tongue or pen," he wrote, "The saddest are these: 'It might have been!'"[132]

CHAPTER SIX

THE RIGHT TO USE
PRIVATE PROPERTY

THE RIGHT TO OWN and use private property is so essential
to freedom that many political philosophers have called it the
most basic of all rights. All freedom, argued John Locke, is basically a kind of property right over ourselves, and when a thief or a
tyrant takes away our possessions, he is taking away a part of ourselves. America's founding fathers considered it a fundamental
part of all freedom, including freedom of speech and religion.
When James Madison sought to explain free speech, the best argument he could think of was to liken it to private property: we own
our thoughts like we own objects, he wrote, and therefore have the
right to express them if we want. The Bill of Rights mentions property more than any other right: protecting our "houses," "papers,"
and "effects," ensuring our rights to "keep" arms and not to have
our "things" seized, guaranteeing our right to compensation when
the government does take our property, and – most importantly –
forbidding the government from taking away property without
due process of law.[1]

Sadly, government today takes away many property rights,
imposing a host of restrictions that bar people from using their
land or building homes or running businesses, and it typically pays

no compensation at all. Zoning laws and permit requirements force people to get permission from bureaucratic agencies before they may use the property that supposedly belongs to them, and this enables bureaucrats to demand extortionate payoffs in exchange for permission to build. In some places, the situation is so bad that, as one California Supreme Court justice wrote, the government acts as though it has confiscated all the property and is selling it back to "owners" in the form of permits. "The government, in effect, says: We have the power; therefore, pay us to leave you alone.... Instead of the government having to pay compensation to property owners, the government now wants property owners to compensate *it* to get back the fair value of property the government took away through regulation."[2]

Zoning: The Power to Sculpt Society

One of the most pervasive intrusions on private property rights in the modern age began in the 1920s when the Supreme Court first upheld the constitutionality of zoning laws. Zoning was invented as a way to bar obnoxious uses of private property, but at the time Progressives had a broad concept of "obnoxious."[3] A rising tide of immigration from Italy, Poland, Russia, and Asia led to a backlash among America's political elites, who sought a way to keep racial minorities concentrated in districts away from the white middle class. Frank B. Williams, a leader of the zoning movement who wrote the New York City Planning Law of 1913, candidly acknowledged in *The Law of City Planning and Zoning* (1922) that the "invasion of the inferior," and particularly "the Chinese or negroes," tended to produce "discomfort and disorder, and has a distinct tendency to lower property values."[4]

By the time he wrote those words, the Supreme Court had declared race-based zoning unconstitutional. In a pathbreaking 1917 decision, *Buchanan v. Warley*,[5] it struck down a Louisville,

Kentucky, ordinance entitled "An ordinance to prevent conflict and ill-feeling between the white and colored races," which barred blacks from white neighborhoods and vice versa. Nobody could deny that there was "a feeling of race hostility" in the country, wrote Justice William Day. "But its solution cannot be promoted by depriving citizens of their constitutional rights and privileges."[6]

That ruling was a profound step toward racial equality, and it became a crucial precedent in the campaign to overrule the court's notorious "separate but equal" decision. Yet *Buchanan* did not end racial zoning. Instead, planners seeking to separate the races began using other factors as proxies for race. For example, because members of minority groups were more likely to rent apartments than to own houses, planners forbade apartment buildings in neighborhoods with single-family homes.

That issue came before the Minnesota Supreme Court in a 1920 case, when it upheld a state law allowing Minneapolis officials to ban apartment buildings from residential districts. The law was valid because it kept neighborhoods looking nice, said the court. "Beauty and fitness enhance values in public and private structures," and the law gave citizens a way "to secure for that portion of a city, wherein they establish their homes, fit and harmonious surround-ings." This "promotes contentment, induces further efforts to enhance the appearance and value of the home, fosters civic pride, and thus tends to produce a better type of citizens. It is time that courts recognized the aesthetic as a factor in life." The government could restrict property rights not just to protect people from dangerous things like dynamite factories, or pollution from mills or power plants, but also to promote "pleasure ... 'even if the pleasure is secured merely by delighting one of the senses.'"[7]

Two dissenting justices made clear what that really meant. "Back of all the suggestion of aesthetic considerations," they wrote, "is the disinclination of the exclusive district to have in its midst those who dwell in apartments. It matters not how mentally fit, or how morally correct, or how decorous in conduct they are, they are unwelcome."⁸ The law "in effect segregates the people into classes founded on invidious distinctions," allowing "one class" to "exclude from their selected neighborhood members of the other classes, and thus deprive them arbitrarily of the free enjoyment of their property, although they may be of equal intelligence and moral standing with those thus temporarily vested with the use of that powerful state weapon."⁹

Four years later, a federal judge in Ohio struck down a zoning ordinance in the Cleveland suburb of Euclid. That law prohibited commercial property uses, and allowed only residences, on a large plot of land that the owner had intended for business development. Although such restrictions are commonplace today, Judge D. C. Westhaver regarded it warily. He agreed that government could restrict the use of property to protect the public, but like the dissenters in the Minnesota case, he feared that such rules might also be imposed for discriminatory purposes. After all, home-based businesses were a common way for the poor to provide for themselves at that time, and buildings that incorporated stores or other businesses on the bottom floors and apartments on upper levels were often used as a form of low-income housing. A law banning all commercial uses therefore had the sort of disproportionate impact – often breaking down along racial lines – that the dissenters on the Minnesota Supreme Court had warned about. The "true object" of the Euclid ordinance, wrote Judge Westhaver, was "really to regulate the mode of living of persons who may hereafter inhabit [the land]. In the last analysis, the result to be accomplished is to classify the population and segregate them according to their income or situation in life." A law prohibiting businesses in a residential neighborhood may seem like an aesthetic regulation, but in reality it "is a matter of income and wealth."

Westhaver admitted that the government had the power to prohibit businesses in the area it wanted to, but it would have to do so through eminent domain, by paying the owner just compensation for taking away his property rights and not by simply issuing a decree forbidding commercial uses. To let the government impose such a ban without compensation could be dangerous – not just because it would create a loophole in the constitutional protections for property owners, but also because that power is often used to persecute disfavored minorities.

Courts, wrote Westhaver, should regard zoning laws skeptically to prevent abuses of that sort. Had the Supreme Court not applied similar skepticism to Maryland's racial zoning ordinance in the *Buchanan* case, "its provisions would have spread from city to city throughout the length and breadth of the land," and "the next step" would have been "to apply similar restrictions for the purpose of segregating in like manner various groups of newly arrived immigrants."[10] There were better ways to protect the public against undesirable uses of property without empowering politically powerful groups to discriminate against poor people. The Euclid restriction had to go.

But when the Supreme Court reviewed the case, it brushed aside these concerns. The opinion by Justice George Sutherland acknowledged the possibility that lawmakers might use zoning to exclude "not only offensive or dangerous industries" but also "those which are neither offensive nor dangerous." But Sutherland thought this was "no more than happens in respect of many practice-forbidding laws which this court has upheld."[11] He made no mention of the possible class- or race-based discrimination that plays a role – sometimes overt, sometimes subtle – in land use regulations. If anything, he hinted that he shared those prejudices. Separating industrial buildings from residential areas would "increase the safety and security of home life," he wrote, and "preserve a more favorable environment in which to rear children." It was especially desirable to ban apartment buildings, which he called "parasite[s]" built "to take advantage of the open spaces and attractive surroundings created by the residential character of [a] district." Apartment complexes ruin neighborhoods, he claimed, "utterly destroy[ing]" their "desirability" by creating "disturbing noises" and increasing traffic, which "depriv[ed] children of the privilege of quiet and open spaces for play."[12]

Such paternalistic attitudes are today often labeled "conservative," but they were a plank in the Progressive platform which Sutherland generally endorsed. Progressivism's socially conservative attitudes were so strong that early twentieth-century Progressives sought to ban divorce, alcohol, and the immoral use of automobiles.[13] Progressives in Congress even passed legislation to deport any immigrant who performed music in a brothel.[14] Sutherland's view that government could improve the society's moral fiber by restricting property uses was therefore at the cutting edge of Progressive opinion.

But the consequences for immigrants and minorities – many of whom lived in ways that did not comfortably mesh with Progressive views about proper family life – were unmistakable. The "foreign-born," wrote one sociologist in 1920, "prefer to build apartments.... It may be bad taste on their part, and possibly bad business also; but so long as such apartments are permitted at all, their segregation within certain areas cuts the foreign-born out of American home neighborhoods as effectively as if they were prohibited from living there."[15]

The disparities caused by zoning persist. More than half a century after the *Euclid* decision, the Supreme Court was forced to address the constitutionality of zoning laws designed to exclude people whom the authorities considered undesirable: laws barring unmarried families from living together[16] or blocking homes for the mentally handicapped.[17] Even zoning restrictions not adopted with racial motives tend to solidify economic divisions that are already inflected with race. A law separating single-family residences from apartment buildings will tend to widen the gulf between those who can afford homes of their own and those who cannot. Laws banning small homes or requiring large "setbacks" on property will ensure that only high-priced homes, beyond the buying power of many immigrants or minority members, are built.

In wealthy, predominantly white communities, "affordable housing" can become a racial euphemism, and the suggestion that a developer might build cheaper homes or apartment buildings is often greeted with horror by neighborhood groups. In 2015, after director George Lucas was denied permission to build a film studio on land he owns in California's upscale Marin County, he proposed instead to build a 224-unit affordable housing project. Furious neighbors accused him of "inciting" class "wafare" as a form of revenge for the denial of his previous request.[18]

"Rational" Planning

Advocates of zoning generally argue that such rules are needed to protect the public from incompatible land uses – to ensure that cities are rationally planned and not constructed haphazardly. As Justice Sutherland memorably phrased it in the *Euclid* decision, nobody wants "a pig in the parlor instead of the barnyard,"[19] and nobody wants a glue factory in a residential neighborhood.

In reality, different people have different needs and different tastes, and what might seem absurd to some people might seem reasonable to others. Allowing government planners to determine what property uses should be allowed and what should not is a recipe not only for discrimination along race and class lines, but also for arbitrary and even corrupt decision-making as well. And because a dynamic economy is always changing, often unpredictably, rules that force property owners to get government permission before they can use their property often retard progress and disrupt economic growth.

Zoning laws are inherently inflexible, one-size-fits-all rules. Knowing that such rules cannot possibly work, zoning boards typically allow for variances or other exceptions that let people use their property in ways that would otherwise be illegal. Also, local governments often enforce zoning restrictions haphazardly, forcing some property owners to comply strictly with the letter of the law and allowing other infractions to slide.

Anyone who thinks that zoning ensures rational planning only needs to take a look at the New York City zoning code.[20] The Big Apple was the first city in the United States to adopt comprehensive zoning. A century later, the city's zoning rules take up more than 3,376 pages, covering such picayune details as section 133-32(d)(1), which mandates that seating in the public areas of the Special Southern Roosevelt Island District be between 16 and 20 inches above the level of the adjacent walking surface. The New York zoning map, meanwhile, is a crazy quilt of land use designations, pockmarked with variances, exceptions, and subcategories. Forty percent of buildings in Manhattan have some sort of variance.[21] Today, land use in the city is just as diverse as it ever was – except that now, exemptions are based on political considerations rather than economic ones.

"The complexity of zoning laws means more power for regulators," wrote law professor Bernard Siegan, who until his death in 2006 was among the nation's leading experts on the subject. "[T]he length and cost of the process gives zoning regulators enormous discretion in determining land plans, building designs, and building materials.... Fighting city hall is very expensive, and developers must necessarily limit such activity if they are to stay in business."[22]

Siegan rose to prominence in 1972 with a breakthrough study of Houston, the only major American city without zoning. The lack of such laws had not brought about any sort of chaos, he argued. Incompatible uses were no more common there than in major cities that do have zoning. There were no dynamite factories located next to schools.

The explanation was simple: Houston *does* have land use controls, just of a different kind. Decisions about how property is to be used are primarily made by private contracts between owners and people affected by the property in question, rather than by bureaucrats. Property owners negotiate privately to form their own agreements about how to use their land, and the city enforces their agreements instead of imposing its own vision from the top down. Market forces still tend to separate the city into industrial and residential areas – gas stations and drive-thru restaurants are found on major streets instead of residential neighborhoods because major streets are where consumers prefer to shop for gas or fast food. Land use decisions are therefore made by mutual exchange, not by government dictate, and without the interference of noisy activist groups who – in communities with government land use planning – often pressure officials into making rules that do not benefit the average citizen.

In cities where zoning boards make decisions about land use, Siegan noted, hearings tend to turn into "theater," with developers, neighbors, lobbying groups, political activists, and labor unions vying for time, each "producing a planner to prove 'conclusively' that its position is the only correct one."[23] Faced with such heated debate, a zoning board is likely make a decision that is *politically* palatable, regardless of whether it reflects the public's actual desires.

But in Houston, the lack of political control means that "[t]he site in question will in all likelihood be developed for the uses that society values the most, thereby satisfying the predominant consumer demand." If a developer thinks consumers want an apartment building, he will build an apartment building. If he is right, he profits. If he is wrong, he will lose money and change the use to something more lucrative. Either way, the decisions of developers, property owners, and consumers – each of whom has a strong incentive to use property in the most efficient way – are much more likely to reflect the public's actual desires than decisions made by political officials, who are not subject to the forces of supply and demand and who risk little if they make a wrong call.

Society, argued Siegan, should not hand decisions about land use over to people "who have no stake in the success of the venture and may even prefer its demise." At many zoning hearings, residents, owners, and activists who lack experience or training in real estate development or environmental science are given more credence than specialists "because they emanate from sources with a powerful weapon: the ability to vote them out of office."[24] Contrary to arguments made by pro-regulation forces, zoning laws often result not in "rational" planning by experts but in inconsistent decisions motivated by politics.

Houston is no libertarian idyll. In recent years, the city has adopted laws that mimic some aspects of zoning, including restrictions on the use of "historic" property, landscaping rules, and ordinances regulating billboards.[25] But Siegan's research showed that the absence of zoning rules reduces the cost of housing and contributes to more efficient decision-making about land use. Better, it respects the rights of owners who might otherwise be deprived of their freedom to choose how to use land that belongs to them. And it reduces the government's tendency to use permit requirements as a way to demand payoffs from property owners.

Want a Permit? Better Pay Up!

Government's power to force people to pay for permits was first addressed by the Supreme Court in a 1987 case called *Nollan v. California Coastal Commission*.[26] The Nollan family owned a one-story home on the shore in Malibu, California. When they wanted to put a second story on the house, they had to get permission not only from city officials but from the Coastal Commission.

Since its creation in 1974, the commission has aggressively limited development along the state's 800-mile coastline, and the Nollans' case was no different. The commission decided that a second story would create a "psychological barrier" to using the beach – the public might not realize there was a beach nearby[27] – and to combat this problem, the family would have to sign over an easement across their land: a path on which any member of the public could walk across their backyard to the ocean.

The Nollans thought this was too much. They sued, lost, and appealed to the Supreme Court, arguing that although the government may restrict development in order to protect the public from pollution, shoddy construction, or other dangers, it could not simply use its powers to force people to give up their property without compensation. Such a trick sliced the Fifth Amendment's promise of just compensation in two – the government, which must pay property owners when it takes land outright, could get the same land for free by demanding it as the price of a building permit.

Local governments had been making such demands – called "exactions" – for years. In 1981, the California Court of Appeal upheld a law that forced developers to give land or pay cash to school districts in exchange for permission to build. "Development is a privilege not a right," the court declared, so these payments were really "voluntary in nature." The fact that a property owner is forbidden to build without a permit did not change things, because "he voluntarily decides whether to develop or not to develop."[28] Five years later, another California court upheld a San Francisco ordinance that forced hotel owners to pay fees for permission to change from long-term rentals to night-to-night tourist hotels. The fee was "not compulsory," the court said. It was only a toll for the "privilege of converting residential hotel units to other uses."[29]

The Supreme Court took a different view in the *Nollan* case. Government can impose conditions on building permits, it ruled, only where those conditions are designed to alleviate some harm caused by the construction itself. For example, if asked to approve construction of a factory that might pollute the air, local officials may require the owner to install filters on the smokestacks or take other steps to curb that pollution. But by the same reasoning, any condition the government imposes that is *not* related to the pollution would pervert the permit system, making it a mere fundraising tool, not a device for protecting the public. "The situation becomes the same as if California law forbade shouting fire in a crowded theater, but granted dispensations to those willing to contribute $100 to the state treasury," wrote Justice Scalia.[30] There must be some connection between the harm a development might cause and the demands government makes of the owner, to ensure that the permit requirement does not become "'an out-and-out plan of extortion.'"[31]

In dissent, Justice William Brennan objected to the idea that the Coastal Commission was engaged in extortion. He saw the use of property not as a right but as a permission the government gives to people and for which it can demand some form of payment. The Nollans had been "allowed" to add a second story to their house, he wrote, and since that was a "benefit" to them, the state could require them to give up something in return. Brennan pointed to an earlier case in which the court had upheld the government's right to force the Monsanto company to disclose certain valuable trade secrets in exchange for a permit to sell pesticides. "Monsanto may not sell its property without obtaining government approval and the Nollans may not build new development on their property without government approval," he wrote. "Obtaining such approval is as much a 'government benefit' for the Nollans as it is for Monsanto."[32] Since allowing people to use their property is only a favor the government does for them, the Coastal Commission "ha[d] not sought to interfere with any pre-existing property interest," and therefore, "no taking has occurred."[33]

Justice Scalia's answer to this argument was sharp: "the right to build on one's own property – even though its exercise can be subjected to legitimate permitting requirements – cannot remotely be described as a 'governmental benefit.'"[34] Developing property that one owns is just one aspect of owning it. To picture the Nollans' rights as privilege extended by bureaucrats was to radically transform the Constitution's protections for property. Building permits are not meant as some special dispensation enabling people to use their land. They are just tools to avert harms that might be caused by development.

The court clarified the point a few years later: not only may the government not demand things unrelated to the harms of a proposed development, it also may not demand extremely valuable things to make up for tiny harms. When Oregon landowner Florence Dolan sought a permit to expand her hardware store and resurface the parking lot, officials in her hometown of Tigard demanded that she hand over property for the city's flood-drain system and for a public bike path – about 10 percent of her property.[35] She sued, and the Supreme Court ruled that although these demands were related to her project – they had the "nexus" required by the *Nollan* decision – there was still no connection between the *amount* the city was demanding and any possible consequence of Dolan's renovations. This meant the city's demands were just a variation on the extortion the court had struck down in the earlier case. The Constitution, wrote the justices, requires government to make "some sort of individualized determination that the required dedication is related *both in nature and extent* to the impact of the proposed development."[36]

The *Nollan* and *Dolan* decisions set powerful limits on the ability of local governments to demand payoffs in exchange for permits. But in many cities, land use bureaucrats found ways to avoid complying with the rules. First, some claimed that these limits only applied when land use decisions were "adjudicative" and not "legislative" – in other words, if a city reviewing a *specific* permit application ordered an owner to hand over property in exchange for that permit, the *Nollan* and *Dolan* precedents would apply, but if the city instead passed an ordinance generally imposing a demand on all permit applicants, those rules would not apply.[37] Some state courts have adopted this legislative/adjudicative distinction, and the Supreme Court has so far not clearly addressed the issue.

Second, many land use bureaucrats claimed that the *Nollan* and *Dolan* rules only applied in cases where the government forced property owners to give up *land*, not in cases in which the government demanded *cash*. Florida developer Coy Koontz learned this lesson in 1994, when he sought permission to develop some

Orange County land he had bought 32 years earlier. Officials at the St. Johns River Management District – an agency that oversees development in a large swath of northeastern and central Florida – had declared the area a "protection zone." Koontz hoped at first to negotiate a deal with the regulators, so he gave in to their demand that he set aside 11 acres as a nature preserve in exchange for being allowed to develop the remaining 3.7 acres. But that was not enough. District bureaucrats also demanded that he pay to repair some drainage culverts – a cost of perhaps $150,000 or $200,000[38] – on the government's own property, located more than four miles from Koontz's land.

Koontz's lawyer was outraged. "How much do you want?" he demanded at a testy hearing. "He's giving up approximately two-thirds of this property.... He's an elderly gentleman. He needs to sell the property, and we're trying to get enough that he can reclaim his investment." For the government to order him to pay the cost of fixing up the district's property, too, was "ludicrous."[39] District officials were unmoved. "[I]t's no fun, but that's the facts of life," said one.[40]

Koontz sued, arguing that the demand broke the *Nollan* and *Dolan* rules. The case bounced back and forth between different judges for decades. Only in 2011 did it reach the Florida Supreme Court, by which time Koontz had died and his children had taken over the lawsuit. The court ruled against them. The *Nollan-Dolan* rules only applied when government demanded land in exchange for a permit – not when it forced landowners to give up "monetary exactions."[41] To hold otherwise might limit the government's "authority and flexibility."[42]

The Koontz family appealed to the U.S. Supreme Court two years later, arguing that there was no difference in principle between forcing property owners to give up land and to give up cash. The court agreed. To apply the *Nollan* and *Dolan* precedents only to cases involving land would make it "very easy for land-use permitting officials to evade the limitations," wrote Justice Samuel Alito.[43]

Regulators could simply offer people the choice of surrendering land or paying cash of equal value. Such an obvious loophole would contradict the Constitution's protections for property owners and once again turn the permit system into a tool of extortion.[44] Finally, in March 2016, more than two decades after their case began, the Koontz family received the just compensation they were owed.[45]

Is Using Property a Privilege or a Right?

As the exchange between Brennan and Scalia shows, the basic conflict of principle behind *Nollan* and later decisions is between those who see private property as a right that all people have and those who envision it as a privilege the government gives people on its own terms. Although Scalia's stern declaration that the right to build on one's own property "cannot remotely be described as a 'governmental benefit'" won the day in *Nollan*,[46] this clash remains a constant source of lawsuits between citizens and the government.[47] If people have a basic *right* to use their property, permit requirements can be used only to prevent dangers to the public, nothing more. But if development is only a *privilege*, then the permit system provides government planners broad power to shape society to their will.

That conflict sparked another exchange between Justice Scalia and the liberal wing of the court in a 1990 case involving a South Carolina law that prohibited development in the state's coastal zone.[48] Property owner David Lucas had planned to develop land there until a new law forbade it and rendered his property essentially worthless. He sued, arguing that the law amounted to a confiscation of his land and that the Fifth Amendment entitled him to just compensation. This raised a complicated problem: states can regulate how property is used, and sometimes prohibit its use entirely, without having to pay. So when, exactly, does a limit on property rights cross the line and require compensation?

In his majority opinion, Justice Scalia gave a brief but somewhat vague answer. A prohibition that eliminates all economically beneficial uses of land "cannot be newly legislated or decreed" without compensation. But if the prohibition is "inhere[nt] in the title itself, in the restrictions that background principles of the State's law of property and nuisance already place upon land ownership," the state can forbid the use of land without paying the owner.

This language invoked the distinction between the nuisance system and the permission system. If the state imposes a development ban that only "duplicate[s] the result that could have been achieved in the courts – by adjacent landowners (or other uniquely affected persons) under the State's law of private nuisance, or by the State under its complementary power to abate nuisances that affect the public generally," no just compensation is owed, because the ban has not deprived the owner of anything to which he had a right.[49] But any restriction that goes further than this interferes with property rights and triggers the Fifth Amendment's just compensation guarantee.

By using nuisance as the baseline protection for property owners, Scalia seemed to be saying that government cannot restrict a property owner's rights unless his use of property risks harming his neighbors. But puzzlingly, he did not cite the traditional phrase of *sic utere* – the common-law rule that allows property owners to do what they wish with their land, so long as they injure nobody else. By using the term "background principles" instead, Scalia caused confusion among lawyers and academics, who have argued ever since about what sorts of restrictions on property use qualify as "background principles."

Scalia likely used that phrase in an effort to protect a role for state autonomy in the law of property regulation. State laws vary, and federal courts have ruled that the "property" protected by the Fifth Amendment is the property recognized by state law. This gives states flexibility to adopt their own nuisance rules. What counts as a nuisance in one state may not in another, and the compensation requirement accordingly varies from state to state. But Scalia's vague phrase risked giving states a tool to escape their constitutional obligation to pay for the property they take. Lawmakers might amend the state's property laws, or judges might conveniently reinterpret them, in ways that seize property by retroactively declaring that it was never legally protected to begin with. Scalia acknowledged this possibility when he warned that state courts were not free to change "background principles" willy-nilly. Only a court decision that adopts "an objectively reasonable application of relevant precedents" may bar the use of property without compensation.[50]

Nevertheless, in the years since, state courts have occasionally tried to create new "background principles" in decisions that announce – surprise! – that state law has always prohibited the development in question, and therefore the owner deserves no compensation even though his land has been rendered worthless. The court has occasionally spoken out against these "judicial takings"[51] but so far has never actually struck one down as unconstitutional.

Some courts have held that a property owner who already has permission to build can be deprived of that right later without just compensation. In one 1990 case, the Ninth Circuit ruled against a company that received a building permit in 1974, only to be ordered in 1981 to seek further approval before building. Quoting Justice Scalia's comment in *Nollan* that the right to develop is not a mere privilege, the company argued that once it got the first permit, it should not have been subjected to further restrictions. But the court declared that "there is no federal Constitutional right to be free from changes in land use laws,"[52] and since the owners had "bought into a heavily regulated situation," they should have known that they might be "subject to further legislation upon the same topic."[53] That meant they had no firm entitlement to build, despite having permits – and yet they were owed no compensation because nothing had been taken from them.

Private property rights cannot have value if they do not include the right to use the property. Owning land without the right to use it is more of a detriment than an advantage, since the owner remains on the hook for the taxes, mortgage, or possible liability if people trip and fall on the property. Yet even when they are not trying to use land but simply trying to protect it – or protect themselves – property owners often run into rigid permit requirements and unsympathetic bureaucrats.

In 2008, homeowners Martin and Janis Burke wanted to repair an old chain-link fence that blocked beachgoers from scaling the treacherous bluffs on their oceanfront property in Torrance, California. Years before, two teenagers had died falling from the steep cliffs, so officials from the city, the State Lands Commission, and the offices of the governor and the attorney general all signed an agreement that allowed the owners to install a fence. But 20 years later, when the Burkes wanted to repair the fence, Coastal Commission officials said no. They admitted that the fence did not block views of the ocean but still refused to allow the repairs because a fence "transforms the experience of the area from one of open space to one of being in the shadow of someone's fenced-in yard."[54]

The situation is no better in cases where people try to protect their land from being damaged. Beachfront property owners often must install seawalls to stop waves and wind from gradually eroding the land and causing their buildings to collapse. But in recent years, the Coastal Commission and similar agencies in other states have adopted a policy called "planned retreat," which holds that property owners should simply accept the natural destruction and "retreat" further inland. California law says that property owners who had seawalls in place before the Coastal Commission was established in 1974 have the right to repair or replace them, but the commission has found ways to bypass this rule, particularly by imposing conditions on seawall permits. In recent years, it has used this power to implement the "planned retreat" strategy.

When Barbara Lynch and her neighbor Thomas Frick sought permits to repair the wall protecting their Encinitas homes, the commission agreed, but only on several conditions: they would have to pay a "mitigation fee" of more than $31,000, and the seawall permit would expire after 20 years, whereupon they would have to come back and request another permit to keep the seawalls in place, and the commission could impose further demands. Also, Lynch would have to remove her 40-year-old stairway to the beach, despite the fact that it was legally exempt from the commission's authority.

Lynch and Frick protested these demands, but while they were waiting for an answer, a severe storm struck the area, and large portions of nearby bluffs collapsed. President Obama declared it a disaster area. Yet six months later, the commission still had not allowed Lynch and Frick to repair their property. They filed a lawsuit to challenge the commission's demands, but worried that the bluffs could collapse before the courts acted, they rebuilt the seawall. Commissioners agreed to let them on condition that they record a deed restriction acknowledging the ongoing dispute about the conditions imposed on their permit. With the signatures in place, they finished the repairs, and when the trial court issued its decision in 2013, they were delighted: the conditions, said the judge, were illegal.

But the next year, a higher court reversed that decision. It ruled that, by rebuilding the wall, Lynch and Frick had waived their rights to sue. Unlike the laws of other states,[55] California law does not allow property owners to accept a permit "under protest" and build before a court rules on the validity of the government's demands. "[A]llowing permit applicants to accept the benefits of a permit while challenging its burdens would foster litigation and create uncertainty in land use planning," the court declared.[56] As to the 20-year time limit on the seawall, this was "reasonable" because although the law entitled them to build, the commission could still "mitigate" for its "impacts."[57] The state Supreme Court agreed to review the case, but it has not yet issued a decision.

That case and others like it are examples of one of the most devastating effects of the permit system: when the government grants a permit subject to conditions that a person considers illegal or unjustified, he or she is usually forced to choose between challenging those conditions in court – which could take years – and giving in to whatever the government demands. Rarely can property owners afford to halt all construction for years, possibly decades, while their case is decided and appealed and decided and appealed again. Certainly Barbara Lynch and her neighbors could not have been expected to wait under the constant threat that their land might crumble into the sea. Given the delay, the expense, and the risk – not to mention the stress – of litigation, most people have no realistic choice but to accede to whatever burdens bureaucrats choose to impose.

In that sense, the court of appeal was right: letting property owners seek court protection against abusive bureaucrats would "foster litigation."[58] But the alternative to fostering litigation is to allow government planners to do whatever they please with impunity. The commission's aggressive use of permit requirements is a prime example of how transforming property from a right into a permission gives bureaucrats extraordinary power to force citizens to comply with their ideas of how society should be organized.

Paying a "Toll" for Freedom

The phenomenon is not limited to land. Today, federal agriculture laws dating back to the 1930s still force farmers to comply with a wide range of anticompetitive rules designed for the express purpose of making food more expensive.

That's right: New Deal planners, believing that the Great Depression had been caused by excessive competition and low prices, passed a series of laws designed to keep food costs higher than they would be in a competitive market, by creating nationwide cartels in agriculture. The Agricultural Adjustment Act, and its successor, the Agricultural Marketing Agreement Act, allowed farmers to band together and limit the amount of crops and what farmers could charge for them. Today, nearly 80 years after the end of the Depression, these laws remain in place, restricting the supply of food and driving prices up.

Somewhere around half of all the raisins in the world are produced in California's fertile Central Valley, but under federal law, farmers who produce raisins are not allowed to sell them. Instead, they must hand over a portion of their crop – usually between a third and half of all their raisins – to the government, which then donates or sells them at a discount and distributes the proceeds (if any) among the farmers. The idea is that by manipulating the supply, the government can keep the market price of raisins steady, even as prices for other goods and services go down.

In 2003, the federal government seized 11,000 tons of raisins from California farmers and the year after, almost 20,000. Raisin farmer Joyce Evans sued, arguing that since the government was taking her property, it owed her just compensation. But the Federal Court of Claims, which hears takings cases against the federal government, viewed it differently. The raisins weren't being *taken*. Instead, Evans was being required to pay for the *privilege* of selling her raisins: "In essence," wrote Judge Charles Lettow, Evans was "paying an admissions fee or a toll – admittedly a steep one – for marketing raisins. The government does not force [farmers] to grow raisins or to market the raisins; rather, it directs that if they grow and market raisins, then passing title to their 'reserve tonnage' raisins to the [government] is their admission ticket."[59]

Two other raisin farmers, Marvin Horne and his wife Laura, had no better success when they went to a different federal court. They were fined when they refused to surrender their raisins, and they challenged the fine on the grounds that it violated their Fifth Amendment right not to give up property without compensation. Once more, the court ruled that the confiscation program did not actually take their property. Likening the Hornes' case to the case in which Monsanto was forced to surrender information in exchange for a pesticide permit, the Ninth Circuit ruled that when the government took their raisins, that was only "a use restriction applying to the Hornes insofar as they voluntarily choose to send their raisins into the stream of interstate commerce."[60]

This was an astonishing conclusion. Throughout history, a farmer's right to sell his produce has been considered a badge of his freedom. The very expression "fruits of his labor" reflects the long-standing connection between the work he puts into growing his crops and his right to sell those crops to provide for himself and his family. The raisin-seizure program essentially forced farmers to work as government sharecroppers, trading part of their produce for the right to sell the rest. And although at one time it might have been regarded as a "privilege" to sell raisins "interstate," court rulings since the 1930s have defined the term "interstate commerce" so broadly that practically everything qualifies. In 2005, the Supreme Court even ruled that a person who obtained marijuana seeds as a gift, grew the plants in her own backyard, and smoked it herself was still engaged in "interstate commerce."[61] Under today's law, Evans or the Hornes could not have sold their raisins *at all*, or even eaten them themselves, without qualifying as engaging in "interstate commerce."

The Supreme Court heard the Hornes' case in 2015. Once again, government lawyers insisted that the program was not a forcible seizure of property, just a toll for the privilege of selling their crops: "The government has not taken the raisins," argued Deputy Solicitor General Edwin Kneedler. "This program operates only when the producer, the grower, has voluntarily submitted – committed the raisins to the stream of commerce."

Justice Scalia balked. "The government can – can prevent you from putting something into the stream of commerce? Can charge you for putting something into the stream?"

When Kneedler answered yes, Justice Samuel Alito was stunned. "Is there any – any limit to that argument?" he asked. "Could the government say to a manufacturer of cellphones, you can sell cellphones; however, every fifth one you have to give to us? Or a manufacturer of cars, you can sell cars in the United States, but every third car you have to give to the United States?"

"I – I think that would present a very different question," stammered Kneedler. "I think that would present a very different question."

"Why would it be different?" Alito demanded.

"Because – because this – this is part of a comprehensive regulatory program that if – that – it – it isn't just acquiring it. It's, in fact – "

Justice Anthony Kennedy jumped in. "So you say if the government took *all* GM's cars, then it would be okay?"

But for Kneedler, the right to sell one's raisins was only a benefit the government could give people when it chose, and it could demand some sort of payment for it. He cited the Monsanto case as his precedent, the same case Justice Brennan invoked three decades earlier in *Nollan* to argue that building permits are a kind of privilege.

That triggered a quick reply from Justice Scalia. He had refused to accept Brennan's argument two decades earlier in *Nollan*. He certainly would not accept it now. "[Y]ou say that introducing raisins into interstate commerce is a government benefit, right?" he challenged. "You're saying the activity, which is subjected to this taking, is the introduction of raisins in interstate commerce. And you say that is something that the benign government can give or withhold."

"It is," answered Kneedler. "It is – it is the permission to do it, which is – "

Scalia was shocked. "Really?"

In its written decision, the Supreme Court resoundingly rejected Kneedler's permission argument. The seizure of the Horne

family's raisins "cannot reasonably be characterized as part of a ...
voluntary exchange," wrote Chief Justice John Roberts. "In one of
the years at issue here, the Government insisted that the Hornes
turn over 47 percent of their raisin crop, in exchange for the 'benefit' of being allowed to sell the remaining 53 percent. The next year,
the toll was 30 percent." Citing *Nollan*, Roberts wrote that the
court had long "rejected the idea that *Monsanto* may be extended
by regarding basic and familiar uses of property as a 'Government
benefit' on the same order as a permit to sell hazardous chemicals.
Selling produce in interstate commerce, although certainly subject
to reasonable government regulation, is similarly not a special governmental benefit that the Government may hold hostage, to be
ransomed by the waiver of constitutional protection."[62]

Property "Takings" and Privilege "Givings"

One of the most extreme versions of the idea that property is a
privilege is a theory called "givings," advanced in a 2001 article by
law professors Abraham Bell and Gideon Parchomovsky.[63] Since
government must pay property owners for "takings," they argue, it
is only logical that owners pay the government when it "gives"
them a benefit by letting them use their property. Whenever the
government issues a business license, grants a zoning variance, or
waives some environmental restriction, the person who benefits
can be required to pay. "Givings," they write, "are ever-present....
Like a reflection in a mirror, the massive universe of takings is
everywhere accompanied by givings."[64]

Bell and Parchomovsky's theory is, indeed, like a reflection in a
mirror – that is to say, backward. By viewing property rights and
economic freedom as state-created benefits, they envision wealth
creation not as the just reward of a person's hard effort, but as a
consequence of the state's magnanimity in "relaxing" its grip on
their freedom. The founding fathers considered individual liberty

as the norm from which any deviation must be justified, but for Bell and Parchomovsky, the baseline is "relative wealth."[65] This means that whenever government takes property from people it must pay, not to make up for having taken their possessions, but to restore the equality of wealth. It follows that government should require people to pay whenever it grants them licenses or permits that enable them to earn more money or enjoy their property more than others.

This "givings" theory, if it were ever adopted, would create a form of prior restraint covering virtually every aspect of life, and would enable the government to impose demands on citizens in exchange for even the most routine activities. A driver's license, a marriage license, even citizenship itself are kinds of permits, after all, that undoubtedly increase a person's relative wealth, since someone who can drive, marry, or vote is better off than someone who cannot. Can people be forced, then, to give up important rights in exchange for these permissions? In fact, if anything that deviates from wealth equality is considered a permission, the government could force people to pay for anything that makes them unequal – their skills, talents, beauty, determination – as well as the wealth these things bring about. Recall Ronald Dworkin's assertion that "differences in talent" are "morally irrelevant" when deciding how government should "distribute" resources.[66]

Bell and Parchomovsky claim that their theory would not require people to pay for every "giving." Following their mirror metaphor, they contend that the government should only demand payment for a "giving" if the inverse of the same act would have been a "taking" – that is, if the benefits of the "giving" are concentrated on one or a few recipients and are not awarded in recognition of some past benefit to society. In other words, the only time citizens should *not* be required to pay for a permit is "when the state bestows an identical benefit on all members of the public, and when we assume that the state is a proxy [for] the entire public."[67]

This is hardly reassuring. *Most* permits are valuable only to specific individuals, and marriage licenses, driver's licenses, and citizenship are not bestowed identically on everybody. True, anybody can *apply* for these things, and generally get them – but they are not available to all, and they do create disparities in wealth and social benefits. Certainly building permits, corporate charters, and licenses to install burglar alarms or run horse races would not be exempt under Bell and Parchomovsky's scheme. Even an admission letter to a state university might require some form of "compensation" to the government – perhaps in the form of compulsory public service by all graduates of state universities.

In fact, some legal scholars have already proposed applying the "givings" theory to driver's licenses. Rapid growth in China in recent years has dramatically increased the number of drivers. Law professors Jianlin Chen and Jiongzhe Cui have therefore suggested that driver's licenses should be regarded as a sort of distribution of publicly owned resources – as "givings" – for which recipients should be forced to pay. Driver's licenses "represent substantial economic value for the select few to whom they are allocated." The government should therefore redistribute the wealth generated by people who get licenses.[68]

Obviously there are some cases in which the government may justly impose restrictions on those to whom it grants privileges. Government can require recipients of certain government benefits to submit to regulation – for example, when it grants a monopoly privilege to a corporation or allows it to use the power of eminent domain. Railroads, or the investors who built toll roads and bridges in the nineteenth century, were privileged against competition – it was often impossible for the public to go to any competing railroad or toll bridge – so the government regulated the owners to prevent them from exploiting that privilege for their private benefit. But regulations of that sort have never been applied to ordinary behaviors or non-monopoly businesses, simply to ensure that anyone who "benefits" from a permit pays the state back for that "privilege." Were the government to impose conditions on ordinary permits in order to ensure that "an identical benefit" is enjoyed by "every member of the public," such conditions would render many permits essentially worthless and transform corporate charters, tax credits, marriage licenses, driver licenses, and other arguable "benefits" into tools for government control over private actions. Officials would then have authority over any behavior they chose to license.

"Taking" Away Voting and Speech Rights

Whether it be racial exclusion, environmental policies, or simply a desire for cash on the barrelhead, bureaucracies use permit conditions to demand things they could never get otherwise. The impact is felt far beyond the economic and social realms. Perhaps the most shocking cases are those in which the government forces people to waive their legal rights in exchange for permits.

In one case, Southern California property owners Craig and Robin Griswold were forced to give up their constitutionally protected right to vote in exchange for permission to build a second story on their home in the San Diego suburb of Carlsbad. Although the state constitution guarantees property owners the right to vote on whether their neighborhoods will be subject to "assessments" to pay for local improvements, the city adopted an ordinance that forced local homeowners to pay an assessment up front – and, if they could not afford it, to sign a waiver giving up their right to vote on future assessments. That waiver applied not just to the owner but to anyone who might buy the property thereafter. When the Griswolds challenged the requirement in court, the Ninth Circuit ruled that because they had gone ahead with construction, they – like Barbara Lynch and Thomas Frick – were barred from challenging these conditions.[69]

Shortly after voters in Arizona approved a ballot initiative giving property owners stronger protections against government regulations of their property, cities across the state began requiring people to waive that right in exchange for building permits. The idea, spearheaded by a coalition of bureaucrats at the Arizona League of Cities, is to require anyone seeking a zoning change or a construction permit to sign away their right to compensation in the event that the government forbids development later on. A sample form posted on the City of Scottsdale's website requires property owners to "agree[] and consent[] to all of the conditions and/or stipulations imposed by the Scottsdale Planning Commission, Development Review Board, city staff, or the City Council" and to "waive[] any right to compensation for diminution of value that may be asserted now or in the future."[70] Grady Gammage, one of the state's leading attorneys representing government in property disputes, admits that these waivers are meant to shield the government from responsibility when it prohibits people from using their property. "Don't do anything unless you can get everyone to sign a waiver of their Prop 207 rights," he advises his clients. "We don't do nothin' without it."[71]

Unfortunately, developers who need a permit to begin construction and to avoid costly delay often have little choice but to agree. "Cities are going to throw up as many obstructions and roadblocks as needed to eviscerate the meaning of the law," says Bob Kerrick, an Arizona lawyer who frequently represents property owners. "Clearly, the waivers violate the spirit of the law."[72] But so far, the state's courts have not addressed whether they are legal.

Government can use permit conditions to restrict other kinds of rights, too – including even property owners' right to self-expression. Under a process called "design review," architects are required to submit their plans for approval, not on the basis of safety or environmental impact but purely on the basis of aesthetics. This lets government officials veto construction simply because they do not like the way a building looks.

This process violates freedom of expression.[73] The Supreme Court has recognized that the First Amendment applies not just to words that articulate "a narrow, succinctly articulable message"[74] but also to artworks that convey "inexpressible emotions,"[75] such as the "painting of Jackson Pollock, music of Arnold Schöenberg, or Jabberwocky verse of Lewis Carroll."[76] Like these things, architecture is an art form – "inhabited sculpture," as the Romanian artist Constantin Brâncuşi put it. Icons like Frank Lloyd Wright, Ludwig Mies van der Rohe, Richard Meier, and Greene and Greene have built monuments every bit as expressive as any sculpture, and nobody can stand inside their great buildings – Fallingwater, the Barcelona Pavilion, the Getty Museum, the Gamble House – without experiencing the feelings that great artists strive to evoke. Congress has recognized architecture as an art form and granted architects copyright protections similar to those enjoyed by other artists.[77]

Yet architectural design review requires architects to obtain bureaucratic approval of the appearance of buildings before construction begins. This is a prototypical prior restraint on speech, which allows officials to dictate how entire towns look and to ban designs they consider too radical or too original based on purely subjective attitudes.

Of course, one of the main reasons zoning laws were invented was to improve the aesthetics of neighborhoods, but what qualifies as "improvement" in one person's eyes may not please another. For instance, postmodernist architect Frank Gehry's extraordinary creations, including Los Angeles's Disney Concert Hall and Prague's Dancing House, have often proven controversial – his proposed monument to President Dwight Eisenhower sparked so much contention that after 15 years of development, it remains unbuilt. But artists are not expected to bow to general tastes. They are supposed to create new images, following their own vision. Laws that force them to conform to the tastes of government bureaucrats – who frequently aim for bland uniformity rather than bold originality – are nothing short of censorship.

In one 1970 case, property owners in Ladue, Missouri, designed an innovative pyramid-shaped house that complied with all of the city's zoning regulations and safety standards, but officials rejected it because they considered it ugly. The owners sued, arguing that banning them from constructing the house for such subjective reasons was beyond the government's power. A state court disagreed. The city could take "the aesthetic factor" into account "when the basic purpose to be served is that of the general welfare of persons in the entire community."[78] Since the pyramid would clash with the Colonial- and Tudor-style houses in the neighborhood, the government could forbid that form of expression.

Nobody wants an ugly building in their neighborhood. But the price of free expression is that we respect how others express themselves, even if it is sometimes unpleasant.[79] In any event, neighborhoods have many ways to prevent the construction of eyesores. Residents can sign contracts or deed restrictions or form homeowners associations. Design review, by contrast, requires conformity to a style decreed by local governments, often with no objective standards to guide the bureaucrats' decisions. For the government to dictate what architectural styles are acceptable, or to ban buildings simply because officials do not like how they look, is to violate the freedom of expression.

The fact that unusual or unattractive buildings might decrease property values cannot justify artistic censorship. As one scholar puts it,

> in an appearance review context property values are nothing more than an attempt to measure (and impose) majoritarian taste. When a community says, "We think a pyramid home will hurt our property values," they are simply saying that "enough people will find your house distasteful that it will make our homes worth less." Even if such a conclusion could be proven, the fact remains that all government is doing is measuring community distaste for the expression of an idea.[80]

Nevertheless, courts have regularly upheld aesthetic restrictions on building. In 1963, an Ohio court allowed regulators to deny a permit for a modern glass and cement house. Nobody claimed it was ugly, but the court ruled that it was "out of keeping with and a radical departure from the structures now standing" in the area.[81] But, asked a dissenting judge, what about the owner's rights? "She feels that the plan submitted calls for a residence of beauty and utility and so does her architect."[82] She should not be forced to sacrifice her views "under the official municipal juggernaut of conformity" or to "sublimate herself in this group and suffer the frustration of individual creative aspirations."[83]

Yet the judge did not cite the First Amendment in his opinion, and no court has yet applied the Constitution to protect architecture against the arbitrary interference of design review boards. Pacific Legal Foundation attorneys argued in 2004 that Lake Tahoe's "Scenic Review Ordinance" – which prescribes the "landscaping, building design, glass treatment, articulation, color, texture," and other details of buildings in the area – violated the free speech rights of homebuilders. But while the judge acknowledged that "residential housing can constitute speech," he ruled that people seeing the houses in question did not think of them as "communicative or expressive," and therefore the First Amendment did not apply.[84]

Whether it be the right of a family to add a new bedroom to their home, a farmer's right to sell the crops he grows, or an architect's freedom of expression, the Permission Society empowers bureaucrats to force people to surrender their rights in exchange for using property that supposedly belongs to them in the first place. By contrast, a society that respects private property as a right instead of a privilege protects each person's freedom of choice. "In a word," wrote James Madison, "as a man is said to have a right to his property, he may be equally said to have a property in his rights."[85]

CHAPTER SEVEN

GUNS, DRUGS, AND SEX

B ECAUSE PERMIT REQUIREMENTS allow the government to choose when people may engage in some activity or other, permits are a powerful tool for officials who want to impose not just economic controls or environmental restrictions, but also their own social attitudes and preferences, on others. In the pursuit of moral rectitude, bureaucrats have often used the power of prior restraints not only to limit competition or property uses but also to restrict the availability of guns, drugs, and, in a sense, even sex.

Prior Restraint and the Second Amendment

Although the Second Amendment was added to the Constitution in 1789, it was not until 2008 that the U.S. Supreme Court decided a case directly interpreting that amendment. The case, *District of Columbia v. Heller*,[1] involved the constitutionality of one of the nation's strictest gun control measures: a D.C. ordinance that essentially barred any person from owning a firearm.

No handgun was legal without a permit, but the city also refused to issue permits, so when Dick Heller applied for permission to keep one at home, his application was denied. Heller worked for the District as a special police officer and carried a pistol as part of his official duties, yet the same government that trusted him to carry a gun for work banned him from keeping one at home for self-defense. He sued, and the trial court threw out his case on the grounds that the Second Amendment does not protect an individual's right to possess a firearm for personal use. Although the amendment promises that "the right of the people to keep and bear arms shall not be infringed," it also speaks of the importance of a "well-regulated militia," and in the judge's view, this meant the amendment protected only a "collective" right to bear arms in conjunction with military service.

The Supreme Court disagreed. In his opinion reinstating the lawsuit, Justice Scalia marshaled detailed historical evidence to show that the authors of the Bill of Rights were sensitive to the importance of "an individual right protecting against both public and private violence."[2] This right could not be regarded as less significant than other constitutionally protected freedoms. "The very enumeration of the right takes out of the hands of government – even the [courts] – the power to decide on a case-by-case basis whether the right is *really worth* insisting upon," he wrote. Likening the Second Amendment to the First, which protects the right to express offensive ideas as well as congenial ones, Scalia concluded that "[a] constitutional guarantee subject to future judges' assessments of its usefulness is no constitutional guarantee at all."[3] The Constitution secures the right to possess a firearm, and it was not for judges to question the value of that protection.

Still, neither *Heller* nor the follow-up case *McDonald v. Chicago*,[4] which held that states as well as Congress must respect the right to own guns, addressed what sorts of licensing and registration requirements the Constitution allows. If the Second Amendment, like the First, guarantees the rights of individuals rather than the abstract interests of society, then it is reasonable to ask whether the rule against prior restraints on speech also bars prior restraints on the possession of guns.

As we have seen, the Supreme Court began in the 1950s to dilute the First Amendment's once-absolute prohibition on prior restraints. Those precedents transformed that prohibition into a set of procedural rules under which a law that requires someone to get a permit before speaking is constitutional as long as there are clear standards for obtaining a permit, some form of judicial appeal, and a time limit within which licensing officials can consider applications.

These rules are a poor substitute for the total prohibition on prior restraints that was once the boast of First Amendment lawyers, but they still provide important safeguards against arbitrary government action. The government cannot simply ban people from speaking for subjective or arbitrary reasons, and it cannot make people wait indefinitely when they apply for a permit. There is no reason why those same protections should not also apply to laws that force people to get permission to exercise any other constitutional right.

In fact, in 1958, the Supreme Court said just this, ruling that any law that "makes the peaceful enjoyment of freedoms which the Constitution guarantees contingent upon the uncontrolled will of an official – as by requiring a permit or license which may be granted or withheld in the discretion of such official – is an unconstitutional censorship or prior restraint upon the enjoyment of those freedoms."[5] While the phrase "prior restraint" is most often found in cases involving speech, the court held, the basic procedural safeguards of clarity, objectivity, and time limits apply to all permit requirements.

Attorney Alan Gura, the constitutional litigator who won both the *Heller* and *McDonald* cases, has pushed judges to apply the same rule to laws that require gun permits. He believes the Second Amendment should be treated "as a normal constitutional right."[6] Courts would never tolerate an arbitrary or subjective licensing requirement that barred people from exercising their freedoms of speech, religion, travel, or even abortion rights without prior approval from the government. The Second Amendment should be treated no differently.

In 2012, Gura argued before the Second Circuit Court of Appeals that a New York law requiring people to show "proper cause" before they may possess firearms was vague and subjective and failed to provide the procedural guarantees required of all prior restraints. The law did not define the term "proper cause," essentially leaving state officials free to decide on their own whether to let people carry guns. Such a rule "comes literally within the definition of a prior restraint," Gura argued.[7] Citing the many precedents that require licensing laws to set forth "narrow, objective and definite"[8] criteria, he contended that "proper cause" was only a vague, nice-sounding term, not susceptible to any objective measurement. It meant whatever bureaucrats said it meant, and if it applied to speech, such a rule would violate the First Amendment. When applied to guns, such a subjective prohibition on the exercise of constitutional freedom also violated the Second Amendment. If anything, he concluded, *Heller* and *McDonald* made clear that "[t]he desire for self-defense" is "all the 'proper cause' required."[9]

The judges disagreed.[10] There might be "analogies" between the First and Second Amendments, they held, but it would be "imprudent" and "incautious" to apply the prior restraint precedents to gun control laws because that "could well result in the erosion of hard-won First Amendment rights."[11] That was a remarkable admission. The judges seemed to be saying that they were so devoted to upholding restrictions on gun rights that they would be willing to sacrifice protections for free speech if necessary.

Gura had more success three years later in a lawsuit challenging a Yolo County, California, ordinance that required a person to demonstrate "good moral character" and prove "good cause" before obtaining a concealed weapon permit. As in New York, the trial court initially rejected Gura's argument, claiming that the prior restraint doctrine only applies to cases involving First Amendment rights.[12] But when the case was appealed, it was heard alongside another case challenging a similar "good cause" requirement in

San Diego.[13] The Ninth Circuit struck both down, likening the requirements to the kinds of prior restraints forbidden by First Amendment law. "To reason by analogy, it is as though San Diego County banned all political speech, but exempted from this restriction particular people (like current or former political figures), particular places (like private property), and particular situations (like the week before an election)." Such exceptions would "preserve small pockets of freedom" but would "do little to prevent destruction of the right to free speech as a whole."[14] A year after declaring the licensing requirement unconstitutional, however, the court reconsidered the case and upheld it instead.[15]

The "good cause" law Gura was challenging is known as "discretionary issue" because it allows officials discretion to choose when to issue gun permits. In recent years, states have increasingly adopted "shall issue" rules instead, which mandate that permits be granted whenever a person meets the specified requirements. About 40 states have adopted "shall issue" laws, motivated by concerns that officials were abusing their powers by denying permits to all, or nearly all, applicants.

There are good reasons for such concerns. Hawaii, which has some of the nation's strictest handgun regulations, grants concealed weapons permits only in "exceptional" cases, "when an applicant shows reason to fear injury to the applicant's person or property," and it issues open-carry permits only if the applicant is "of good moral character" and demonstrates "urgency" or "need."[16] These rules are so strict that although Hawaii's population is about 1.4 million, only 183 people are licensed to carry handguns.[17]

The idea of applying prior restraint theory to the Second Amendment is not original to Gura.[18] In a 1997 article, law professor Donald Dowd discussed the idea, only to reject it on the grounds that the First Amendment protects different values than the Second, and laws limiting gun possession should be presumed valid – a presumption never given to the government in cases involving free speech.[19] But these arguments are unpersuasive. In fact, the "values" protected by the two amendments are remarkably similar. Both speech and gun possession promote social as well as individual interests. At an individual level, free speech enables people to express themselves – literally to "defend" themselves against misrepresentation, misunderstanding, or false accusations – just as the possession of firearms enables them to defend themselves against others who might want to harm them physically. At a social level, freedom of speech fosters public deliberation – but so does the right to own guns. An armed minority can resist bullying and compel others to respect them and talk politely instead. And an armed majority can protect democratic principles from abuse by public officials or invasion by hostile forces.

The First and Second Amendments thus reinforce each other: self-defense is valuable to someone who expresses unpopular views – as racial minorities were often forced to defend themselves if they spoke out against Jim Crow. Southern racists tried to disarm blacks in the years following the Civil War because they knew that a disarmed and unpopular minority is vulnerable. Frederick Douglass, recognizing that risk, argued that equal citizenship rests on "three boxes": "the ballot box, the jury box, and the cartridge box."[20] Black Americans needed all three to defend their freedom.

During the Civil War, Douglass urged Abraham Lincoln to admit black soldiers into the Union army, not merely as a step toward abolishing slavery but as a move toward equal democratic citizenship as well. He believed that black veterans could not be denied the right to speak, vote, and possess guns when the war was over. He turned out to be wrong: with the end of Reconstruction in the 1870s, southern states progressively disarmed, disenfranchised, and terrorized black Americans, leading to virtual re-enslavement.[21] A century later, Malcolm X would insist on the right to possess firearms, arguing that "where the government has proven itself either unwilling or unable to defend the lives and the property of Negroes, it's time for Negroes to defend themselves." The Second Amendment, he said, "provides you and me the right to own a rifle or a shotgun.... If the white man doesn't want the black man buying rifles and shotguns, then let the government do its job."[22]

In his article, Professor Dowd rejected the parallel between the First and Second Amendments, writing that opinions "are formed and laws are made by the effect of words, not guns."[23] But this is not a notion that vulnerable minorities have the luxury of sharing. When they are denied the tools of self-defense, unpopular minorities have no means of insisting upon their right to an equal share in democracy, and no shield against the tyranny of the majority. On the other hand, responsible gun ownership is as much a part of American citizenship as voting. That is why Akhil Reed Amar, one of the nation's foremost scholars of the Bill of Rights, considers the First and Second Amendments twinned: both preserve the values of "populism and federalism," and both are focused on securing the Constitution's "great principle of popular sovereignty and its concomitant right to alter or abolish the national government."[24]

The McMinn County War

It's not just the national government. An extraordinary example of the way firearms possession, like free speech, can protect democratic institutions can be found in a little-known conflict called the "Battle of Athens" or the "McMinn County War" of 1946. That battle began when a group of soldiers returning to their Tennessee hometown after World War II became fed up with the corruption and brutality of the county's Democratic political machine. Under the leadership of boss E. H. Crump, the machine dominated politics by intimidating, assaulting, and outlawing the opposition – in one instance, abolishing the independent judicial review of election results and giving the job of counting ballots to the Sheriff's Department, which was run by Crump's cronies.

The sheriff's office operated on a fee system whereby deputies were paid for each citation they issued and suspect they booked.

Deputies often cited or arrested citizens on falsified charges for a quick buck – sometimes more than $100 per week – and frequently stopped buses on their way through the county in order to charge every sleeping passenger with public drunkenness. Others demanded payoffs from local businesses to ignore gambling or prostitution on the premises.

Political protests against these practices did no good, because deputies bribed or intimidated voters, stole ballot boxes, or paid minors to vote and because many state officials were themselves members of the Crump gang. Federal attorneys brought corruption charges against local officials, but judges and juries were too fearful to stem the abuse.

Finally, frustrated veterans decided to act. They met secretly to form their own political party, the "G.I. Ticket," which included a veteran candidate for each countywide office, and issued a platform promising that under their leadership, "every ballot will be counted." Knowing the danger they faced, the group asked the governor and the federal Department of Justice for protection. All refused. On August 1, election day, the sheriff brought in 200 armed "special deputies" to menace the voters. One G.I. Ticket poll watcher was arrested when he disputed whether a voter was qualified.[25] Other veterans were kidnapped by deputies who took them to the county jail or dropped them off naked in the woods to keep them from reaching the polls.[26] At one precinct, officers pulled guns on G.I. observers, who fled by leaping through a plate-glass window.[27] Later, a group of officers led by a deputy named Windy Wise beat black veteran Tom Gillespie with brass knuckles when he came to vote. When Gillespie tried to run away, Wise shot him in the back.[28]

When the polls finally closed, sheriff's deputies confiscated the ballot boxes and took them to the county jail, to "count" the ballots in secret. Twenty-one-year-old Marine veteran Bill White then spoke up. He would not let Crump's lackeys steal the election, he told his friends. He had "faced a thousand bullets for democracy" fighting the Japanese and had been awarded two Purple Hearts.

Now he was ready to "fight fire with fire."[29] He and 60 other G.I.s marched to the local armory, where they seized guns and explosives before heading to the county jail to liberate their wrongfully arrested allies and stop the sheriff from manipulating the ballots.

With the men surrounding the jail, White shouted at the guard towers: "Would you damn bastards bring those damn ballot boxes out here or we are going to set siege against the jail and blow it down?"[30] Gunfire erupted. The G.I.s kept up the siege for hours, blasting away with their rifles and blowing up sheriff's cars with dynamite. The sheriff asked the governor to dispatch the National Guard, but the Guard's commanding general refused to aid the corrupt local officials. At last the G.I.s blew down the jail door and the deputies surrendered. The soldiers marched them around the town square to the cheers of the townspeople. Some locals attacked the captured deputies, especially Wise, who was badly beaten before being arrested and charged for shooting Gillespie. He was later sentenced to three years in prison.

When the ballots were counted, the G.I. Ticket had won by a landslide, and the county sheriff promptly resigned in favor of his G.I. challenger. Among those who cheered the soldiers' uprising was former First Lady Eleanor Roosevelt. "If we want to continue to be a mature people who, at home and abroad, settle our difficulties peacefully and not through the use of force," she wrote in her syndicated newspaper column, "then we will take to heart this lesson and we will jealously guard our rights.... The decisive action which has just occurred in our midst is a warning, and one which we cannot afford to overlook."[31]

While the McMinn County War dramatized the way Second Amendment rights can protect First Amendment freedoms, a more personal case in 2011 demonstrated how interconnected these rights can be. Paul Dorr, a member of the Taxpayers Association in Osceola, Iowa, had complained about what he considered the exorbitant salaries paid to county officials. Soon after he handed out leaflets protesting Sheriff Douglas Weber, he learned that the sheriff had rejected his application for the renewal of his gun permit. "Concerns from Public. Don't trust him," Weber wrote on Dorr's application.[32] Although Weber could cite no specifics about why Dorr might be untrustworthy, Iowa's law included a lax "discretionary issue" rule, which gave the sheriff the power to enforce his own personal attitudes. "Paul was granted permits by Sheriff Weber and his predecessor for five years without incident," a federal judge later wrote, "but then was denied a renewal of his permit only after he became associated with the Osceola County Taxpayers Association and engaged in advocating its position that Sheriff Weber and other county officials were overpaid."[33] Such retaliation violated Dorr's First Amendment rights.

Freedom of speech and the right to own guns thus share in serving social, as well as individual, interests: the First Amendment promotes the democratic goals of deliberation and persuasion, while the right to self-defense enables people to defend themselves against social upheavals such as riots, terrorism, or persecution – as well as against the corruption of public officials. Both amendments support the republican vision of the founding fathers, ensuring a socially responsible citizenry whose freedom is intertwined with their willingness to defend their rights. The violation of either right undermines the stability of democratic institutions – and the government should not be allowed to force citizens to get its permission before exercising either freedom.

In arguing that the rule against prior restraints should not apply to gun rights, Professor Dowd claimed that the risk that such restraints might impose a "chilling effect" on the exercise of constitutional rights "is hardly applicable to the Second Amendment."[34] But this is untrue. Laws restricting firearms deter people from exercising their right to buy a gun for self-defense. Some resort to illegal gun ownership. Others just do without and hope for the best – sometimes in vain. After she was threatened by her abusive ex-boyfriend, Carol Bowne of Berlin Township, New Jersey, got a restraining order against him and in April 2015 applied for a permit to carry a pistol. But it takes months for permits to be granted, and hers was still pending when her ex stabbed her to death in her home. She had called the police department only days before to ask about the status of her application.[35] Now she is one of myriad victims who find that relying on 911 in an emergency is often too little, too late. Given that the Supreme Court has repeatedly ruled that police officers have no legal duty to protect citizens,[36] gun ownership is a sensible and responsible alternative for citizens who want to defend themselves and their neighbors against violence.

Dowd's argument, therefore, that the rule against prior restraints on speech should not also apply to Second Amendment rights because "[t]he possibility of harm coming from the possession of a press is quite different from the possibility of harm from possession of a gun,"[37] frames the issue wrongly. The real issue is the potential harm of *not having a gun when it is needed*. As law professor Glenn Reynolds, a noted gun-rights advocate, puts it, when every second counts, the cops are minutes away. In major cities, average police response times in life-threatening situations are often 10 minutes or more.[38] Any homeowner who confronts an intruder but cannot defend herself thanks to laws restricting gun ownership knows that the need for faithful enforcement of Second Amendment rights is *greater* than the need for protecting freedom of speech.

After *Heller* and *McDonald*, the question is no longer whether the possession of firearms is desirable. It is a constitutional right and should receive the same safeguards that apply to all such rights. The Constitution forbids all permit requirements that allow officials to curtail a person's freedom for arbitrary, unpredictable, and unprincipled reasons. Whatever the right in question – free speech or gun ownership – basic rules of fairness require that the government set out clear and objective guidelines when it regulates the exercise of those rights.

* * *

Permission to Take Pills

Medical prescriptions today are a type of government license that allow people to possess "controlled substances." This was not always the case. Before 1914, a doctor's prescription was merely a note to a pharmacist or a written reminder for the patient. But one of the major reform efforts of Progressivism was to regulate the safety of food and medicine at the national level, and a new era was born with the enactment of the 1906 Pure Food and Drug Act and then the 1914 Harrison Act, the first federal law banning drugs. The Harrison Act prohibited the sale of opium or coca drugs without a signed doctor's prescription, and the law was later interpreted as prohibiting physicians from prescribing drugs to addicts.[39] Predictably, this created a black market, to which Congress responded with the Marijuana Tax Act of 1937, which essentially banned that drug as well. When that act was declared unconstitutional in 1969, Congress replaced it with the comprehensive Controlled Substances Act of 1970, the centerpiece of federal drug regulation today.

That law divides drugs into different categories, or "Schedules," with those considered most dangerous occupying Schedule I (incongruously grouped with marijuana[40]). Less potent drugs reside on lower levels in the hierarchy, down to certain cough syrups on Schedule V. Schedule I substances are forbidden; drugs in the other schedules may be obtained only with a doctor's permission. Prescriptions thus act as a kind of license or prior restraint on the possession of drugs. Combined with the requirement that doctors be licensed by the government to practice their profession, this means that prescription requirements also operate as a prior restraint on the practice of medicine. Federal regulators can control how doctors throughout the country treat their patients, and they have sometimes used that power not to protect patient safety but to promote the moral preferences of those in power.

Contraception is a revealing example. For decades, Americans have debated whether birth control pills or the "morning after" pill should be available without a prescription. Hormonal birth control has medical risks, and patients are wise to seek a doctor's advice before taking it, but it is no more dangerous than many other medicines that are already available over the counter. Yet since the Pill's introduction a half century ago, the federal government has required women to get a prescription for it. Efforts are under way to end this rule, and some 70 percent of Americans now favor over-the-counter availability, including the American College of Obstetricians and Gynecologists.[41] Many opponents of birth control who dread seeing it become more readily available still prefer dropping the prescription requirement because doing so would allow doctors with moral qualms to avoid being involved in the process. As one Catholic doctor explained, "Catholic OBGYNs would not need to materially cooperate with evil."[42]

The primary opponents of over-the-counter birth control now are doctors themselves. They do not deny that the Pill is safe, but many prefer to keep the prescription requirement in place because it gives them the ability to force patients to show up for annual physicals. Recent research has shown that annual exams are unnecessary, possibly counterproductive, and needlessly drive up medical costs.[43] Still, physicians are understandably conservative about such things, and requiring an annual doctor's note for the Pill gives them a gentle way to coerce patients each year. When two prominent gynecologists published an editorial against efforts to eliminate the prescription requirement for this reason, *Mother Jones* writer Stephanie Mencimer had an apt reply: "Women don't need to have their birth control pills held hostage to get needed cancer screenings," she wrote. "After all, men are never required to, say, have a colonoscopy as a condition of getting blood pressure medication, Viagra, or even a vasectomy, even though men are much worse about going to the doctor and getting checkups than women are."[44]

Much more controversial was the decades-long effort to make

Plan B, or the "morning after" pill, available without a prescription, and that conflict proved how easily prescription requirements can be used to control behavior instead of protecting patients.

Reproductive rights groups filed a petition in 2001 asking the FDA to allow over-the-counter sales of Plan B, arguing that it was safe enough that consumers could be trusted to read and understand the directions. But the agency did nothing for years until it at last rejected the petition in 2006. The groups sued, and three years later, federal judge Edward Korman ruled that the FDA had "bowed to political pressure from the White House and anti-abortion constituents despite the uniform recommendation of the FDA's scientific review staff to approve over-the-counter access."[45] Detailing the many unorthodox steps the agency took in reviewing the request to eliminate the Plan B prescription requirement, Judge Korman found that Bush administration officials overrode the judgment of FDA scientists and broke the agency's own rules to delay the request – and, when sued, used obstruction tactics to postpone a court decision. All of this, Korman ruled, proved that the FDA had "acted in bad faith and in response to political pressure."[46] The agency appealed that ruling and lost again. But it was not until 2013, after the Second Circuit Court of Appeals upheld Korman's order,[47] that the Obama administration accepted the ruling and authorized sales without a prescription.

Even without such overt political pressure, the FDA's monopoly over medicine is the determinative factor for how Americans receive health care. Since 1962, the agency has been charged with judging not only whether drugs and treatments are safe but also whether they are effective – a much more complicated and time-consuming evaluation and a much harder call to make. Safety and efficacy are quite different: no patient wants to take an unsafe drug, but many – especially the terminally ill – are willing to give investigational medicines a try. Their ability to do so, however, is curtailed by federal laws that impose a prior restraint on the availability of potentially life-saving drugs.

The Abigail Alliance, a group named for 21-year-old cancer patient Abigail Burroughs, sued the FDA in 2004 asking a federal court to declare those laws unconstitutional. Burroughs died of cancer while waiting for approval to try a medicine called Erbitux, which her doctor thought might save her life but which had not received final FDA approval. The Abigail Alliance contended that laws that bar people from taking unapproved medicines violate the Constitution's protections for liberty – which, they argued, includes the right to defend one's life by taking medicines of one's choice.

There was much merit to this argument. The Constitution forbids government from taking away a person's "life" without "due process of law," and a patient prohibited from taking potentially life-saving drugs, not because she has done anything wrong but because unelected bureaucrats think the drug will not work, has not received due process of law.[48] The Supreme Court has already said that people may refuse potentially life-saving treatment if they choose[49] and that they cannot be subjected to medical procedures against their will.[50] It seems only logical that patients, not the government, should have the right to decide what sorts of investigational medicines are worth the risk.

The D.C. Circuit Court of Appeals ruled in favor of the Abigail Alliance in 2006. Everyone has the right "to decide for herself whether to assume any known or unknown risks of taking a medication that might prolong her life," it said. "If there is a protected liberty interest in self-determination that includes a right to refuse life-sustaining treatment, even though this will hasten death, then the same liberty interest must include the complementary right of access to potentially life-sustaining medication, in light of the explicit protection accorded 'life.'"[51] But a year later, the court reconsidered the case and changed its ruling. The right to access medicines to save one's life "is not fundamental," it decreed, and the interests of patients were easily trumped by the government's authority to regulate drugs.[52]

Sadly, the FDA's approval process is so slow that every year, countless patients die awaiting treatments that could save their lives. "Countless" is literally the word, since it is impossible to say for certain how many lives the FDA costs by blocking access to medicine and treatments. Some scholars estimate that pre-approval requirements lead to between 21,000 and 120,000 unnecessary deaths per decade, while those rules protect about 10,000 per decade against unsafe drugs.[53] These numbers are speculative, but all scholars who have tried to quantify the costs of FDA regulation have agreed that it hurts more than it helps, and these costs cannot be shrugged off as the inevitable price of drug safety. As bioethicist Julian Savulescu writes, "[t]o delay by 1 year the development of a treatment that cures a lethal disease that kills 100,000 people per year is to be responsible for the deaths of those 100,000 people, even if you never see them."[54]

The FDA does allow some patients to access investigative medicines before they are officially approved for sale through a process called "Compassionate Use," but the Compassionate Use system is so burdensome that many patients find it offers them only false hope. Although the agency approves most Compassionate Use requests, approval takes so long that it comes too late for many, and the rules for applying are so stringent that innumerable patients find it impossible even to apply.[55]

The 2013 film *Dallas Buyers Club* dramatized the desperation of patients who collide with the FDA's bureaucracy and paternalism. In one scene, an administrator explains to a crowd of AIDS sufferers, "The FDA's standard procedure to approve a new drug is eight to twelve years – "

An audience member interrupts: "We're dying here!"

"We are looking to fast track – "

"We need it now!"

"We're working closely with the FDA to make sure every effort is made – "

"The hell, if it works even a little, we'll take the chance!"

Fortunately, in the real-life story on which the film was based, many people did get that chance. But for thousands of others, the opportunity to access potentially life-saving medicines is beyond their reach, thanks to government's permission-style regulation of medicine. Like Ron Woodroof, the real man on whom *Dallas Buyers Club* was based, many Americans are even forced to travel to other countries, at great expense, to obtain medicines approved for sale there but unavailable in the land of the free.

That was the case with Diego Morris. Diagnosed with osteosarcoma at the age of 11, Diego seemed doomed until his family learned of a promising new bone cancer treatment called mifamurtide. But the treatment was not available in the United States: while it was undergoing the third stage of the FDA's lengthy review and approval process, the manufacturer had gone out of business, and the test results were never completed. This meant that although mifamurtide had been approved for safety during the first phase of testing, it had not received federal approval. When Diego's doctor begged the agency to let him treat Diego with mifamurtide, the FDA refused. Fortunately for Diego, his family could afford to move to London, where the treatment was legal. After dozens of treatments, Diego began to improve – and his life was saved. "Thank God we were able to make that decision," his mother Paulina reflected. "So many people can't."[56]

Nobody should be forced to move to a foreign country, or organize a social media campaign, to have access to these safe medicines that offer the chance of saving a life. That's why more than half of the states have now enacted laws called "Right to Try," which provide terminally ill patients with the legal right to use treatments that the FDA has approved for safety, but not yet for efficacy. The laws also exempt drug makers from liability if they provide those medicines. Right to Try doesn't allow patients to use unsafe treatments – they simply allow patients to use medicines that are already approved for safety, and which are already being given to patients in FDA-approved clinical settings, but have not yet received final approval for sale. "If you have the Right to Die, you have the Right to Try," notes Darcy Olsen, president of the Goldwater Institute, which has spearheaded this legal reform. "And you don't have to wait for Washington to secure it."[57]

Opponents of Right to Try claim that the FDA's review process protects patients from ineffective treatments. But that ignores the many effective treatments that are delayed or stifled while needy patients suffer. Worse, such paternalistic attitudes clash with the principle of patient autonomy, a cornerstone of medical ethics, which holds that decisions about treatment are ultimately for the patient to make – not bureaucrats in a federal building thousands of miles away. Clinical testing is a valuable technique for determining whether drugs work, but that cannot justify depriving people of the freedom to choose their own medical care. The rights of patients must take priority over rigid bureaucratic protocols.

Prior Restraints on Doctors

The paternalism of government control over medicine is nowhere more obvious than on the battlefield of America's hopeless War on Drugs. That war does not just take place on the streets of inner cities. Federal and state regulators also monitor physicians to ensure that they are not participating in drug abuse by writing prescriptions for addicts or dealers. Because chronic pain is especially hard to test objectively, officials are particularly suspicious of prescriptions for pain medicines. A doctor accused of prescribing too much may find it impossible to prove otherwise, and such an accusation can cost him his license. Fearful of investigation or censure, doctors sometimes suspect their patients of faking or exaggerating their symptoms and resist prescribing opiates that are the only hope for people who suffer chronic, even crippling pain. Doctors have a word for this phenomenon: opiophobia.

After his death in 1987, the family of cancer patient Henry

James sued the hospital that had treated him for skimping on the morphine he was prescribed. The jury ruled in their favor after the nursing supervisor testified that she cut his doses out of fear that he might become addicted. The nursing staff had experienced a case of opiophobia, which caused James unnecessary agony before he died. "By perpetuating such attitudes, the war on drugs obstructs pain relief," writes journalist Jacob Sullum. "[P]rescription monitoring has a chilling effect on the practice of medicine."[58]

Meanwhile, marijuana is the safest psychoactive substance known to science. Bad reactions to aspirin or Tylenol, though exceedingly rare, kill thousands of Americans annually, while there are no reliable records of anyone dying from the physical effects of marijuana use.[59] Nevertheless, it remains on Schedule I, alongside serious drugs such as heroin and LSD. A growing number of doctors have spoken out in favor of its potential medical benefits, primarily for people who find oral painkillers ineffective, such as cancer patients whose chemotherapy makes them vomit up their medication and whose veins are too fragile for IVs. In 1996, California became the first state to legalize marijuana for medical use, so that although the drug remains illegal under federal law, state officials are now barred from bringing criminal charges against patients who possess it – if they have prescriptions.

Shortly before the election on the California initiative, the Clinton administration's attorney general, Janet Reno, joined FDA administrator Barry McCaffrey in warning that any doctor who issued such a prescription would face federal charges. A group of doctors filed a lawsuit, asking for an injunction to bar federal officials from penalizing them if they recommended marijuana to patients.[60] They argued that Reno's threat was a prior restraint that violated their First Amendment rights. Relying on the "professional speech" doctrine that gives government broad powers to limit what doctors may say, the court issued an ambiguous ruling which said that while doctors do have the right to *converse* with patients about the risks and benefits of marijuana use, actually *recommending* it could be prosecuted.[61] The Ninth Circuit disagreed. In a separate case, it upheld an injunction blocking Reno from prosecuting doctors who recommended marijuana. "Being a member of a regulated profession does not, as the government suggests, result in a surrender of First Amendment rights," the judges declared.[62] Given the confusion over the free speech rights of professionals, it's not surprising that these conflicting opinions have never been sorted out.

The FDA has also used its power to stifle speech of which it disapproves in cases that do not involve controlled substances. Doctors sometimes suggest that patients use medicines for conditions other than those that the FDA had in mind when it approved the medicines for sale. For example, it may have approved a drug for use against a sleep disorder that also works well against muscle problems, and a physician might prescribe it for the muscle problem instead of the sleep disorder. Prescribing drugs for these "off-label" uses is legal, and it is legal to use drugs for such purposes. Medicare even pays for such off-label uses.[63] But it is illegal to *promote* a drug for off-label uses, and the penalties can be severe.

Orphan Pharmaceutical sales representative Alfred Caronia was brought up on criminal charges when he told a doctor that the sleep-disorder drug Xyrem could also work for chronic pain and muscle disorders. "Right now the indication is for narcolepsy," Caronia said, "but because of the properties that . . . it has it's going to insomnia, Fibromyalgia, periodic leg movement, restless leg."[64] These statements were all true, but because the FDA had not approved Xyrem for those conditions, Caronia was convicted of a crime for uttering true statements about the legal use of a safe and legal drug.

Caronia appealed the case, arguing that he had a First Amendment right to communicate truthful information, and the Second Circuit agreed with him. "[P]rohibiting off-label promotion by a pharmaceutical manufacturer while simultaneously allowing off-label use," the court concluded, "'paternalistically' interferes with the ability of physicians and patients to receive potentially relevant treatment information."[65] Such paternalism could be dangerous "in the fields of medicine and public health, 'where information can save lives.'"[66]

Although the *Caronia* case involved criminal charges, a New York trial court held three years later that the same rule barred the FDA from censoring off-label drug promotion. Recognizing the "therapeutic – indeed, sometimes life-saving – value of off-label uses," the court noted that physicians often write off-label prescriptions.[67] "For a doctor treating a cancer patient, the option of waiting years for possible FDA approval of a new use for an existing drug will often be untenable," leaving the doctor with few other options. Punishing people for truthfully promoting those uses violated the First Amendment.

Despite these rulings, paternalism remains the hallmark of drug regulation, at both the federal and state levels. Since California's 1996 liberalization of marijuana restrictions, 22 other states and the District of Columbia have legalized the medical use of cannabis, and Colorado has even legalized it for recreational use. But implementation of these new laws has often met resistance from government officials. There are certainly valid concerns about the proper locations of marijuana dispensaries, and because it remains illegal under federal law, those dispensaries inhabit a legal twilight zone. That fact gives local bureaucrats who oppose legalization an opportunity to use their powerful tools of business licensing and zoning restrictions to block legalization in their communities.

Arizona voters approved a ballot initiative authorizing medical marijuana in 2010, but officials in Maricopa County have since refused to issue permits for the opening of marijuana dispensaries. Knowing that any outright denial would allow a property owner to at least ask a court to intervene, the county does not actually *reject* such applications; it simply refuses to act, using the excuse that as long as federal law still prohibits marijuana, they can neither grant nor deny permits. Nothing in federal or state law actually says this, but county attorney Bill Montgomery, an extreme opponent of legalization, claimed that permitting dispensaries would make county bureaucrats liable to federal prosecution and ordered the county not to authorize dispensaries until this threat "is conclusively removed."[68]

Federal drug enforcement officers do sometimes enforce federal prohibition, and occasionally raid dispensaries that break the rules, but they have never punished county officers for issuing zoning permits pursuant to state law, and the Obama administration has adopted an explicit policy of accommodating the laws of states that allow medical marijuana. Montgomery's rationale for withholding permits is simply a delaying tactic designed to keep in place a ban of which he personally approves but which the state's voters have rejected. Challenged at a public debate by a Vietnam veteran who uses marijuana, Montgomery made his attitude clear enough: "I have no respect for you," he sneered, "for someone that tried to claim you served this country and took an oath to uphold the Constitution and defend against all enemies foreign and domestic, because you're an enemy."[69]

In 2012, property owners wanting to open a dispensary sued the county for refusing to act on their permit application. Montgomery's office replied that the county could do nothing until the owners submitted documents proving that their operations were legal, which they could not do on account of federal prohibition. Stuck for years in bureaucratic limbo, the owners at last asked a judge to order the county to do *something*, and the judge agreed, ruling that Montgomery's "categorical refusal to examine whether Plaintiff's proposed site meets zoning requirements" was "unlawful."[70] When the county responded with a new zoning ordinance restricting the rights of dispensaries, the judge declared it "a transparent attempt to prevent the implementation of the Arizona Medical Marijuana Act."[71]

Such obstructionist tactics might seem pointless – and in the end, they are – but business owners are still forced to go through the tedious, frustrating process of applying for permits, waiting, and eventually suing. If they were to try simply opening a dispensary without a permit, as an act of civil disobedience, they would be subject to criminal prosecution under both state and federal law and could face lengthy jail terms for illegally selling a Schedule I narcotic. In short, while Arizona voters have approved partial decriminalization, the state's largest county has effectively used permit requirements to nullify that vote.

Prior Restraints on Sex?

Rape is among the most serious crimes there is. But in recent years, efforts to combat sexual violence, especially on college campuses, have led to the adoption of a new kind of law which goes beyond preventing crime. These rules, called "affirmative consent," or "yes means yes," actually operate as a kind of prior restraint on sex itself. They require people to obtain explicit permission before engaging in any sexual contact, forbid people from presuming consent on the basis of silence or acquiescence, and allow a person to withdraw consent at any time. In the abstract, these rules may sound reasonable. But in practice, they actually embody the impossible "Devil's proof" standard, because they presume that a person accused of sexual assault is guilty unless he can prove his innocence.

Responding to a purported epidemic of rape on college campuses,[72] California adopted a "yes means yes" law in 2014. It mandates that the state's colleges revise their disciplinary standards to define sexual contact – including kissing or touching – as a form of assault unless both parties expressed an "affirmative, conscious, and voluntary agreement" beforehand. The law makes quite clear that "silence," or "[l]ack of protest or resistance," or "[t]he existence of a dating relationship" do not qualify as consent.[73] Instead, a person must "take reasonable steps" to determine whether the other person consents. That consent "must be ongoing throughout a sexual activity" and "can be revoked at any time." And the law specifies that the ordinary criminal law standard of "beyond a reasonable doubt" does not apply. Instead, the accused is guilty if "the elements of the complaint" are "demonstrated [by] the *preponderance of the evidence*," a standard far easier for prosecutors to satisfy.[74]

Although this law is not a criminal statute and does not govern all Californians, it does apply to the students in virtually all of the state's colleges and universities. College disciplinary proceedings result in a form of punishment – expulsion, which can make it extremely difficult to be admitted to another college – and can damage a person's reputation for life. That is why federal and state courts have long held that disciplinary procedures by government-funded schools must abide by constitutional rules, including due process of law.[75] "Yes means yes" abandons the presumption of innocence, one of the central tenets of due process, and presumes guilt unless the accused can demonstrate that the other person expressly consented and did not "revoke" that consent "at any time."

Such a vague law creates a treacherous risk of false accusations, which can destroy an innocent student's reputation and future. It's easy to imagine how such an injustice might take place. A couple, walking through the quad one evening after a party, stop in the moonlight. He is interested – more so than she. He leans in for a kiss, hoping the spontaneous moment will sweep her off her feet .... He has already committed sexual assault by failing to "take reasonable steps" to ensure that she has consented to the kiss beforehand. Or consider another couple, who have dated for a year. They wake up together; he leans over to kiss her good morning – again, he has already broken the law. Neither the existence of their relationship nor her previous acquiescence, are enough to prove consent. She can revoke her consent "at any time," and he must ask first before any kiss.

In these and other easily imaginable scenarios, the accused faces humiliation and expulsion under circumstances that make it practically impossible for him to defend himself. As Robert Shibley of the Foundation for Individual Rights in Education writes, "yes means yes" puts the burden "on the accused to prove to a college panel or a single administrator that [he] received continuous consent to any and every sexual act in question. If a student can't produce that proof, he or she is a rapist. It doesn't matter whether the accuser *did* want the sexual act to happen, it only matters whether the accused can convince the school that they indicated as much.... It's hard to see how this can be described as fair, even if the procedures are scrupulously followed."[76]

Simply put, the "affirmative consent" rule imposes a form of prior restraint on sex. Obviously, unwanted sexual contact can be a serious crime, deserving stiff punishment. But that is just why the law has always required that the accused be convicted by objective evidence that proves guilt beyond a reasonable doubt. Until that proof is given, the law presumes in favor of the accused, not the accuser – to protect the innocent from undeserved punishment.[77]

Yet the most egregious aspect of "yes means yes" – its reversal of the presumption of innocence – is just what has gained it the strongest applause from supporters. "The California law removes perpetrators' ability to plead confusion," wrote *Salon's* Jenny Kutner, "and it prevents schools from pleading ignorance to their crimes."[78] But the law does not apply to "perpetrators." It applies to people who are *accused* of being perpetrators – people who have not been convicted of perpetrating anything – and it denies them the protections afforded by centuries of legal precedent. When *New York Magazine* writer Jonathan Chait expressed concern that it might result in wrongful convictions, another *Salon* writer, Katie McDonough, shot back with an accusation of sexism: "When will women's lives and safety matter more than abstractions?"[79] Yet the presumption of innocence is not just an abstraction – it is the cornerstone of an impartial justice system long committed to the maxim that it is better for a guilty person to go free than for an innocent person to be condemned. McDonough dismissed this principle too, spurning those who "side with the 'resolution' that leaves women vulnerable to repeat victimization – once through assault, then a second time through a system that ignores and all but condones the violence."[80]

Contrary to McDonough's implication, concern for the due process rights of the accused is not proof of insensitivity. Instead, experience has tragically proven that accusations of rape are especially prone to abuse, probably because they involve such personal and intimate details and the facts can be so hard to prove in court. Vague rules and presumptions of guilt have a shameful history as tools of oppression. In the Jim Crow South, a white woman's word was often enough to send a black man to prison or even get him the death penalty for rape. In 1952, a Georgia jury convicted a black man of rape despite the fact that when the crime occurred, he had been in another part of town recovering from a circumcision.[81] The following year, another black man was convicted of rape after he simply looked at a 17-year-old white girl from 75 feet away.[82] Even defendants fortunate enough to be acquitted often fell victim to lynching. At a time when even consensual relationships between the races could bring ostracism or violent retribution, white women caught in affairs with black men sometimes escaped censure by claiming they had been raped.

Julie Lavonne Novkov describes one such case in her book *Racial Union: Law, Intimacy and the White State in Alabama*. Clarence Story, a black man, was accused of rape in 1912 by a white woman named Beatrice McClure. She hired Story to drive her from a train station to the place where she was staying – which, according to one witness, was a brothel. After a drunken fight there, she left, only to meet Story a few days later. He drove her to a friend's house to find some whiskey. McClure later claimed that, after about three hours of drinking and carousing, Story raped her.

In court, Clarence Story's lawyer tried to prove that McClure was a prostitute, had had sex with several other black men that week, and had only accused Story after being arrested for vagrancy herself. That tactic, shocking today, was likely Story's only hope: although it is generally considered improper nowadays to introduce evidence of a woman's sexual history when she accuses a man of rape, Novkov explains that Story's lawyer, knowing the overwhelming racial bias against his client, may have thought this was the only way he could persuade the jury to "permit itself to believe the word of a black man over the word of a white woman." Without such evidence, "the jury would not take that step, instead accepting McClure's account of the events." But the judge refused to allow the testimony, and the jury sentenced Story to 35 years in prison. His conviction was later overturned on appeal.[83]

Obviously nobody will ever know what really happened between Story and McClure, but that is just the point: in the absence of objective evidence, race and class prejudices were given free rein. A culture profoundly biased toward preserving the virtue of women, who were presumed sinless and whose word was accepted without question, was willing to ignore even overwhelming evidence in a defendant's favor. Often, the consequence was a heinous perversion of justice.

Today's advocates of "yes means yes" may not be that extreme, but recent incidents of false rape accusations make clear that the problem still exists. In 2006, three white male students at Duke University were falsely accused of raping a black woman at a party. A year of accusations, publicity, and protests followed, with national talk show hosts and their own professors denouncing them. At last, when it became apparent that the accuser had invented the story, the prosecution was forced to drop the charges.[84]

In late 2014, *Rolling Stone* magazine published a sensational story in which a female student using the alias "Jackie" claimed that seven members of a University of Virginia fraternity gang-raped her atop of a pile of broken glass as part of an initiation ritual. Despite the implausibility of the story, university officials suspended the fraternity, protest marches were organized, newspaper columnists and television personalities denounced the students, and rocks and bottles were thrown through the fraternity house's windows. Not until the following spring did the magazine retract the story.[85]

In an article on the website *Thought Catalog*, writer Janet Bloomfield assembled 13 instances of women who falsely accused men of rape to find out why they did it.[86] One lied to cover up cheating on her husband. Another lied when her mother caught her looking at porn. A third lied because she felt guilty about sleeping with the son of a friend. Some lie because they are mentally ill, others for sympathy. False accusations are not always the result of conscious lying – they can result from faulty memories, miscommunications, or overzealous prosecutors. The infamous McMartin Preschool trial, still the longest criminal trial in California history, dragged on for three years despite the fact that the accusations – that the McMartins had raped children, flushed children down toilets, and engaged in bestiality and witchcraft rituals in subterranean caverns beneath the school – were obviously fantasies whipped up by bewildered children, hysterical parents, and obsessive prosecutors.[87]

Whatever their cause, false accusations ruin lives. In 2015, Britain's *Daily Telegraph* published an article by a man using the pseudonym James Robinson, who had been investigated after a false allegation of rape. Robinson was never arrested or officially charged, but the ordeal still haunted him. "I withdrew from my social life," he explained. "I had no interest in sex whatsoever, just stultifying amounts of drink." His accuser was given free counseling, but "I, obviously, got nothing. How angry would that have made you? With me, the answer was 'angry to the point that it felt like it would eat me whole.'" Terrified of relationships, Robinson finally gave up on dating. "Me attempting to form romantic relationships is like trying to paint with a broken arm."[88]

Advocates of "yes means yes" often claim that false accusations are rare, but real evidence one way or the other is impossible to find.[89] Many rape accusations are quickly retracted. Of those that are not, most are settled by plea bargain, so the evidence is never weighed. Only half of all accused rapists are convicted, whether by plea bargain or trial, so it seems likely that the number of false accusations is large. As attorney Edward Greer notes, a significant fraction of convicted *murderers* turn out to be innocent, and there is no reason to think the percentage of false rape charges is smaller. Yet the "yes means yes" policy depends on the assumption that false accusations are rare. Otherwise, that policy would "surely raise the conviction rate toward the ninety-eight percent benchmark," says Greer. Because "at her sole discretion, the woman could imprison any current or former sexual partner."[90]

Actually, given the virtual impossibility of proof, the result would be not universal convictions but an increase in selective and arbitrary enforcement. So many sexual interactions fall into a gray zone – or can be made to seem that way in retrospect – that prosecutors would have plentiful grounds on which to charge people essentially at will and use that power as leverage over people who fear the ordeal of a public trial. Prosecutors often use such advantages to get people to plead guilty to lesser offenses, to testify against other suspects, to agree to searches, or even to become informants.

It is precisely to avoid these problems that the criminal law presumes innocence and requires overwhelming proof of guilt. Advocates of "yes means yes," motivated by compassion for the victim rather than concern for the rights of the accused, wave away hard-won legal protections and replace them with a vague, inherently retroactive standard that presumes guilt, forces the accused to prove after the fact that he obtained overt consent at every moment of sexual activity, and punishes based on a relaxed "preponderance of the evidence" standard. These advocates, including the *New York Times*, which editorialized in support of "yes means yes," hope to see it adopted nationwide and perhaps made the basis of a general revision of criminal law.[91] But by imposing a sort of prior restraint on sex, this law is a frightening step toward a society in which a mere accusation – of something often impossible to prove one way or the other – can permanently scar one's life.

Ironically, another *Times* editorial, published when a small private school called Antioch College adopted a similar policy 20 years before, put the point best. Obviously schools should take sexual crimes seriously, the *Times* declared then,

> [b]*ut adolescence, particularly the college years, is a time for experimentation, and experimentation means making mistakes. No policy will ever be able to protect all young people from those awful mornings-after that are accompanied by the dreadful feeling: "Oh my God! What have I done?" It's from such moments, accompanied by "I'll never let that happen again," that people learn.*[92]

While it's right to enforce clear rules that protect the rights of all students, and actual rapists should be severely punished, overly intrusive laws will only inflict hurt and intimidate the innocent.

CHAPTER EIGHT

The Future of Permission

T HE BASIC PRINCIPLE of the Permission Society is that free-dom is a privilege the government may give or take away as it sees fit. This idea gives those in power a forceful tool to demand that citizens conform or to compel people to surrender their free-dom or property in exchange for the permits or licenses they need. For centuries, that device has been used to control private prop-erty, freedom of speech, and people's religious, economic, and even medical choices. Today, government requires permits for a vast number of activities – everything from building a house to taking medicine – and the number is increasing.

Voters in Santa Monica were recently asked to pass an initiative that would impose strict new permit requirements for any building project taller than 32 *feet.*[1] The City of Berkeley has considered requiring a permit to release balloons.[2] Even such trivial, day-to-day activities as cutting down trees sometimes requires permission from the government. Homeowners who do not know about such rules, or who break them, face severe penalties. In 2007, firefight-ers in Glendale, California, warned Mike and Ann Collard that the oak and sycamore trees surrounding their home were a fire hazard. But the couple failed to get a permit before cutting the trees back. The city fined them $347,600. Only quick work by a lawyer and publicity in the newspaper got them off the hook.[3]

Some countries, including Germany, Sweden, Japan, and Iceland, require parents to get permission to name their babies. Iceland's Personal Names Act creates a national Naming Committee, with members appointed by the country's Minister of Justice, which maintains an official list of pre-approved names. Parents who want to give their child a name not on the list must submit a request and pay a fee. The committee will reject a name if it applies to the "wrong" gender or does not conform to Icelandic grammar rules. In the United States, too, the law sometimes allows the government to decide what people may call themselves. A New York man named Stephen Bobrowich, wishing to express his anger that he had been "treated like a slave" all his life, asked a court in 2003 to change his name to "Steffi Owned Slave." An indignant judge refused because the name was "offensive" and denounced him for insulting the memories of actual slaves who suffered in bondage and those who died to liberate them.[4] The judge had a point, but restricting what Bobrowich could name himself nevertheless intruded on his freedom of expression.

The reason permit requirements are so prolific is that there is no human activity that cannot somehow fit within the logic of the Permission Society. Every act has *some* potential to cause *some* sort of harm to others or to society in the abstract. Driving creates a risk of collisions. Building a house creates a risk that it could fall down. Freedom of speech creates a danger that people might lie, defraud, defame others, or divulge secrets. Letting people cut trees means a neighborhood might lose shade. Letting people name their babies what they like means some people will give kids silly names, or names derived from a foreign language, thus contributing to the dilution of native culture. And because risks can never be perfectly predicted, the idea that we should require people to justify acting before they do so seems like a sensible way to minimize the possibility of harm. Still, imposing a pre-approval requirement on risky activities creates a dangerous potential for abuse, reinforces inequality, deters innovation, and intrudes on personal freedom.

Consider the raising of children. An educated populace is essential in a democracy, and many people think government should guarantee that all citizens have some basic schooling to protect society from the doleful effects of ignorance and illiteracy. But in the Progressive Era, reformers tried to go further and to ban private schools out of a belief that they perpetuated insular attitudes – German parents only sent kids to German schools, Italians to Italian schools – and a fear that parents might teach children poor English skills, might not emphasize math or critical thinking, and might pass along their prejudicial or chauvinistic attitudes. Why not, then, presume that the government will raise children unless parents prove themselves capable?

Oregon legislators agreed with that argument in 1922 and passed a law to compel parents to send children to government-run schools unless they got a special permit. The Supreme Court struck the law down. "The child is not the mere creature of the state," the justices declared.[5] Parents have the right to direct the upbringing of their children – including sending them to private schools if they prefer – without asking for government permission.

Nevertheless, officials in many communities still make it hard for parents to send children to schools of their choice.[6] As homeschooling has become more common in recent decades, parents have sometimes been forced to defend their rights against laws requiring them to get teaching permits before they may educate their own sons and daughters. Several Michigan parents were convicted in the 1980s of teaching their children at home without official certification. They appealed, and in 1992, the state supreme court threw out their convictions. States can require that children be adequately taught, the court said, but the evidence showed that these parents were doing a fine job.[7] The state's decision to prosecute them suggested that bureaucrats were focusing "not [on] ensuring that the goals of compulsory education are met" but instead on a "narrow interest in maintaining the certification requirement."[8] The court rejected that narrowness: as long as children are learning, that is enough – the state may not force parents to get licenses to teach.

Some writers have proposed that the government require licenses before people have children at all. Philosophy professor Hugh Lafollette has argued that people should be barred from reproducing without permits, and he employed the typical arguments used to justify licensing any occupation or activity: parents might be incompetent; their children, and society, might suffer as a result; we already require licenses to drive or to take certain jobs, so why not forbid procreation except for those who prove they are worthy? "[P]eople do not automatically have rights to rear children," Lafollette asserted. Instead, the government should only let them do so if they "meet[] certain minimal standards of child rearing."[9]

This idea is not so farfetched. During the Progressive Era, many states imposed laws that barred the "unfit" from marrying or having children. This eugenics movement gained many adherents in the United States. Some states held competitions to reward couples who had healthy and intelligent children. Other states forced the "unfit" to undergo surgery to render them sterile. In 1927, the Supreme Court upheld compulsory sterilization laws, in an opinion by Justice Oliver Wendell Holmes. The government can draft men into the army against their will, he reasoned, so it might as well force women to give up their right to procreate.[10] These laws remained on the books in the United States until 1956 and in Europe until the 1970s. Today, China's "one child" policy still forbids parents from having children without government permission. Those who violate the policy face fines, seizure of property, loss of employment, or worse. Local officials sometimes force violators to undergo abortions.[11]

The point is not that government has often made mistakes or that some countries still abuse their powers. It is that the permit system is what software engineers call "scalable." The argument for the Permission Society – the idea that future actions might be dangerous, and therefore we should have to ask the government before acting – can just as easily apply to anything humans do: speak, write, read, pray, build, work, raise children, even name babies. Whatever the issue may be, the heart of darkness in all permit systems is that they regard government control as the norm and freedom as the exception. They regard rights as privileges the government can sell to us at its own price.

As more and more realms of freedom are walled off by prior restraints, government's power grows larger, which gives politically influential groups more power to exploit the rules for their benefit. People who lack that influence and are forced to obtain approval from their political or social superiors become increasingly submissive and less likely to innovate or to buck the system. This was the phenomenon Alexis de Tocqueville warned about when he wrote that one of democracy's great dangers was its tendency to take "each citizen in turn in its powerful grasp" and "shape[] him to its will" by imposing "a network of petty, complicated rules" on society, which "men of the greatest originality and most vigorous temperament" cannot escape. This soft despotism does not force people to act, "but often inhibits action; it does not destroy anything, but prevents much from being born; it is not at all tyrannical, but it hinders, restrains, enervates, stifles, and stultifies." In the end, it reduces people to "a flock of timid and hardworking animals with the government as its shepherd."[12]

The Precautionary Principle

One basic assumption behind the Permission Society is the idea that when an activity might harm others, the person wishing to act must justify doing so. Scholars call this the "precautionary principle," and it appeals to our intuition to "look before you leap." But the precautionary principle imposes dangerous risks of its own.

First, without knowing how much risk is too much, the principle can easily become an absolute prohibition on any activity. As

St. Thomas Aquinas observed, if a captain's only concern were the safety of his ship, he would never leave port.[13] Safety cannot be our overriding consideration, particularly because there is no way to be certain that even innocuous activities might not bring about terrible consequences. If we peg the threshold of acceptable risk at zero, the precautionary principle will always lead to the conclusion that it's best to wait and see. Yet waiting and seeing has risks, too, and many of these are impossible to measure.[14] In effect, the precautionary principle contradicts itself.

Risk is usually measured by multiplying the potential downside of an action by the likelihood that it will happen. So, for example, if there is a 50 percent chance that moving an antique sculpture might break it, costing $5,000, then the risk can be calculated as $2,500. But this simple formula is often inapplicable to real-life scenarios, where there are myriad variables, most of which cannot be measured accurately. And efforts to calculate them can mislead because the numbers on which such efforts depend are often only "guesstimates." What does it mean, for instance, to say there is a 50 percent chance the sculpture might break? If it only means that it will either break or it won't, then the number really reveals nothing. Calculating the risks of more complicated undertakings – whether a ship leaving port will reach its destination, whether a factory will pollute the local groundwater, whether a new product will succeed or fail – is often impossible.

Worse, people tend to rely on guesstimates, which bias their own perceptions despite their awareness that the number is only a guess. As Gregory N. Mandel and James Thuo Gathii observe, "[t]he quantitative appearance of cost-benefit analysis lures unsuspecting decision makers to believe that it offers far more than it can actually provide." It is rare for planners to have reliable figures with which to predict the future. But "once cost-benefit analysis spits out a number, people attach to it, even when they are aware that it is highly unreliable."[15] The consequences can be worse than simply admitting our ignorance.

Nobel Prize–winning physicist Richard Feynman encountered a striking example of this phenomenon while investigating the explosion of the space shuttle *Challenger* in 1986. One engineer he interviewed told him that NASA calculated the failure rate of the space shuttle's engines as 1 in 100,000. Feynman instantly recognized this number as absurd. "That means you could fly the shuttle every day for an average of 300 years between accidents – every day, one flight, for 300 years – which is obviously crazy!"[16] It took weeks to find the source of this number: NASA administrators had simply made it up to appease a Congressman who demanded a number. Knowing it is impossible to quantify the possibility that a machine as complex as the space shuttle would fail, engineers had refused to answer. But when politicians insisted on a number – any number at all – an unknown NASA administrator fabricated the 1 in 100,000 figure. Once it was in place, it evolved from meaningless to dangerous. Scientists who thought the shuttle less reliable than that were told that their calculations must be wrong, and their warnings went unheeded because the "official number" showed it was safer.[17]

In short, the advice to look before you leap makes sense if you know what you are looking for, but most of the time we do not. And *not* leaping when you should has costs, too – costs that can be harder to calculate because they are often "unseen": the opportunities that *might* have led to prosperity, discovery, success, and happiness if only they had been allowed to materialize. A law that imposes costly delays on drug companies before they can sell medicines, for example, costs lives that *might* have been saved, but it is impossible to measure that cost accurately; nobody knows who could have been saved or how. Nor can we ever know what secondary innovations might have come about if the first had been allowed. A law that requires entrepreneurs to undergo a complicated, expensive licensing process to start a new company deprives society of the products and services that *might* have been created, as well as the further innovations their innovation *might* have inspired. No cost-benefit analysis can factor in such invisible costs.

Even when we stretch our imaginations, we inevitably underestimate the costs of not innovating relative to the potential benefits. Genetically modified foods, for instance, are a safe and effective means of improving nutrition and public health, but, like everything, they are not risk-free. When the European Union banned genetically modified supplements because scientists could not "guarantee" that they pose "no risk to human health," one scientist was indignant: it "cannot be emphasized enough," he wrote, that "it can never be proven that (micro)nutrient food supplements do not pose any risks to any consumers."[18] To require proof that they are entirely risk-free means requiring proof of a negative – the same "Devil's proof" that haunts the permit system in all its forms.

"Trying to preemptively plan for every hypothetical worst-case scenario means that many best-case scenarios will never come about," writes economist Adam Thierer in his book, *Permissionless Innovation.* "That is, the benefits that accompany freedom to experiment will necessarily be sacrificed if fear paralyzes our innovative spirit. Progress and prosperity will be stifled as a result."[19] The one thing the precautionary principle is not is a *principle*. It is, at best, vague advice to be careful. That is certainly wise, but it is of little value in deciding how to act in a world full of complicated risks and hidden costs. Yet it is routinely used to justify the permit system, which prohibits innovation and potentially risky new ventures unless people prove to the government's satisfaction that the change is justified. When we consider the costs of blocking change – including the unseen costs – we can get a sense of the immense danger that the Permission Society poses to innovation and freedom.

"Privilege"

Leftist political thinkers have offered a still more virulent argument for envisioning rights as permissions. This idea, called "Privilege Theory," originated in a 1988 essay by Wellesley College professor Peggy McIntosh, and it focuses on the degree to which "unacknowledged privilege" unfairly elevates some people over others.[20]

According to McIntosh, those who are "privileged" unconsciously foster "conservative assumptions about the inevitability of present gender [or race] relations and distributions of power."[21] There is an element of truth to this: some people are born wealthy, others poor – some strong, others weak – and it is easy to forget that some people don't have it as good as others. But Privilege Theory goes further. By employing vague language about the alleged power structures that shape society – structures that are conveniently "elusive and fugitive"[22] – Privilege theorists blur distinctions that are critical for understanding justice and treat inequality as a *per se* wrong that government should rectify. Ignoring the fact that many people are better off because they and their families worked hard, made responsible choices, and developed habits and virtues that raised them to prosperity, advocates of Privilege Theory typically regard disparities of wealth or social position as proof of unfair advantage and characterize individual rights as just another benefit that society gives to the wealthy and powerful at the expense of the "underprivileged."

Privilege theorist Ezra Rosser, for example, argues that because previous generations of white Americans had more property than blacks and left that property to their descendants, whites today enjoy an unfair advantage. "[R]arely do whites consider that their houses, or the houses of their parents, may be citadels perpetuating prior discriminatory policies," he writes.[23] Legal protections for private property are therefore just another way that society perpetuates inequality. But it is not only inheritance that Rosser opposes: even *earning* new property is tainted by unconscious racial bias. "Once acquisition is stripped of deservedness and merit, once whites recognize the systematic advantages that their ancestors enjoyed, and that they enjoy currently, the ownership status quo is harder to defend."[24]

For this reason, Rosser and other Privilege theorists advocate not merely wealth redistribution but also vandalism and theft as ways to resist the invisible injustice that pervades society. "Property disobedience," he writes, "would seem a natural way for those disadvantaged by this history to respond to these acquisition issues."[25] Because "violations of property law" play a "positive role" in "ensuring that the law matches our values," political leaders should allow "space ... for disobedience." Concerned about the "danger of property rights overenforcement and rule-breaking overdeterrence," Rosser criticizes other Privilege Theory advocates for not doing more to encourage vandalism, theft, riots, and other property crimes – which he euphemistically calls "radical breaks from existing law and associated inequality in the distribution of property."[26] More simply, stealing or breaking other people's things is justified because wealthy people have enjoyed too much "acquisition" privilege.

Another Privilege Theory enthusiast, University of Minnesota law professor john a. powell (who writes his name in lowercase to signify that we are "part of the universe, not over it"[27]) applies the same logic to freedom of speech. As with property, society also unjustly privileges some "narratives" over others, including the "narrative" that supports the value of free expression. According to the "freedom" narrative, "people assert[] their autonomy through participation, free thought, and self-expression," and people who embrace this conception of free speech are "nervous about any government or community constraint" on speech. But another narrative, which powell calls the "equality" narrative, "tells a story of a government that, until recently, actively engaged in efforts to exclude, and now passively stands by while private actors and powerful social forces continue to shut the door to full membership in society." Those who embrace the "equality" narrative are likely to support restrictions on speech that aim at remedying these alleged inequalities.[28]

Blanket prohibitions on censorship, such as the First Amend-

ment, should therefore be abandoned, because they "privilege[]
the free speech narrative" so that "the claims of [the] equality
[narrative] with regard to harm cannot be heard."[29] Powell particularly objects to court decisions striking down college speech codes
that censor racist, sexist, or other offensive expression because
these decisions focus exclusively on whether the rules abridge
speech and do not ask whether "the purpose of the regulation" is
benign, such as "end[ing] discrimination" or "eradicat[ing] imped-
iments to the provision of an equal education to groups who have
been historically denied educational opportunity."[30] Good intentions make a prohibition of speech not censorship, only a different,
equally valid "narrative" of speech. Powell does not mean that the
"equality" approach is *better* than the "liberty" approach. In his
view, there is "no transcendental standard by which one can determine if a form of speech should be regulated."[31] The question of
whether speech should be punished by the government is not to be
answered by "closed or abstract logic" but by "an open, dialogical
process."[32]

It's easy to dismiss arguments like powell's as faddish nonsense,
but they actually represent a serious new spin on an old theme:
rights are only privileges society gives people, and because it par-
cels out those rights in an unequal way, government should make
things more equal by redistributing rights. Powell is explicit on
this point: "There may be strong arguments for assigning liberty
rights to the individual," he writes, "but this is a social question
that must be resolved through social balancing."[33] In times past,
freedom of speech, private property, and other rights were unjustly
"assigned" without such balancing: "Indeed, part of the function of
calling something a liberty is to avoid this calculus." Privilege Theory, by deconstructing this ironclad conception of liberty, aims to
"balance" society by redistributing not just wealth but all rights.[34]

Still more extreme is the work of philosophers Harry Brighouse
and Adam Swift, who argue that the very existence of families is a
form of unfair privilege because children fortunate enough to be

raised by loving parents end up better off than those who are not. Throughout their 2014 book *Family Values*, Brighouse and Swift contend that the benefits conferred on kids by caring, functional families make the family a presumptively unjust institution, which society should only allow if people can prove its benefits. "The egalitarian challenge demands an account of why families should be permitted to create inequalities between children," they write, "and what kinds of familial interactions, creating what kinds of inequalities, are indeed justified."[35] Where Hugh Lafollette would require people to get a permit to have children as a way of preventing child *abuse*, Brighouse and Swift would require parents to get permission to treat their children *well*.

Because "the freedoms liberals value tend to disrupt the equality egalitarians value," the state should parcel out those freedoms, including the freedom to care for one's child, only to those who can justify deviating from the basic assumption of equality. To the question of why parents have any right "generally to benefit their children," they answer that the state has "a duty" *not* to "permit" such benefits if "permitting them conflicts with other children's interest in favor of equality of opportunity."[36] While Brighouse and Swift consider some forms of parental caring justifiable, others, including private schools, should be abolished. "I don't think parents reading their children bedtime stories should constantly have in their minds the way that they are unfairly disadvantaging other people's children," Swift told an interviewer in 2015, "but I think they should have that thought occasionally."[37]

As Brighouse, Swift, Rosser, and powell demonstrate, Privilege Theory seeks to attain equality by classifying individual rights as privileges society assigns or "allows," and then fashioning a formula for assigning those privileges in a more desirable way. In the service of equality or "social balancing," even the violation of individual rights – vandalism, theft, censorship, and the breaking of the parent-child bond – is justifiable.

* * *

Rescuing Liberty

We have seen how the permit system in various guises gives government extraordinary power to control individual lives. We have seen also that the permit system has several significant drawbacks:

Rent-seeking: When permits become valuable, they encourage people to devote time and money to getting permits and blocking their competitors from getting them. Moving companies that can use Competitor's Veto laws, for example, try to succeed not by providing better service to customers but by obtaining favors from the government and preventing new companies from starting.

The Knowledge Problem: The permit system is premised on the notion that government knows what should and should not be permitted. But there is rarely good reason to assume this, and often good reason to doubt it. The founding fathers eliminated prior restraints on freedoms of religion and speech in part because the government does not know the "truth" about religion or politics and cannot be trusted to ensure that only true things are preached or published. But government is no better at managing our economic choices, the uses of property, the practice of medicine, or our family relationships than it is at managing those things.

Vagueness: The standards a person must meet in order to get a permit are often written so vaguely that nobody can know what they really mean – which gives bureaucrats the ability to impose whatever restrictions they want. Broadcasters regulated under the ambiguous "public interest" standard often found that their freedom of speech existed only at the mercy of the FCC, and architectural design review, which enables officials to block the construction of buildings they find unattractive, allows them to impose their own aesthetic tastes on neighborhoods.

Demanding payoffs: The power to give someone permission allows the government to make demands of people in exchange for permits. When property owners request a permit to improve their property, the permitting agency has the leverage to force them to give up land or cash. And because the government can deprive doctors of the ability to practice medicine or prescribe treatment, it can restrict their rights to free speech and the rights of patients to access medicine they need.

The double-layer effect of permits: Because violating a permit requirement is illegal, even if the permit requirement itself is invalid, citizens have little opportunity to resist illegal restrictions of their freedom. A property owner, for example, who thinks the government is abusing its authority must hold off construction, often for years, while a court reviews the case – a prospect many people cannot afford. Officials often use delay and financial pressure to get their way.

Stifling innovation: Permit requirements essentially force a person to prove that something is a good idea before he can give it a try. But in many areas of life, particularly in economics, it is simply not possible to know whether something will prove to be a good idea without trying it first. As Friedrich Hayek wrote, competition is a "discovery procedure"[38] – a tool for learning what innovations will or will not prove beneficial. But the permit system bars competition and discovery and often scares entrepreneurs away from trying new ideas that might otherwise have made everybody better off.

Government as superior: Because the permit system requires government approval of things a citizen would like to do, it essentially establishes a Permission Society – a system of superiors and inferiors, in which those who grant permission stand on a higher plane than those who must ask for it. This contradicts the basic principle of equality and gradually corrupts the spirit of self-reliance on which healthy democracies depend. Instead of equal citizens who together establish and run the government for the benefit of all, the Permission Society regards citizens as subjects or children, who can be told what they may do with their property, what they may read or say, what sorts of medicine they may take, and even what sort of sexual and family relationships are permissible.

What other option is there? The ubiquity of permit requirements leads many people to assume that they are the only way to regulate potentially dangerous activities. But the traditional system of nuisance – with its fundamental principle of *sic utere*, or "do as you will with what's yours, but harm nobody else" – provides a ready alternative that respects equality and freedom of choice. People need not ask permission before acting but must pay damages to anyone their actions harm.

This method of regulation is already widely used in many areas of life. With some exceptions, people are not required to get licenses before speaking, but if they defraud or libel people, they can be sued or punished. No license is required to buy poisons, knives, or certain explosives. People can ski, skydive, or play football without licenses. They can use power tools, build campfires, or run scientific experiments with dangerous chemicals, without licenses, even though all these things pose a risk of harm to oneself or others. In all these cases, the threat of punishment in the event that one hurts others is considered sufficient to deter wrongdoing.

The primary drawback to the nuisance system is that it is generally reactive. Rather than checking harm, nuisance law requires compensation when someone is injured, or prevents injury only when it is imminent. But this shortcoming is easily fixed – indeed, it already is, through private certification and insurance requirements.

Private certification or "seals of approval" enforce industry standards and provide the same benefits to consumers that licensing laws are supposed to provide – informing them of what businesses are safe, qualified, and honest. The advent of social media has given consumers plentiful ways to make informed choices. People today are far more likely to turn to Yelp! or Angie's List, or the reviews on Amazon.com than to ask whether a product or service has passed some government inspection.

Businesses are more responsive to the needs of consumers than bureaucrats anyway. As Judge Brown put it in her ruling striking down Washington, D.C.'s licensing requirement for tour guides, private industry "already has strong incentives to provide a quality consumer experience – namely, the desire to stay in business and maximize a return on its capital investment."[39] Business owners strive to provide customers with satisfactory services not because they fear losing their licenses but because they want to succeed economically. Contractors build buildings that do not fall down not to satisfy government officials but because if their buildings collapse, they will be liable for damages and nobody will hire them again. Pharmaceutical companies produce medicines that do not poison people because otherwise they would be taken to court and patients would distrust their products in the future. People do not use their freedom of speech to defame others because if they do, they will be punished and others will shun them as bad people.[40]

The Federal Trade Commission (FTC) has recommended private certification as a better way to provide consumers with the benefits of licensing without restricting competition, raising prices, and depriving entrepreneurs of the opportunity to innovate. In

2015, the White House agreed, in a lengthy report that urged states to use voluntary certification instead of mandatory licensing because it "provides information to consumers while allowing them to choose the quality they can afford ... without limiting the workers' access to the occupation."[41] Or, as the FTC report put it, certification lets people "choose either a lower priced, noncertified professional or a higher priced, certified one," but since it does not punish people for practicing the trade without approval, it allows for innovation and opportunity. The FTC quoted Nobel laureate Milton Friedman: "If the argument is that we are too ignorant to judge good practitioners, all that is needed is to make the relevant information available. If, in full knowledge, we still want to go to someone who is not certified, that is our business."[42]

Private certification alone will not protect against all problems: laws prohibiting fraud and requiring practitioners to pay for any injuries they cause are also essential, but these rules already exist. Insurance companies already require their clients to comply with certain standards and, in many cases, to obtain private certification as a condition of being insured. They also require inspections or physical exams to make sure their clients are not taking unwise risks. Insurers often examine buildings to check whether they are adequately maintained and require basic safety equipment like smoke or carbon monoxide detectors. They hire investigators to detect fraud and track down thieves. Some perform surprise inspections of restaurants and other businesses they insure, to make certain their clients are not engaging in dangerous behavior that might expose them to liability. Such requirements play the role that permit rules now play, without the legal restrictions that violate individual freedom and inhibit competition and innovation. In fact, the government itself sometimes relies on the standards established by the insurance industry when it tries to predict risk or write safety rules. Because insurers bear the brunt of injuries their clients sustain, they have a natural incentive to create and maintain meaningful safety requirements, and the insurance industry is therefore best suited to formulate rules that will protect people with the least sacrifice of innovation and productivity.

The idea of relying on insurers to play this role might discomfit some people, given that insurance companies are often regarded with skepticism and fear. But while insurance companies sometimes act in greedy and dishonest ways, government has often proven greedy and dishonest, too. Whatever reasons there might be to distrust private industry, government is far less reliable because it has less of an incentive to serve people well. Customers unhappy with the way one company does business can shop somewhere else. But they have much less bargaining power relative to the government. They cannot fire it, refuse to pay it, or (much of the time) even sue it. And because most permit laws are enforced by administrative agencies instead of elected officials, the power to vote has little meaningful impact on the way such laws are administered.

It is often said that a smaller government operating more on the nuisance principle than the permit principle may have made sense in the past, when society was simpler and less interdependent than today, but in the complex, interdependent world in which we live now, more government control is needed to rationally organize society. In fact, the opposite is true. As economic and social life becomes increasingly sophisticated, the notion that any central bureaucratic agency can organize and plan the innumerable relationships between citizens and provide for their needs becomes far less plausible. The more intricate and fast-paced our society, the more we depend upon alternatives to government: private institutions that can devise new ways to protect consumers while allowing people to make their own choices, as opposed to tedious bureaucratic controls overseen by office-holders who have little incentive to find the most efficient solutions for social problems.

Given the many disadvantages that permit requirements create, such as rent-seeking and vagueness, government intervention becomes increasingly counterproductive as government gets more

THE FUTURE OF PERMISSION

deeply involved. Nobody knows whether, say, Missouri or Kentucky need new moving companies, and nobody *can* know. Nobody knows what medical innovations should or should not be allowed, or what ideas should be published, or who really needs a gun, or who should be free to have children. Government bureaucrats are probably the *least* qualified to answer such questions. The only way to find out the answers is to let people make their own choices, enjoying the rewards of wise decisions and paying the price for bad ones.

Steps Toward Freedom

Some states have begun taking steps to limit the growth of licensing and permit requirements. One device, called "Sunrise Review," is already law in Arizona,[43] Washington state,[44] Colorado,[45] Maine,[46] Vermont,[47] and elsewhere. Sunrise Review requires lawmakers to determine whether there is a genuine need to impose a licensing requirement on a business before they adopt such a law. A typical sunrise rule declares that the government may regulate professions only to protect consumers, not private interests, and that the state may only impose a licensing requirement if the unregulated practice of that profession would clearly endanger the public. Before passing a licensing law, the legislature must submit to a tough analysis of whether the benefits of a new regulation exceed the costs and whether those benefits cannot be achieved by private certification or other alternatives.

Obviously a legislature can jump over such a hurdle if it truly wants to, but procedural requirements like this can at least slow the process down and inform voters about possible abuses. In 2000, the Colorado legislature relied on its sunrise law to reject the effort of the American Society of Interior Designers to force that state's interior designers to be licensed. The sunrise report showed that there was no need for such a law: evidence from states that do require interior designers to be licensed showed that consumers hardly ever made complaints and that the law was generally only used by existing companies to block competition. "There is no reason to expect that the Colorado experience will be any different," the report found.[48] Since there was "no persuasive evidence" that unlicensed interior designers were a "measurable harm" to the public, the report recommended against requiring licensure. Lawmakers agreed and voted down the bill.

Still more effective are laws that limit the power of administrative agencies to adopt new permit requirements. The Arizona legislature enacted a law in 2015 that forbids agencies from adopting "any new rule that would increase existing regulatory restraints or burdens on the free exercise of property rights or the freedom to engage in an otherwise lawful business or occupation" unless that new rule is part of a "comprehensive effort to reduce regulatory restraints or burdens" or is required by a court order. The only exception is for rules adopted out of an "immediate need" to prevent a "catastrophic event."[49] This law limits unelected bureaucracies to the enforcement of existing law and leaves the power to make law in the hands of elected legislators.

But in the end, the only way to stop America's descent into a Permission Society is for citizens to realize the high stakes involved. Freedom is something all people enjoy because we are people. It is not a privilege the government gives to us. If the blessings of liberty are to remain a reality, they must be regarded as *rights*, not as permissions. Whether it be the freedom to build a home, start a business, advertise, or take medicine or own guns to protect our lives, we must not allow politicians to treat our freedoms as gifts they bestow upon us out of their magnanimity.

AFTERWORD

AT THE NUREMBERG TRIALS in 1946, Supreme Court Justice
Robert Jackson, serving as the chief prosecutor of Nazi war
criminals, sought words to express the idea of freedom that he
hoped would rise from the ashes of Europe. He found those words
in an 1899 poem by Rudyard Kipling entitled "The Old Issue":

> *All we have of freedom, all we use or know,*
> *This our fathers bought for us, long and long ago.*
> *Ancient Right unnoticed – as the breath we draw.*
> *Leave to live by no man's leave, underneath the law.*[1]

Leave to live by no man's leave. The freedom to decide and to
act without first asking leave of kings or bureaucrats is the crucial
difference between those who are free and those who are not. As
government takes increasing control over aspects of our lives –
economic, political, social, and personal – our nation is more in
danger of losing all we have of freedom.

It is sometimes said that we owe it to future generations to pass
the world on to them at least as good as we found it, because future
generations may be unable to fix the messes we make. How much
more crucial is it, then, to pass on to them the protections for liberty written into our Constitution – protections which, if betrayed,

215

whittled away, or abandoned, might never be restored? Perhaps the most crucial principle Americans have inherited, and which they must preserve, is the idea that freedom means not having to ask permission. Today, however, America is slowly becoming a Permission Society instead of the free society that our highest law calls us.

Yet the Permission Society's basic assumption – that people cannot be trusted with freedom, that they are therefore not free unless government says they are – is not only its most offensive element but also its silliest. *Of course* people can be trusted with freedom. We do it all the time. And if we do not, then we must ask the question: Whom can we trust with *ours*?

ACKNOWLEDGMENTS

THIS BOOK was inspired by conversations with Jack Armstrong, Joe Getty, Alan Gura, and Christina Sandefur. Thanks also to George F. Will for his kind encouragement. Earlier versions of portions of this book appeared in the *Cato Supreme Court Review*, the *George Mason University Civil Rights Law Journal*, the *Harvard Journal of Law & Public Policy*, *Nexus: A Journal of Opinion*, the *Notre Dame Journal of Law, Ethics & Public Policy*, the *NYU Journal of Law & Liberty*, and *Regulation*. Other material originated in lawsuits or briefs I filed as an attorney with the Pacific Legal Foundation and the Goldwater Institute, and particularly my litigation on behalf of Raleigh Bruner and Michael Munie, discussed in chapter 5. I am grateful for the assistance of Alan Gura, Daniel Himebaugh, M. Reed Hopper, Larry Salzman, Barbara Siebert, Christina Sandefur, Pagona A. Stratoudakis, and Joshua P. Thompson – and particularly Deborah J. La Fetra for much editorial assistance on this and other works over more than a decade. But the opinions expressed herein do not necessarily represent those of the Goldwater Institute, the Pacific Legal Foundation, or their staff, supporters, or clients.

NOTES

INTRODUCTION

1   Walt Whitman, "Song of the Open Road," in Michael Warner, ed., *The Portable Walt Whitman* (New York: Penguin, 2004), p. 139.

2   John Locke, *Second Treatise* § 57, in Peter Laslett, ed., *John Locke: Two Treatises of Government* (New York: Oxford University Press, rev. ed., 1963), p. 348.

3   George Smith, *The System of Liberty* (New York: Cambridge University Press, 2013), p. 138.

CHAPTER ONE

1   Jack Rakove, ed., *James Madison: Writings* (New York: Library of America, 1999), p. 502.

2   William Blackstone, *Commentaries on the Laws of England* (London: A. Strahan, 1809), vol. 1, p. 49.

3   Ibid.

4   Ibid., p. 161.

5   Ibid., p. 162.

6   Kermit L. Hall & Mark David Hall, eds., *Collected Works of James Wilson* (Indianapolis: Liberty Fund, 2007), vol. 2, pp. 1057-58.

7   Noel B. Gerson, *The Edict of Nantes* (New York: Grosset & Dunlap, 1969), p. 150.

8   John Stetson Barry, *The History of Massachusetts*, 4th ed. (Boston: John Barry, 1856), vol. 1, p. 490.

9   Gordon Wood, ed., *John Adams: Revolutionary Writings 1755-1775* (New York: Library of America, 2011), p. 397.

10   Declaratory Act of 1766, 6 Geo. III c. 12, *Statutes at Large* (Danby Pickering, ed., 1767), vol. 27, pp. 19-20.

11   U.S. Declaration of Independence, 1 Stat. 1 (1776).

12   The term "pie crust promises" is probably best known from the film *Mary Poppins*, in which Mary uses the term to refer to promises "easily made, easily broken." But the term is much older. In her 1861 poem "Promises Like Pie Crust,"

Christina Rossetti urges her beau to "Promise me no promises, / So I will not promise you: / Keep we both our liberties, / Never false and never true."

13   Virginia Declaration of Rights ¶ 1 (1776).

14   Richard A. Epstein, *Bargaining with the State* (Princeton: Princeton University Press, 1993), pp. 28–29.

15   Ibid., p. 29.

16   *Writings of Thomas Jefferson* (New York: Riker, Thorne & Co., 1855), vol. 2, p. 404 (spelling corrected).

17   Edmund Powell, *The Practice of the Law of Evidence* (Philadelphia: T. & J.W. Johnson & Co., 1858), p. 114.

18   William Briggs, *A Manual of Logic* (London: University Tutorial Press, 1905), vol. 2, p. 286.

19   Bertrand Russell, "Is There a God?" in John G. Slater, ed., *The Collected Papers of Bertrand Russell* (London: Routledge, 1997), vol. 11, pp. 547–48.

20   Although an acquitted defendant cannot be tried again for the same offense, he can be held civilly liable, or, at the very least, shunned by polite society.

21   Am. Fed'n of State, Cnty. & Mun. Employees Council 79 v. Scott, 717 F.3d 851, 882 (11th Cir. 2013), *cert. denied*, 134 S. Ct. 1877 (2014).

22   Merrill Peterson, ed., *Thomas Jefferson: Writings* (New York: Library of America, 1984), p. 1517.

23   Declaration of the Causes and Necessity of Taking Up Arms (1775), in *Journals of the Continental Congress* (Washington, D.C.: Government Printing Office, 1905), vol. 2, p. 140.

24   Henry Fairlie, "What Europeans Thought of Our Revolution," *The New Republic*, July 4, 2014, http://www.newrepublic.com/article/118527/american-revolution-what-did-europeans-think.

25   David Armitage, *The Declaration of Independence: A Global History* (Cambridge, MA: Harvard University Press, 2007), p. 77.

26   Ibid., p. 174.

27   *Works of Bentham* (Edinburgh: William Tait, 1843), vol. 2, p. 501.

28   Ibid., vol. 11, p. 7.

29   Ibid., vol. 9, p. 217.

30   Ibid.

31   Ibid.

32   Ibid., p. 221.

33   Richard A. Posner, ed., *The Essential Holmes* (Chicago: University of Chicago Press, 1992), p. xxv.

34   Ibid., p. 181.

35   Ibid., p. 116.

36   H. L. A. Hart, *The Concept of Law*, 2nd ed. (New York: Oxford University Press, 1961), pp. 19–23.

37   Lon L. Fuller, *The Law in Quest of Itself* (Boston: Beacon Press, 1966), p. 110.

38   Lawrence v. Texas, 539 U.S. 558, 578 (2003) (emphasis added).

39   It would probably be best to distinguish between "rights," "liberties," and "freedom," as Anthony de Jasay takes care to do in *Justice and Its Surroundings* (Indianapolis: Liberty Fund, 2002), p. 256–57. Jasay defines "rights" as obligations on others to do or not do a certain thing, "liberty" as the absence of any sort of constraint or obligation, and "freedom" as the group of liberties we have "after unfreedoms have been identified as such by confronting them with the rules of justice and 'blotted out' as inadmissible." Ibid., p. xxvi.

40   Tom G. Palmer, *Realizing Freedom*, 2nd ed. (Washington, D.C.: Cato Institute, 2009), p. 76.

41   *Works of Bentham*, vol. 2, p. 501.

42   Ibid., vol. 9, p. 223.

43   *Collected Works of James Wilson*, vol. 2, p. 1058.

44   *Works of Bentham*, vol. 2, p. 502. As political philosopher Hannah Arendt put it, "the Rights of Man, supposedly inalienable, proved to be unenforceable" in the Holocaust. Hannah Arendt, *The Origins of Totalitarianism* (Orlando: Harvest Books, 1976), p. 293.

45   W. H. Auden, *Collected Poems* (New York: Vintage, 1991), p. 264.

46   Lon Fuller, *The Morality of Law* (New Haven: Yale University Press, 1969), p. 61. See also Rinat Kitai, "Presuming Innocence," *Oklahoma Law Review* vol. 55 (2002): 281–82.

47   Peterson, *Thomas Jefferson: Writings*, pp. 120–21.

48   Oliver Wendell Holmes, "Natural Law," *Harvard Law Review* vol. 32 (1918): 41.

49   John Chipman Gray, *The Nature and Sources of the Law* (New York: Columbia University Press, 1909), § 656, p. 291.

50   In his recent book, *Is Administrative Law Unlawful?* (Chicago: University of Chicago Press, 2014), p. 493, Professor Philip Hamburger puts the point well. Although the administrative agency system created by Progressive Era thinkers is "widely said to be a novelty, which developed in response to the necessities of modern life," it is actually "as ancient as the desire for consolidated power outside and above the law" and a throwback "to the absolute prerogative" of the medieval monarchy.

51   Ronald Dworkin, *Taking Rights Seriously* (Cambridge, MA: Harvard University Press, 1978), p. 273.

52   Taken from Robert Nozick, *Anarchy, State, and Utopia* (New York: Basic Books, 1974), pp. 161–63.

53   *Federalist* No. 10, J. Cooke, ed. (Middletown: Wesleyan University Press, 1961), p. 58.

54   Ronald Dworkin, *A Matter of Principle* (Cambridge, MA: Harvard University Press, 1985), p. 199.

55 Anthony de Jasay, "Slicing the Cake Nobody Baked," in *Justice and Its Surroundings*, pp. 186–96.

56 Dworkin was relying on the philosopher John Rawls for this point. See John Rawls, *A Theory of Justice* (Cambridge, MA: Belknap, 1971).

57 Wallace Matson, *Uncorrected Papers* (New York: Humanity Books, 2006), p. 116.

58 Dworkin, *Taking Rights Seriously*, p. 274.

59 Ibid., p. 273 (emphasis added).

60 Dworkin, *Matter of Principle*, p. 353.

61 Dworkin, *Taking Rights Seriously*, p. 276.

62 Dworkin, *Matter of Principle*, p. 362.

63 Ibid., pp. 360, 414n16.

64 Ibid., p. 205.

65 Ibid., p. 199.

66 Ibid., p. 206.

67 Dworkin, *Taking Rights Seriously*, p. 277.

68 Ibid., p. 278.

69 See David E. Bernstein, *Rehabilitating Lochner* (Chicago: University of Chicago Press, 2011).

70 Lochner v. New York, 198 U.S. 45, 61 (1905).

71 *Id.* at 57.

CHAPTER TWO

1 Elmer E. Smead, "*Sic Utere Tuo Ut Elienum Non Laedas*: A Basis of the State Police Power," *Cornell Law Quarterly* vol. 21 (1936): 276–92.

2 In 1937, the city imposed a maximum of 16,900 licensed taxicabs in the city. That number fell, then rose again, and at present there are 13,237. Dana Rubinstein, "The Curse of the New York City Taxi Medallion," *Capital New York*, Jan. 31, 2013, http://www.capitalnewyork.com/article/politics/2013/01/7399052/curse-new-york-city-taxi-medallion?page=all.

3 Leonard Read, *I, Pencil* (first published 1958), Library of Economics and Liberty, http://www.econlib.org/library/Essays/rdPncl1.html.

4 Montgomery Nat. Bank v. Clarke, 882 F.2d 87, 88 (3d Cir. 1989).

5 *Id.* at 88–89 (emphasis original).

6 Id. at 90 (quoting Elizabeth Federal Savings & Loan Association v. Howell, 30 N.J. 190, 194 (1959) (per curiam)).

7 Arendt, *Origins of Totalitarianism*, p. 244.

8 Chevron, U.S.A., Inc. v. Natural Res. Def. Council, Inc., 467 U.S. 837 (1984).

9 Gualala Festivals Comm. v. California Coastal Comm'n, 183 Cal. App. 4th 60 (2010).

10 "Sebelius: 'I Don't Work For' People Who Want Me to Resign," *National*

Review Corner, Oct. 24, 2013, http://www.nationalreview.com/corner/362166/sebelius-i-dont-work-people-who-want-me-resign-nro-staff.

11 Shuttlesworth v. City of Birmingham, 394 U.S. 147 (1969).

12 Walker v. City of Birmingham, 388 U.S. 307, 318–21 (1967).

13 James M. Washington, ed., *A Testament of Hope* (New York: Harper Collins, 1986), p. 542.

14 As with so many purported Franklinisms, this may be apocryphal. Seymour L. Chapin, "A Legendary Bon Mot? Franklin's 'What Is the Good of a Newborn Baby?'" *Proceedings of the American Philosophical Society* vol. 129, no. 3 (Sept. 1985): 278–90; I. Bernard Cohen, "Faraday and Franklin's 'Newborn Baby,'" *Proceedings of the American Philosophical Society* vol. 131, no. 2 (June 1987): 177–82.

15 16 U.S.C. § 1532(20).

16 Andrew P. Morriss & Richard L. Stroup, "Quartering Species: The 'Living Constitution,' the Third Amendment, and the Endangered Species Act," *Environmental Law* vol. 30 (2000): 787.

17 Barton H. Thompson Jr., "The Endangered Species Act: A Case Study in Takings & Incentives," *Stanford Law Review* vol. 49 (1997): 317.

18 John Copeland Nagle, "Playing Noah," *Minnesota Law Review* vol. 82 (1998): 1184–85.

19 Thompson, "Endangered Species Act," pp. 317–18.

20 Jacob Goldstein, "How Corruption Affects the Time It Takes to Do Business," NPR, Feb. 5, 2015, http://www.npr.org/2015/02/05/384119672/how-corruption-affects-the-time-it-takes-to-do-business.

21 Hernando de Soto, "Bureaucracy and Corruption," in *The Power of the Poor*, http://www.thepowerofthepoor.com/concepts/c7.php.

22 Frederic Bastiat, "What Is Seen and What Is Not Seen," in David Boaz, ed., *The Libertarian Reader* (New York: Free Press, 1997), p. 265.

23 Avik Roy, "Stifling New Cures: The True Cost of Lengthy Clinical Drug Trials," Manhattan Institute Project FDA Report No. 5, Apr. 2012, http://www.manhattan-institute.org/html/fda_05.htm.

24 John Alvis, ed., *Areopagitica and Other Political Writings of John Milton* (Indianapolis: Liberty Fund, 1999), p. 7.

25 Nicholas Pocock, ed., *The History of the Reformation of the Church of England* (Oxford: Clarendon Press, 1865), vol. 5, p. 194.

26 Blackstone, *Commentaries on the Laws of England*, vol. 2, p. 52.

27 Ibid., p. 53.

28 Eric Foner, ed., *Thomas Paine: Collected Writings* (New York: Library of America, 1995), p. 482 (emphasis original).

29 John Rhodehamel, ed., *George Washington: Writings* (New York: Library of America, 1997), p. 767.

30 Quoted in Robert S. Alley, "The Despotism of Toleration," in Robert S. Alley,

ed., *James Madison on Religious Liberty* (Amherst, NY: Prometheus Books, 1985), p. 147.

31 Peterson, *Thomas Jefferson: Writings*, p. 286.

32 Ibid., p. 285.

33 Ibid.

34 Ibid., p. 346.

35 Rano Turaeva-Hoehne, "Propiska Regime in Post-Soviet Space: Regulating Mobility and Residence," Central Asian Studies Institute Working Paper, Oct. 2011, https://www.academia.edu/2052850/Propiska_regime_in_post-Soviet_space_regulating_mobility_and_residence.

36 Vasily Grossman, *Life and Fate* (New York: New York Review Books, 2006), pp. 120–33.

37 David K. Shipler, *Russia: Broken Idols, Solemn Dreams* (New York: Penguin, 1989), pp. 171–78.

38 Jane R. Zavisca, *Housing the New Russia* (New York: Cornell University Press, 2012), p. 133; Georgy Bovt, "The Propiska Sends Russia Back to the U.S.S.R.," *Moscow Times*, Jan. 17, 2013, http://www.themoscowtimes.com/opinion/article/the-propiska-sends-russia-back-to-the-ussr/474085.html.

39 Richard Pipes, *Russia Under the Bolshevik Regime* (New York: Vintage, 1995), p. 296.

40 Ibid., p. 313.

41 Katherine Bliss Eaton, *Daily Life in the Soviet Union* (Westport, CT: Greenwood Press, 2004), p. 63.

42 Caroline Humphrey, *The Unmaking of Soviet Life: Everyday Economies after Socialism* (New York: Cornell University Press, 2002), p. 26.

43 *The Rise and Fall of the Berlin Wall*, History Channel (Nov. 7, 2009).

44 Dred Scott v. Sandford, 19 How. (60 U.S.) 393, 407 (1856).

45 H. Lee Cheek, ed., *John C. Calhoun: Selected Writings and Speeches* (Washington, D.C.: Regnery, 2003), p. 681.

46 Ibid., p. 31.

47 George Fitzhugh, *Sociology for the South, or, The Failure of a Free Society* (Richmond: A. Morris, 1854), p. 182.

48 Ibid., p. 83.

49 George Hickox, *Legal Disabilities of Married Women in Connecticut*, Connecticut Woman Suffrage Association Tract No. 1 (1871), p. 5.

50 R. Farquharson Sharp, trans., *Four Great Plays by Henrik Ibsen* (New York: Bantam, 1981), p. 14.

51 Ibid., p. 63.

52 Ibid.

53 Louise Ballerstedt Raggio, *Texas Tornado: The Life of a Crusader for Women's Rights and Family Justice* (New York: Citadel Press, 2003), p. 3.

54 208 U.S. 412 (1908).

55 *Lochner*, 198 U.S. at 61.

56 Nancy Woloch, *Muller v. Oregon: A Brief History with Documents* (Boston: Bedford Books, 1996), p. 33.

57 *Muller*, 208 U.S. at 421.

58 *Lochner*, 198 U.S. at 57.

59 Michael McGerr, *A Fierce Discontent: The Rise and Fall of the Progressive Movement in America, 1870–1920* (New York: Free Press, 2003), p. 132.

60 Adkins v. Children's Hospital, 261 U.S. 525 (1923).

61 *Id.* at 553.

CHAPTER THREE

1 A thorough history of prior restraint is Michael I. Myerson, "The Neglected History of the Prior Restraint Doctrine: Rediscovering the Link Between the First Amendment and the Separation of Powers," *Indiana Law Review* vol. 34 (2001): 295–342.

2 Anna Beer, *Milton: Poet, Pamphleteer, and Patriot* (New York: Bloomsbury Press, 2008), pp. 133–73.

3 Alvis, *Areopagitica and Other Political Writings of John Milton*, p. 7.

4 Ibid., pp. 31–32.

5 Ibid., p. 34.

6 Ibid., p. 39.

7 Ibid., p. 17.

8 Ibid., p. 35.

9 Ibid., p. 27.

10 Thomas I. Emerson, "The Doctrine of Prior Restraint," *Law & Contemporary Problems* vol. 20 (1955): 650–71.

11 *The Works of Lord Macaulay* (London: Longmans, Greene, & Co., 1875), vol. 4, p. 125.

12 Blackstone, *Commentaries*, vol. 4, p. 152.

13 Sedition Act, 1 Stat. 596 (1798).

14 Rakove, *James Madison: Writings*, pp. 645–48.

15 St. George Tucker, *Blackstone's Commentaries* (Philadelphia: William Young Birch & Abraham Small, 1803), vol. 5, pp. 28–29.

16 Ibid., p. 30.

17 283 U.S. 697 (1931).

18 376 U.S. 254 (1964).

19 *Near*, 283 U.S. at 713.

20 Hadley Arkes describes the case particularly well in his book *Constitutional Issues and Anchoring Truths* (New York: Cambridge University Press, 2010), ch. 5.

21 Ibid., pp. 119–20.

22 New York Times Co. v. United States, 403 U.S. 713, 714 (1971) (citations and quotation marks omitted).

23 Geoffrey R. Stone, *Perilous Times: Free Speech in Wartime* (New York: Norton, 2005), p. 512.

24 Rakove, *James Madison: Writings*, p. 515.

25 Peterson, *Thomas Jefferson: Writings*, p. 346.

26 Gitlow v. New York, 268 U.S. 652 (1925).

27 250 U.S. 616 (1919).

28 Andrew Cohen, "The Most Powerful Dissent in American History," *The Atlantic*, Aug. 10, 2013, http://www.theatlantic.com/national/archive/2013/08/the-most-powerful-dissent-in-american-history/278503/.

29 163 U.S. 537, 552–64 (1896) (Harlan, J., dissenting).

30 478 U.S. 186, 199–214 (1986) (Blackmun, J., dissenting).

31 83 U.S. (16 Wall.) 36, 83–111 (1873) (Field, J., dissenting).

32 *Lochner*, 198 U.S. at 65–74 (Holmes, J., dissenting).

33 *Abrams*, 250 U.S. at 630 (Holmes, J., dissenting).

34 *Id.* at 627.

35 Galliard Hunt, ed., *The Writings of James Madison* (New York: G.P. Putnam's Sons, 1910), vol. 9, pp. 570–71.

36 Lynne Cheney, *James Madison: A Life Reconsidered* (New York: Viking, 2014), pp. 371–83. There is one possible exception. Richard Brookhiser notes that Madison may have looked the other way when a mob of supporters in Baltimore destroyed the offices of an antiwar newspaper. Nevertheless, Brookhiser praises Madison for resisting efforts to enact a new law against sedition. *James Madison* (New York: Basic Books, 2011), p. 198.

37 Peterson, *Thomas Jefferson: Writings*, p. 346.

38 Compare the words of the Socialist writer Sidney Webb, a contemporary of Holmes, who observed that while prior generations of socialists had sought to "nationalize both rent and interest by the State becoming the sole landowner and capitalist," his own generation had realized that this "arrangement would ... leave untouched the third monopoly, the largest of them all, the monopoly of business ability.... The more recent Socialists strike, therefore, at this monopoly also, by allotting to every worker an equal wage, whatever the nature of his work. This equality has an abstract justification, as the special ability or energy with which some persons are born, is an unearned increment due to the struggle for existence upon their ancestors, and consequently having been produced by Society, is as much due to Society as the 'unearned increment' of rent." Quoted in Henry John Wixton, *Socialism: Being Notes on A Political Tour* (London: MacMillan & Co., 1896), p. 83.

39 Posner, *Essential Holmes*, p. 235.

40 Max Lerner, ed., *The Mind and Faith of Justice Holmes* (New York: Modern Library, 1943), p. 431.

41 Pennsylvania Coal v. Mahon, 260 U.S. 393 (1922). Although *Mahon* is often considered favorable to property owners, in fact it fundamentally undermined property rights by treating the difference between eminent domain and the police power as one of degree instead of a difference in principle. The law of "regulatory takings" has never recovered from the resulting confusion. See Richard A. Epstein, *Supreme Neglect* (Oxford: Oxford University Press, 2008), p. 107.

42 Tyson & Bro.–United Theatre Ticket Offices v. Banton, 273 U.S. 418, 446 (1927) (Holmes, J., dissenting) ("the Legislature may forbid or restrict any business when it has a sufficient force of public opinion behind it.").

43 Interstate Consol. St. Ry. Co. v. Commonwealth of Massachusetts, 207 U.S. 79, 86–87 (1907) ("constitutional rights … are matters of degree, and … the great constitutional provisions for the protection of property are not to be pushed to a logical extreme, but must be taken to permit the infliction of some fractional and relatively small losses without compensation, for some, at least, of the purposes of wholesome legislation.… [S]tates … must be allowed a certain latitude in the minor adjustments of life, even though by their action the burdens of a part of the community are somewhat increased.").

44 Posner, *Essential Holmes*, p. 321 ("I don't believe in [free speech] as a theory.… [O]n their premises it seems to me logical in the Catholic Church to kill heretics and the Puritans to whip Quakers – and I see nothing … wrong with it from our ultimate standards.").

45 Buck v. Bell, 274 U.S. 200 (1927).

46 *Lochner*, 198 U.S. at 76 (Holmes, J., dissenting).

47 Holmes, "Natural Law," pp. 42–44.

48 Truax v. Corrigan, 257 U.S. 312, 376 (1921) (Brandeis, J., dissenting).

49 Cass R. Sunstein, *Democracy and the Problem of Free Speech* (New York: Free Press, 1995), p. 28.

50 Nicholls v. Mayor & Sch. Comm. of Lynn, 297 Mass. 65, 71 (1937).

51 310 U.S. 586, 596 (1940).

52 *Id.* at 598.

53 *Id.*

54 *Id.* at 597–98.

55 See, for instance, the chilling account of the Nazi *Volkssturm* – the last-ditch resistance of the Hitler Youth against Allied soldiers in World War II's final days – in Max Hastings, *Armageddon* (New York: Vintage, 2004), pp. 160–61, 469–75.

56 319 U.S. 624 (1943).

57 *Id.* at 638.

58 *Id.* at 647 (Frankfurter, J., dissenting).

59 Sunstein, *Democracy and the Problem of Free Speech*, p. 17.

60 Ibid., p. 18.

61 Ibid., p. 241.

62 Ibid., p. 247.

63 Ibid., p. 28.

64 Ibid., p. 85.

65 Ibid., p. 84.

66 Ibid., p. 83.

67 Ibid., p. 87.

68 Ibid., p. 82.

69 Ibid., pp. 100–01.

70 Ibid., p. 7.

71 Cass R. Sunstein, *Why Societies Need Dissent* (Cambridge, MA: Harvard University Press, 2005), p. v.

72 Ibid., p. 213.

73 Cass R. Sunstein, "Unity and Plurality: The Case of Compulsory Oaths," *Yale Journal on Law & the Humanities* vol. 2 (1998): 111.

74 Ibid., p. 108.

75 Sunstein, *Democracy and the Problem of Free Speech*, p. 27. Sunstein uses these phrases to characterize the views of Justice Louis Brandeis, but in context, Sunstein makes clear that he endorses the view he attributes to Brandeis. See also ibid., p. 251 (contrasting Brandeis and Holmes and concluding that it is "most unfortunate" that "Holmes's view is clearly ascendant").

76 *Nicholls*, 297 Mass. at 66.

77 Jerome Kohn, ed., *Responsibility and Judgment* (New York: Shocken Books, 2003), p. 44.

78 Knox v. Serv. Employees Int'l Union, Local 1000, 132 S. Ct. 2277, 2290 (2012).

79 Tom McGinty & Brody Mullins, "Political Spending by Unions Far Exceeds Direct Donations," *Wall Street Journal*, July 10, 2012, http://www.wsj.com/articles/SB10001424052702304782404577488584031850026.

80 Horace Cooper, "Do Free Speech Rights Apply to Union Members, Too? In Knox v. SEIU, Supreme Court Soon to Rule on SEIU Funding Gimmicks," National Center for Public Policy Research Policy Analysis No. 637, June 2012, http://www.nationalcenter.org/NPA637.html.

81 431 U.S. 209 (1977).

82 *Id.* at 235.

83 *Id.* at 238.

84 475 U.S. 292 (1986).

85 Office & Professional Employees International Union, 331 N.L.R.B. 48 (2000).

86 Shea v. Int'l Ass'n of Machinists & Aerospace Workers, 154 F.3d 508, 515 (5th Cir. 1998).

87 N.A.A.C.P. v. Alabama, 357 U.S. 449, 462–63 (1958).

88 Bob Williams, "WEA-PAC Donations Drying Up: Teachers Taking Their Political Dollars Elsewhere," Evergreen Freedom Foundation, July 6, 1998, http://archive.myfreedomfoundation.com/causes/publication/detail/wea-pac-donations-drying-up-teachers-taking-their-political-dollars-elsewhere.html.

89 Davenport v. WEA, 551 U.S. 177 (2007).

90 Knox v. California State Employees Ass'n, Local 1000, Serv. Employees Int'l Union, AFL-CIO-CLC, 628 F.3d 1115, 1117 (9th Cir. 2010).

91 *Id.* at 1127.

92 *Knox,* 132 S. Ct. at 2277.

93 *Id.* at 2283.

94 *Id.* at 2290.

95 *Id.* at 2283.

96 *Id.*

97 Two years after the *Knox* case, in Harris v. Quinn, 134 S. Ct. 2618 (2014), the court again criticized *Abood* but again stopped short of overruling it. The court then agreed to hear another case, Friedrichs v. California Teachers Association (No. 14-915), to consider whether to overrule *Abood,* but after Justice Scalia's death in early 2016, the court divided 4–4 and issued a single-sentence ruling that set no precedent.

98 Stephen Breyer, *Active Liberty* (New York: Vintage, 2006), p. 48.

99 Ibid.

100 Ibid., p. 49.

101 Nixon v. Shrink Missouri Government PAC, 528 U.S. 377 (2000).

102 *Id.* at 387–88.

103 *Id.* at 397.

104 *Id.* at 405 (Kennedy, J., dissenting) (citations omitted).

105 *Id.* at 406.

106 *Id.* at 410 (Thomas, J., dissenting).

107 *Id.* at 400 (Breyer, J., concurring).

108 *Id.* at 401.

109 *Id.* at 402.

110 *Id.*

111 2 U.S.C. § 30101.

112 Citizens United v. Fed. Election Comm'n, 558 U.S. 310, 335–36 (2010).

113 Thomas v. Collins, 323 U.S. 516, 540 (1945).

114 Coal. for Secular Gov't v. Gessler, 71 F. Supp. 3d 1176 (D. Colo. 2014).

115 Independence Inst. v. Coffman, 209 P.3d 1130, 1134 (Colo. App. 2008).

116 Coal. for Secular Gov't v. Williams, No. 14-1469, 2016 WL 814814, at *12 (10th Cir. Mar. 2, 2016).

117 Delaware Strong Families v. Attorney Gen. of Delaware, 793 F.3d 304 (3d Cir. 2015). Similar to campaign registration requirements are rules that require political groups or non-profits to disclose the identities of their supporters.

Such requirements raise the concern that supporters could face retaliation or discrimination, and the Supreme Court held in the 1950s that they violate the First Amendment unless there is good reason to require disclosure. *N.A.A.C.P.*, 357 U.S. at 462–63. In John Doe No. 1 v. Reed, 561 U.S. 186, 197 (2010), the Supreme Court held that states could require political groups to disclose the identities of their supporters in order to "preserv[e] the integrity of the electoral process." In 2015, however, the attorney general of California went further and demanded that *all* non-profit groups, including those not engaged in any political activities, disclose the names and addresses of supporters who contribute more than $5,000. The Ninth Circuit Court of Appeals upheld this requirement on the grounds that it increased the attorney general's "investigative efficiency," and the Supreme Court chose not to review the case. Ctr. for Competitive Politics v. Harris, 784 F.3d 1307, 1311 (9th Cir. 2015), *cert. denied*, No. 15-152, 136 S. Ct. 480 (2015).

118 Owen M. Fiss, "Free Speech and Social Structure," *Iowa Law Review* vol. 71 (1986): 1425.

119 Actually, there is little evidence support the frequently heard charge that large amounts of spending on political campaigns is a decisive factor in elections. Although most Americans tell pollsters they think there is too much money in politics, relatively little money goes to political campaigns in the United States. Some $4 billion was spent on running for federal office in 2014 – about one-fifth of what Americans spend on pet food each year. Raymond J. La Raja, Small Change: Money, Political Parties, and Campaign Finance Reform (Ann Arbor: University of Michigan Press, 2008), p. 3; "Americans Spent a Record $56 Billion on Pets Last Year," CBS News, Mar. 13, 2014, http://www.cbsnews.com/news/americans-spent-a-record-56-billion-on-pets-last-year/. Taking inflation into account, the 2000 Bush presidential campaign spent around the same amount as William McKinley did in 1896. True, spending on campaigns is going up, but that is largely a function of the growth of government – more offices, and more government programs that redistribute wealth, inevitably mean more lobbying and more intense efforts to gain control over the power to tax and spend. Yet voters do not appear to be swayed to supporting candidates they dislike simply as a result of spending. Sean Trende, "Is the Value of Campaign Spending Overstated?" Real Clear Politics, Nov. 14, 2013, http://www.realclearpolitics.com/articles/2013/11/14/is_the_value_of_campaign_spending_overstated_120667.html; Bradley A. Smith, "Campaign Finance Regulation: Faulty Assumptions and Undemocratic Consequences," Cato Institute Policy Analysis No. 238, Sept. 13, 1995, http://www.cato.org/publications/policy-analysis/campaign-finance-regulation-faulty-assumptions-undemocratic-consequences. Wealthy candidates are frequently defeated at the polls, despite outspending their rivals. Jeb Bush outspent his rivals in the 2016 Republican presidential primary,

only to be resoundingly rejected. Fredreka Schouten, "Spending Heavily, Jeb Bush Super PAC Lobs Last-Minute Attacks," *USA Today*, Jan. 15, 2016, http://www.usatoday.com/story/news/2016/01/13/jeb-bush-super-pac-lobs-last-minute-attacks-marco-rubio/78750792/. California voters rejected Michael Huffington in his 1994 Senate race, at that time the most expensive non-presidential campaign ever waged. Twenty years later, they rejected Meg Whitman as a candidate for governor, despite her spending $140 million of her own money. Ruben Navarrette Jr., "How Meg Whitman Spent a Fortune – And Lost," CNN, Nov. 3, 2010, http://www.cnn.com/2010/OPINION/11/03/navarrette.california.whitman/index.html. Tom Cotton won his Arkansas Senate race against Mark Pryor in 2014, and that same year, a little-known candidate named David Brat defeated House Majority Leader Eric Cantor in Virginia's Republican primary, despite the fact that Cantor outspent him by a factor of 40 to 1. Jon Greenberg, "Rare Feat: Cantor Spent More at Steakhouses than Opponent Did on Campaign," *Tampa Bay Times*, June 11, 2014, http://www.politifact.com/punditfact/statements/2014/jun/11/chuck-todd/rare-feat-cantor-spent-more-steakhouses-opponent-d/. In all these campaigns, wealthy candidates learned that voter enthusiasm matters more than money.

120 Austin v. Michigan Chamber of Commerce, 494 U.S. 652, 660 (1990).

121 Bradley A. Smith, "Campaign Finance Reform: Searching for Corruption in All the Wrong Places," *2002–2003 Cato Supreme Court Review*: 187–222.

122 Richard Hofstadter, *The Age of Reform* (New York: Vintage, 1955), p. 247.

123 Jordan Rau, "California Elections Roundup; Mel Gibson Joins Fight on Prop. 71," *L.A. Times*, Oct. 29, 2004, p. B1; Steve Young, "No Sacrifice Is Too Small for Rep. Dreier: Legislator's Attack on Talk Radio Appears as Phony as It Does Ironic," *Daily News of L.A.*, Nov. 3, 2004, p. N21.

124 Timothy Sandefur, "What Part of 'No Law' Don't You Understand? Getting Government Out of the Politics Business," *Nexus: A Journal of Opinion* vol. 12 (2007): 143–44.

CHAPTER FOUR

1 Mut. Film Corp. v. Indus. Comm'n of Ohio, 236 U.S. 230 (1915).

2 *Id.* at 244–45.

3 *Id.* at 243–44.

4 *Id.* at 242.

5 "Constitutional Law," *Columbia Law Review* vol. 15 (1915): 546.

6 "Recent Important Decisions," *Michigan Law Review* vol. 13 (1915): 516.

7 Pathe Exch. v. Cobb, 195 N.Y.S. 661, 665 (App. Div. 1922), *aff'd*, 236 N.Y. 539 (1923).

8 *Id.*

9   Message Photoplay Co. v. Bell, Comm'r of Licenses, 167 N.Y.S. 129, 132 (Sup. Ct.), *rev'd sub nom.* Message Photo-Play Co. v. Bell, 166 N.Y.S. 338 (App. Div. 1917).

10 *Id.*

11 *Id.*

12 *Message Photo-Play*, 166 N.Y.S. at 344.

13 *Id.* at 343.

14 United States v. Paramount Pictures, 334 U.S. 131, 166 (1948).

15 Joseph Burstyn, Inc. v. Wilson, 343 U.S. 495, 501 (1952).

16 *Id.* at 505–06.

17 *Near*, 283 U.S. at 713.

18 Times Film Corp. v. City of Chicago, 365 U.S. 43, 49 (1961).

19 Laura Wittern-Keller, *Freedom of the Screen: Legal Challenges to State Film Censorship, 1915–1981* (Lexington: University Press of Kentucky, 2008), ch. 2.

20 Freedman v. State of Md., 380 U.S. 51, 58–59 (1965).

21 Southeastern Promotions, Ltd. v. Conrad, 420 U.S. 546, 559 (1975).

22 Jon M. Garon, "Entertainment Law," *Tulane Law Review* vol. 76 (2002): 645.

23 Kingsley Books, Inc. v. Brown, 354 U.S. 436 (1957).

24 *Id.* at 441–42 (quoting Paul Freund, "The Supreme Court and Civil Liberties, Supreme Court and Civil Liberties," *Vanderbilt Law Review* vol. 4 (1951): 539.

25 Red Lion Broadcasting Co. v. F.C.C., 395 U.S. 367, 389–90 (1969).

26 *Id.* at 390.

27 Brandywine-Main Line Radio, Inc. v. F.C.C., 473 F.2d 16, 42 (D.C. Cir. 1972).

28 *Id.* at 47–48.

29 *Id.* at 48.

30 *Id.* at 47.

31 Red Lion Broadcasting Co. v. F.C.C., 381 F.2d 908, 929 (D.C. Cir. 1967) (opinion of Tamm, J.).

32 Gregory P. Magarian, "Substantive Media Regulation in Three Dimensions," *George Washington Law Review* vol. 76 (2008): 853.

33 Dick M. Carpenter II, *Designing Cartels: How Industry Insiders Cut Out Competition* (Institute for Justice, Nov. 2007), p. 1, http://www.ij.org/images/pdf_folder/economic_liberty/Interior-Design-Study.pdf.

34 Byrum v. Landreth, 566 F.3d 442, 447 (5th Cir. 2009).

35 *Id.* at 448.

36 Cal. Bus. & Prof. Code § 2903.

37 Cal. Bus. & Prof. Code § 2908.

38 Donald K. Routh, *Clinical Psychology Since 1917: Science, Practice, and Organization* (New York: Springer, 1994), pp. 138–39.

39 Nat'l Ass'n for Advancement of Psychoanalysis v. California Bd. of Psychology, 228 F.3d 1043, 1052 (9th Cir. 2000).

40 *Id.* at 1056.

41 See, for example, Riley v. Nat'l Fed'n of the Blind of N. Carolina, Inc., 487 U.S. 781 (1988); Sorrell v. IMS Health, 131 S. Ct. 2653 (2011).

42 Paul Sherman, "Occupational Speech and the First Amendment," *Harvard Law Review Forum* vol. 128 (2014): 183.

43 Rosemond v. Markham, No. CV 13-42-GFVT, 2015 WL 5769091 (E.D. Ky. Sept. 30, 2015).

44 Kagan v. City of New Orleans, 957 F. Supp. 2d 774, 777 (E.D. La. 2013).

45 Kagan v. City of New Orleans, 753 F.3d 560, 562 (5th Cir. 2014), *cert. denied*, 135 S. Ct. 1403 (2015).

46 Edwards v. D.C., 755 F.3d 996, 1005–06 (D.C. Cir. 2014).

47 Nev. Rev. Stat. § 648.012.

48 Nev. Rev. Stat. § 648.018.

49 State v. Tatalovich, 309 P.3d 43 (Nev. 2013).

50 Defendants' Motion to Dismiss, Castillo v. Ingram (D. Nev. No. 2:14-cv-00332-GMN-PAL, p. 18 (June 10, 2014).

51 Timothy Sandefur, "Victory in Nevada: You Can Furnish Information without Getting a Government License!" *PLF Liberty Blog*, June 23, 2015, http://blog. pacificlegal.org/victory-in-nevada-you-can-furnish-information-without-getting-a-government-license/.

52 Thomas v. Collins, 323 U.S. 516, 536–37 (1945).

53 *Id.* at 531, 540.

54 *Id.* at 544.

55 472 U.S. 181 (1985). Another case, Planned Parenthood v. Casey, 505 U.S. 833 (1992), has sometimes been cited as a third professional speech precedent, thanks to three sentences in which three justices – O'Connor, Kennedy, and Souter – upheld a law requiring doctors to disclose information about abortion to patients, notwithstanding the First Amendment. While doctors' free speech rights were "implicated," they wrote, their speech was "only [a] part of the practice of medi- cine," and that practice was "subject to reasonable licensing and regulation by the State," so there was "no constitutional infirmity in the requirement."

56 *Lowe*, 472 U.S. at 229–30.

57 *Id.* at 232.

58 Timothy Sandefur, "Free Speech for You and Me, but Not for Professionals," *Regulation* (Winter 2015–16): 48–53.

59 Pickup v. Brown, 728 F.3d 1042 (9th Cir. 2013); King v. Governor of New Jersey, 767 F.3d 216 (3d Cir. 2014).

60 *Pickup*, 740 F.3d at 1221n12 (O'Scannlain, J., dissenting from denial of rehear- ing *en banc*).

61 The first law review article on the topic of professional speech was not pub- lished until 1999. Daniel Halberstam, "Commercial Speech, Professional Speech, and the Constitutional Status of Social Institutions," *University of Pennsylvania Law Review* vol. 147 (1999): 771–874.

62   Stuart v. Camnitz, 774 F.3d 238, 243 (4th Cir. 2014), *cert. denied sub nom.* Walker-McGill v. Stuart, No. 14-1172, 135 S. Ct. 2838 (2015).
63   *Id.* at 246.
64   *Id.* at 251.
65   *Id.* at 248.
66   *Id.* at 245.
67   *Id.* at 255.
68   *Id.* at 252.
69   Texas Med. Providers Performing Abortion Servs. v. Lakey, 667 F.3d 570 (5th Cir. 2012).
70   Planned Parenthood Minnesota, N. Dakota, S. Dakota v. Rounds, 530 F.3d 724, 735 (8th Cir. 2008).

CHAPTER FIVE

1   Morris M. Kleiner & Alan B. Krueger, "Extent and Influence of Occupational Licensing on the Labor Market," *Journal of Labor Economics* vol. 31, no. 2 (2013): S173–S202.
2   Schware v. Board of Examiners, 353 U.S. 232, 238–39 (1957).
3   Timothy Sandefur, *The Right to Earn a Living: Economic Freedom and the Law* (Washington, D.C.: Cato Institute, 2010), ch. 7.
4   See William K. Jones, "Origins of the Certificate of Public Convenience and Necessity: Developments in the States, 1870–1920," *Columbia Law Review* vol. 79 (1979): 427 ("The essence of the certificate of public convenience and necessity is the exclusion of otherwise qualified applicants from a market because, in the judgment of the regulatory commission, the addition of new or expanded services would have no beneficial consequences or, in a more extreme case, would actually have harmful consequences.").
5   See Colon Health Centers of America, LLC v. Hazel, 733 F.3d 535 (4th Cir. 2013).
6   The facts described in this chapter were obtained through discovery in the *Bruner* and *Munie* cases. The discovery was limited to the five-year period before the cases were filed, in order to make the paperwork manageable, but there is no reason to believe that the Kentucky or Missouri CON laws operated any differently at any other period.
7   Ky. Rev. Stat. § 281.6251(1) (2012).
8   Ky. Rev. Stat. § 281.625(1) (2012).
9   The only effort Kentucky courts had made to define "inadequacy" was Eck Miller Transfer Co. v. Armes, 269 S.W.2d 287, 289 (Ky. 1954), which held that the word meant "substantial inadequacy" and added that this "inadequacy" must be due to a deficiency that manifests "an inability or unwillingness

to render adequate service." In Combs v. Johnson, 331 S.W.2d 730, 733–34 (Ky. 1959), the court reiterated *Armes*'s circular definition of the term while admitting that "[i]nadequacy and public need are relative terms."

10   The phrase "present or future public convenience and necessity" does appear in the laws of some other jurisdictions, including the Interstate Commerce Act. But federal courts have often remarked on the vagueness of the term and upheld its constitutionality only because federal regulations specify objective factors the agency must use, and standards parties must prove, in order to make valid findings. See, for example, Ass'n of Am. R.R.s v. I.C.C., 846 F.2d 1465, 1467 (D.C. Cir. 1988) (describing "public convenience and necessity" as "vague" but noting that the Interstate Commerce Commission had promulgated regulations that guided its discretion). In Burlington Truck Lines, Inc., v. I.C.C., 194 F. Supp. 31, 50 (S.D. Ill. 1961), *rev'd on other grounds*, 371 U.S. 156 (1962), the district court recognized that "[f]uture need is an uncertainty in all instances," so that predicting "future" public convenience is a dangerously vague proposition, requiring officials to "exercise a prophetic vision." But it ruled that the vagueness was limited by regulations that established "evidentiary guidelines" specifying objective standards that applicants had to prove to the ICC. See also Artus Trucking Co., Inc. v. I.C.C., 377 F. Supp. 1224, 1230–31 (E.D.N.Y. 1974) (citing *In re.* John Novak Contract Carrier Application, 103 M.C.C. 555, 557 (1967)). Kentucky had no such regulations.

11   Deposition of Jesse Rowe, Bruner v. Zawacki (No. 3:12-cv-00057-DCR), p. 18 (on file with Pacific Legal Foundation).

12   Timothy Sandefur, "State 'Competitor Veto' Laws and the Right to Earn a Living: Some Paths to Federal Reform," *Harvard Journal of Law & Public Policy* vol. 38 (2015): 1035.

13   See 601 Ky. Admin. Regs. 1:030(4)(1)(d) (2012).

14   601 Ky. Admin. Regs. 1:031(1) (2012).

15   Pacific Legal Foundation, Munie v. Koster Litigation Backgrounder, http://www.pacificlegal.org/old-site/document.doc?id=445, p. 1.

16   For a thorough analysis and perceptive critique of the Missouri statute, see Paul H. Gardner Jr., "Entry and Rate Regulation of Interstate Motor Carriers in Missouri: A Strategy for Reform," *Missouri Law Review* vol. 47 (1982): 693–743.

17   Mo. Rev. Stat. § 390.051(4).

18   In State ex rel. Ozark Elec. Coop. v. Pub. Serv. Comm'n, 527 S.W.2d 390, 394 (Mo. Ct. App. 1975), the court of appeals acknowledged that "[f]or some reason, either intentional or otherwise, the General Assembly has not seen fit to statutorily spell out any specific criteria to aid in the determination of what is 'necessary or convenient for the public service.'"

19   Mo. Rev. Stat. § 390.051(5).

20   Timothy Sandefur, "What Abolishing Missouri's Mover Licensing Cartel Has Meant," *PLF Liberty Blog*, Mar. 14, 2013, http://blog.pacificlegal.org/what-abolishing-missouris-mover-licensing-cartel-has-meant/.

21   Jones, "Origins of the Certificate of Public Convenience and Necessity," p. 439.

22   Ibid., p. 428.

23   See Alfred E. Kahn, *The Economics of Regulation* (New York: Wiley, 1971), vol. 2, pp. 221–23.

24   Herbert Hovenkamp & John A. Mackerron III, "Municipal Regulation and Federal Antitrust Policy," *UCLA Law Review* vol. 32 (1985): 761n240.

25   "The Civil Service and the Statutory Law of Public Employment," *Harvard Law Review* vol. 97 (1984): 1619–32.

26   See, for example, Gabriel Kolko, *The Triumph of Conservatism* (Chicago: Quadrangle Books, 1963), pp. 13–14. One example is found in David Syme, *Outlines of an Industrial Science* (London: Kegan Paul & Co., 1876), p. 56: "Every one knows that excessive competition produces enormous waste, and that it leads to the perpetration of fraud, the extent of which is generally in proportion to the intensity or keenness of competition."

27   Syme, *Outlines of an Industrial Science*, p. 61 (using railroad example).

28   Friedrich Hayek, "Competition as a Discovery Procedure," *Quarterly Journal of Austrian Economics* vol. 5, no. 3 (Fall 2002): 9–23.

29   Joseph Schumpeter, *Capitalism, Socialism, and Democracy* (New York: Harper, 1975), ch. 7. Some contemporary economists argue that there might be some cases in which free competition could be harmful, even they admit that such circumstances are exceedingly rare: only when start-up costs are high and products or services are homogenous can competition be "excessive," according to that theory. Kotaro Suzumura, "Excess Entry Theorems after 25 Years," *Japanese Economic Review* vol. 63 (2012): 152–70. Other economists dispute this, but however that may be, start-up costs for moving companies are low (just get a truck and paint "Mover" on the side) and their services are not homogenous: some movers provide highly skilled services moving delicate scientific equipment, and others provide no-frills packing and loading.

30   Richard A. Posner, "Natural Monopoly and Its Regulation," *Stanford Law Review* vol. 21 (1969): 611–12.

31   Friedrich Hayek, "The Use of Knowledge in Society," *American Economic Review* vol. 35 (1945): 519–30.

32   Matt Haig, *Brand Failures: The Truth about the 100 Biggest Branding Mistakes of All Time* (Philadelphia: Kogan Page, Ltd., 2011), pp. 8–14.

33   James Buchanan & Gordon Tullock, *The Calculus of Consent* (Ann Arbor: University of Michigan Press, 1962), esp. ch. 19.

34   Samantha Allen, "The Mysterious Way Uber Bans Drivers," *Daily Beast*, Jan. 27, 2015, http://www.thedailybeast.com/articles/2015/01/27/the-mysterious-way-uber-bans-drivers.html.

35 Jim O'Sullivan, "Boston Ordered to Revise Regulations on Taxis, Ride-Hailing Services," *Boston Globe*, Mar. 31, 2106, http://www.bostonglobe.com/metro/2016/03/31/boston-ordered-revise-regulations-taxis-ride-hailing-services/YtU60YoIl8TiEGbQu82qsL/story.html?event=event25; Ken Yeung, "Class-Action Lawsuit Filed Against Uber by San Francisco Taxi Drivers for Unfair Competition," *The Next Web*, Nov. 14, 2012, http://thenextweb.com/insider/2012/11/14/class-action-lawsuit-filed-against-uber-by-san-francisco-taxicab-drivers-citing-unfair-business-competition//.

36 Graham Rapier, "New York City Has Seized 496 Uber Cars for Illegal Pick-ups," *Business Insider*, June 17, 2015, http://www.businessinsider.com/496-uber-cars-seized-by-new-york-city-authorities-2015-6.

37 Arjun Kharpal, "UberPOP Suspended in France after Riots," CNBC, July 3, 2015, http://cnbc.com/2015/07/03/uberpop-suspended-in-france-after-violence.html.

38 Cf. Juarez Gas Co. v. FPC, 375 F.2d 595, 599 (D.C. Cir. 1967) ("an affected competitor ... is deemed to be in position to advance matters which are relevant and material for consideration by the" agency considering the CON application).

39 See, for example, Mo. Rev. Stat. § 390.051(5) (2011) ("In cases where persons object to the issuance of a certificate, the diversion of revenue or traffic from existing carriers shall be considered."); Nev. Rev. Stat. § 705.391(2) (2012) ("[T]he Authority shall grant the certificate or modification if it finds that ... the operation ... will foster sound economic conditions within the applicable industry[,] ... will not unreasonably and adversely affect other carriers operating in the territory ... [and] will benefit and protect ... the motor carrier business.").

40 See, for example, *In re.* Application of BAMN Enterprises, LLC, Ky. Transp. Docket No. 08-135 (July 11, 2008), p. 2 (on file with Pacific Legal Foundation).

41 Margaret's Moving, which was deemed unfit because it had operated illegally before applying for a CON, could be considered an exception, but the division later reversed this determination.

42 Defendants' Response to Plaintiffs' Interrogatories, Set One, Bruner v. Zawacki, No. 3:12-CV-00057-DCR (Apr. 1, 2013), pp. 19–20 (on file with Pacific Legal Foundation).

43 Report and Recommended Order Granting Authority, *In re.* Application of Little Guys Movers, Inc., Ky. Transp. Cabinet Docket No. 12-061 (Oct. 19, 2012) (on file with Pacific Legal Foundation). The same occurred in the cases of Big O Movers – which applied for a new certificate on January 28, 2011, suffered two protests, withdrew its application, and then successfully applied for permission to buy a CON from Rivertown Moving & Storage, which had protested Big O's initial application; see Ky. Transp. Docket Nos. 11-016, 12-019 (on file with Pacific Legal Foundation) – and Margaret's Moving.

44 *In re.* Application of Michael Ball, Ky. Transp. Cabinet Docket No. 12-091.

45 See Notice of Protest, *In re.* Application of Michael Ball, Ky. Transp. Cabinet Docket No. 12-091 (Oct. 12, 2012) (on file with Pacific Legal Foundation).

46 Transcript of Hearing, *In re.* Application of Michael Ball, Ky. Transp. Cabinet Docket No. 12-091, p. 46 (on file with Pacific Legal Foundation).

47 *Id.*

48 Report and Recommended Order Denying Application, *In re.* Application of Michael Ball, Ky. Transp. Cabinet Docket No. 12-091 (on file with Pacific Legal Foundation), p. 9.

49 *Combs*, 331 S.W.2d at 733.

50 *Id.* at 734.

51 Jones v. Webb Transfer Line, Inc., 328 S.W.2d 407, 411 (Ky. 1959).

52 *Combs*, 331 S.W.2d at 733.

53 Protest, *In re.* Application of BAMN, LLC, Ky. Transp. Cabinet Docket No. 08-135 (July 11, 2008) (on file with Pacific Legal Foundation).

54 See Report and Recommended Order, *In re.* Application of BAMN Enterprises, LLC, Ky. Transp. Cabinet Docket No. 08-135 (Sept. 22, 2009), at 12 (on file with Pacific Legal Foundation).

55 *Id.* at 15.

56 Deposition of Jesse Rowe, p. 53.

57 Report and Recommended Order on Motor Carrier Application, *In re.* Application of BAMN Enterprises, LLC, Ky. Transp. Docket No. 09-163 (July 27, 2010) (on file with Pacific Legal Foundation).

58 Final Order Granting Authority on Motor Carrier Application, *In re.* Application of BAMN Enterprises, LLC, Ky. Transp. Cabinet No. 09-163 (Aug. 12, 2010) (on file with Pacific Legal Foundation).

59 Plaintiffs' Statement of Uncontroverted Facts, Munie v. Skouby, No. 4:10-CV-01096-AGF, ¶¶ 59, 62 (on file with Pacific Legal Foundation). The government provided copies of 75 such applications in response to the plaintiff's evidentiary requests. A 76th, All Metro Movers, was discovered just before the hearing on motions for summary judgment. In the *Munie* and *Bruner* cases, the plaintiffs sought evidence regarding CON applications filed within the previous five years. This time period was chosen to avoid unduly burdening the defendants. There was no reason to believe the process worked differently at any other time.

60 Sixteen such firms were identified during discovery (*id.*, ¶59), but the All Metro Movers application was discovered prior to the summary judgment hearing.

61 Mo. Rev. Stat. § 390.020(4) (2011).

62 Statement of Uncontroverted Facts, ¶ 101.

63 *Id.*, ¶ 113.

64 Deposition of Barbara Hague, Munie v. Koster, No. 4:10-CV-01096-AGF, p. 36 (on file with Pacific Legal Foundation).

65 Declaration of Billy Holloway, Jr., in Support of Plaintiffs' Motion for Summary Judgment, Munie v. Koster, No. 4:10-CV-01096-AGF (on file with Pacific Legal Foundation).

66 *In re.* D. Gaines, Inc., No. 05-0227 MC, 2005 Mo. Admin. Hearings LEXIS 73 at **12–16 (2005). The commission also found that no evidence had been presented regarding Gaines's net profits, net worth, and other financial matters which would have shown his "fitness" under the statute. *Id.* at **13–14.

67 *In re.* Application of All Metro Movers, LLC, No. 07-1835 MC, 2008 Mo. Admin. Hearings LEXIS 299 at **1, 23–24 (2008).

68 F.C.C. v. Beach Commc'ns, Inc., 508 U.S. 307, 315 (1993).

69 Clark Neily, *Terms of Engagement* (New York: Encounter Books, 2013), p. 56.

70 Quoted in Gideon Kanner, "'(Un)equal Justice Under Law': The Invidiously Disparate Treatment of American Property Owners in Taking Cases," *Loyola of Los Angeles Law Review* vol. 40 (2007): 1146n68.

71 Craigmiles v. Giles, 312 F.3d 220 (6th Cir. 2002).

72 *Id.* at 224.

73 St. Joseph Abbey v. Castille, 712 F.3d 215, 222 (5th Cir. 2013), *cert. denied*, 134 S. Ct. 423 (2013).

74 Merrifield v. Lockyer, 547 F.3d 978 (9th Cir. 2008).

75 *Id.* at 991n15.

76 Powers v. Harris, 379 F.3d 1208 (10th Cir. 2004), *cert. denied*, 125 S. Ct. 1638 (2005); Sensational Smiles v. Mullen, 793 F.3d 281 (2d Cir. 2015), *cert. denied*, (No. 15-507, Feb. 29, 2016).

77 Dent v. West Virginia, 129 U.S. 114 (1889).

78 *Schware*, 353 U.S. at 232. Most of the court's decisions involving CON restrictions have, of course, involved public utilities. See, for example, Northwest Cent. Pipeline Corp. v. State Corp. Comm'n, 489 U.S. 493 (1988); Pac. Gas & Elec. Co. v. State Energy Res. Conservation & Dev. Comm'n, 461 U.S. 190 (1983). A particularly helpful article on early CON law cases is Michael J. Phillips, "Entry Restrictions in the *Lochner* Court," *George Mason Law Review* vol. 4 (1996): 405–55.

79 Buck v. Kuykendall, 267 U.S. 307, 315–16 (1925). *Buck* was decided along with a companion case, Bush Co. v. Malloy, 267 U.S. 317 (1925), which invalidated a similar Maryland law on the same grounds.

80 Frost v. Railroad Commission, 271 U.S. 583, 591–92 (1926).

81 285 U.S. 262 (1932). See further Hadley Arkes, *The Return of George Sutherland* (Princeton: Princeton University Press, 1994), pp. 54–61.

82 New State Ice Co. v. Liebmann, 42 F.2d 913, 917–18 (W.D. Okla. 1930).

83 *Id.* at 918.
84 Southwest Utility Ice Co. v. Liebmann, 52 F.2d 349 (10th Cir. 1931).
85 *Id.* at 351–52.
86 *Id.* at 354.
87 *New State Ice*, 285 U.S. at 278. In Munn v. Illinois, 94 U.S. (4 Otto) 113 (1877), the Supreme Court held that although the grain silos at issue did not meet the definition of monopoly or utility, they were nevertheless in a unique market position such that they were "affected with a public interest," and thus were similar to monopolies and could be regulated on that account. *Id.* at 126. In dissent, Justice Stephen Field argued that this theory unduly expanded the concept of monopoly. *Id.* at 140 ("If this be sound law, if there be no protection, either in the principles upon which our republican government is founded, or in the prohibitions of the Constitution against such invasion of private rights, all property and all business in the State are held at the mercy of a majority of its legislature."). But Field did not dispute that actual natural monopolies or franchises could be closely regulated by the government. See Paul Kens, *Stephen Field: Shaping Liberty from the Gold Rush to the Gilded Age* (Lawrence: University of Kansas Press, 1997), ch. 5.
88 *New State Ice*, 285 U.S. at 278–79. As Michael Phillips observes ("Entry Restrictions in the *Lochner* Court," pp. 443–47), Justice Brandeis's argument in favor of the law in his dissent is notably weak. Brandeis essentially admitted that it was private interest legislation designed to establish a cartel: "Trade journals and reports of association meetings of ice manufacturers bear ample witness to the hostility of the industry to such competition, and to its unremitting efforts, through trade associations, informal agreements, combination of delivery systems, and in particular through the consolidation of plants, to protect markets and prices against competition of any character." *New State Ice*, 285 U.S. at 292–93 (Brandeis, J., dissenting).
89 Nebbia v. New York, 291 U.S. 502, 537–38 (1934). *Nebbia*, however, maintained that "arbitrary or discriminatory" laws would still be unconstitutional under the Fourteenth Amendment. *Id.* at 537.
90 H. P. Hood & Sons v. DuMond, 336 U.S. 525, 531 (1949).
91 *Id.* at 533.
92 Colon Health Ctrs. of Am., LLC v. Hazel, 2012 WL 4105063 at *5 (E.D. Va. Sept. 14, 2012).
93 *Id.* at *6.
94 *Hazel*, 733 F.3d 535.
95 Washington, *A Testament of Hope*, pp. 440–41.
96 Taylor Branch, *Parting the Waters* (New York: Simon & Schuster, 1989), p. 146.
97 352 U.S. 903 (1956) (mem.), *aff'g* Browder v. Gayle, 142 F. Supp. 707 (M.D. Ala. 1956).

98 Timothy Sandefur, "Can You Get There from Here? How the Law Still Threatens King's Dream," *Law & Inequality* vol. 22 (2004): 1–6.

99 Mo. Rev. Stat. § 390.051(3).

100 Sandefur, "What Abolishing Missouri's Mover Licensing Cartel Has Meant."

101 Bruner v. Zawacki, 997 F. Supp. 2d 691, 699 (E.D. Ky. 2014).

102 *Id.* at 697.

103 *Id.* at 700.

104 *Id.*

105 *Id.* at 702 (quoting *Craigmiles*, 312 F.3d at 229).

106 See also Robert L. Woodson, "Race and Economic Opportunity," *Vanderbilt Law Review* vol. 42 (1989): 1041–43.

107 Foner, *Thomas Paine: Collected Writings*, p. 471.

108 I borrow this term from Deirdre N. McCloskey, *The Bourgeois Virtues: Ethics for an Age of Commerce* (Chicago: University of Chicago Press, 2006). McCloskey identifies the bourgeois virtues as courage, justice, temperance, prudence, faith, hope, and love.

109 See Walter Isaacson, *Benjamin Franklin: An American Life* (New York: Simon & Schuster, 2003), pp. 471–75; Harvey C. Mansfield, "Liberty and Virtue in the American Founding," in Peter Berkowitz, ed., *Never a Matter of Indifference: Sustaining Virtue in a Free Republic* (Stanford: Hoover Institution Press, 2003), pp. 3, 9–15.

110 J. A. Leo Lemay, ed., *Benjamin Franklin: Writings* (New York: Library of America, 1987), pp. 1305, 1329.

111 Ibid., p. 1369.

112 Alexis de Tocqueville, *Democracy in America* (J. P. Mayer, ed., and George Lawrence, trans., New York: Harper Perennial, 1969), pp. 550–51.

113 There is no better literary depiction of this phenomenon than the "bum's speech" in Ayn Rand, *Atlas Shrugged* (New York: Random House, 1957), 661–72.

114 Meadows v. Odom, 360 F. Supp. 2d 811 (M.D. La. 2005), *vacated as moot*, 198 Fed. App'x 348 (5th Cir. 2006).

115 Institute for Justice, "Let a Thousand Florists Bloom: Uprooting Outrageous Licensing Laws in Louisiana," http://ij.org/case/meadows-v-odom/.

116 The facts of this case are described in Institute for Justice, "Let a Thousand Florists Bloom," and in Clark Neily, Remarks at the Cato Institute Book Forum, *"The Right to Earn a Living*: How Government Stifles Initiative and Harms Economic Growth," Cato Institute (Sept. 20, 2010), http://www.cato.org/events/right-earn-living.

117 *Meadows*, 360 F. Supp. 2d at 823.

118 Memorandum of Points and Authorities in Support of Plaintiffs' Motion for Summary Judgment at 29–30, Meadows v. Odom, No. 03-960 (M.D. La. Dec. 28, 2004) (on file with Pacific Legal Foundation).

119 *Meadows*, 360 F. Supp. 2d at 823–24 (holding the law was "rationally related to the state's desire that floral arrangements will be assembled properly in a manner least likely to cause injury to a consumer and will be prepared in a proper, cost efficient manner").

120 Neily, Cato Institute Book Forum. Because the plaintiffs in the case left Louisiana in the wake of Hurricane Katrina, the case was deemed moot and the decision vacated by the appeals court. 198 Fed. App'x 348 (5th Cir. 2006).

121 Department of the Treasury Office of Economic Policy, Council of Economic Advisers, and Department of Labor, *Occupational Licensing: A Framework for Policymakers* (July 2015), https://www.whitehouse.gov/sites/default/files/docs/licensing_report_final_nonembargo.pdf.

122 See Bastiat, "What Is Seen and What Is Not Seen," p. 265; see also Henry Hazlitt, *Economics in One Lesson* (New York: Random House, 1979).

123 Lester J. Cappon, *The Adams-Jefferson Letters* (Chapel Hill: University of North Carolina Press, 1959), pp. 387, 388.

124 See David E. Bernstein, "Licensing Laws: A Historical Example of the Use of Government Regulatory Power Against African-Americans," *San Diego Law Review* vol. 31 (1994): 98.

125 Michael Argyle, *The Psychology of Social Class* (London: Routledge, 1994), pp. 182–84; Eric Jensen, *Teaching with Poverty in Mind: What Being Poor Does to Kids' Brains and What Schools Can Do About It* (Alexandria, VA: Association for Supervision & Curriculum Development, 2009), pp. 29, 113; Kenneth L. Dion, "Responses to Perceived Discrimination and Relative Deprivation," in James M. Olson et al., eds., *Relative Deprivation and Social Comparison: The Ontario Symposium* (New York: Psychology Press, 1986), vol. 4, p. 159; John Mirowsky et al., "Instrumentalism in the Land of Opportunity: Socioeconomic Causes and Emotional Consequences," *Social Psychology Quarterly* vol. 59 (1996): 322–37; Lois Powell, "Factors Associated with the Underrepresentation of African Americans in Mathematics and Science," *Journal of Negro Education* vol. 59 (1990): 294 (describing a "learned helplessness model for conceptualizing the poor performance of African Americans in mathematics and science which will show how cultural expectations of failure frequently become self-fulfilling prophesies").

126 See Federal Reserve System & the Brookings Institution, "The Enduring Challenge of Concentrated Poverty in America: Case Studies from Communities Across the U.S." (2008), http://www.frbsf.org/cpreport/index.html.

127 William Julius Wilson, *When Work Disappears: The World of the New Urban Poor* (New York: Vintage, 1996).

128 See, for example, Calvin C. Johnson & Chanchalat Chanhatasilpa, "The Race/Ethnicity and Poverty Nexus of Violent Crime: Reconciling Differences in Chicago's Community Area Homicide Rates," in Darnell F. Hawkins, ed., *Vio-

NOTES

lent Crime: Assessing Race and Ethnic Differences (Cambridge: Cambridge University Press, 2003), p. 89; Steven F. Messner & Scott J. South, "Economic Deprivation, Opportunity Structure, and Robbery Victimization: Intra- and Interracial Patterns," *Social Forces* vol. 64, no. 4 (1986): 978.

129 *Slaughter-House*, 83 U.S. (16 Wall.) at 110 (Field, J., dissenting).

130 Evan Baehr et al., *Government Regulation in the Sharing Economy*, Federalist Society for Law and Public Policy (Feb. 10, 2015), http://www.fed-soc.org/multimedia/detail/government-regulation-in-the-sharing-economy-event-audio.

131 *The Complete Poetical Works of John Greenleaf Whittier* (Boston: Houghton, Mifflin, 1904), p. 58.

CHAPTER SIX

1   See Timothy Sandefur, *The Conscience of the Constitution* (Washington, D.C.: Cato Institute, 2015), ch. 2 and 3.

2   San Remo Hotel L.P. v. City & County of San Francisco, 27 Cal. 4th 643, 697–98 (2002) (Brown, J., dissenting).

3   Martha A. Lees, "Preserving Property Values? Preserving Proper Homes? Preserving Privilege? The Pre-*Euclid* Debate over Zoning for Exclusively Private Residential Areas, 1916–1926," *University of Pittsburgh Law Review* vol. 56 (1994): 409–13.

4   Frank B. Williams, *The Law of City Planning and Zoning* (New York: Macmillan, 1922), p. 200.

5   245 U.S. 60 (1917).

6   *Id.* at 80–81.

7   State v. Houghton, 144 Minn. 1, 20 (1920) (quoting Com. v. Boston Adver. Co., 188 Mass. 348, 351 (1905)).

8   *Id.* at 22 (Brown, C.J., and Dibell, J., dissenting).

9   *Id.* at 23.

10   Ambler Realty Co. v. Vill. of Euclid, Ohio, 297 F. 307, 312–13 (N.D. Ohio 1924).

11   Vill. of Euclid, Ohio v. Ambler Realty Co., 272 U.S. 365, 388 (1926).

12   *Id.* at 393–95.

13   Covey Drive Yourself & Garage v. City of Portland, 157 Or. 117, 132 (1937); City of San Antonio v. Besteiro, 209 S.W. 472, 473–74 (Tex. Civ. App. 1919). The federal Mann Act prohibited the transportation of a woman across state lines for immoral purposes. Although not limited to automobiles, the act was largely aimed at their use.

14   McGerr, *A Fierce Discontent*, p. 271.

15   Quoted in Lees, "Preserving Property Values?," p. 387.

16   Moore v. City of E. Cleveland, Ohio, 431 U.S. 494, 510 (1977).

17   City of Cleburne, Tex. v. Cleburne Living Ctr., 473 U.S. 432 (1985).

18 Norimitsu Onishi, "Lucas and Rich Neighbors Agree to Disagree: Part II," *N. Y. Times*, May 21, 2012, http://www.nytimes.com/2012/05/22/us/george-lucas-retreats-from-battle-with-neighbors.html?_r=1.

19 *Euclid*, 272 U.S. at 388.

20 NYC Department of City Planning, "Zoning Map Table," http://www1.nyc. gov/site/planning/zoning/zoning-map-table.page.

21 Quoctrung Bui et al., "40 Percent of Buildings in Manhattan Could Not Be Built Today," *N. Y. Times*, May 20, 2016.

22 Bernard Siegan, *Property and Freedom* (New Brunswick, NJ: Transaction Publishers, 1997), p. 189.

23 Bernard Siegan, "Non-Zoning Is the Best Zoning," *California Western Law Review* vol. 31 (2004): 129–30.

24 Ibid.

25 J. Brian Phillips, "Houston, We Have a (Zoning) Problem," *Objective Standard* vol. 4, no. 1 (2008).

26 483 U.S. 825 (1987).

27 *Id.* at 828–29, 835.

28 Trent Meredith, Inc., v. City of Oxnard, 114 Cal. App. 3d 317, 328 (1981).

29 Terminal Plaza Corp. v. City & Cnty. of San Francisco, 177 Cal. App. 3d 892, 906–07 (1986).

30 *Nollan*, 483 U.S. at 837.

31 *Id.* at 837 (quoting J. E. D. Associates, Inc. v. Atkinson, 121 N.H. 581, 584 (1981)).

32 *Id.* at 860n10 (Brennan, J., dissenting).

33 *Id.* at 856 (Brennan, J., dissenting).

34 *Id.* at 833n2 (majority opinion).

35 Dolan v. City of Tigard, 512 U.S. 374, 380–81 (1994).

36 *Id.* at 391 (emphasis added).

37 Inna Reznik, "The Distinction Between Legislative and Adjudicative Decisions in *Dolan v. City of Tigard*," *N. Y. U. Law Review* vol. 75 (2000): 242–81; Lauren Reznick, "The Death of *Nollan* and *Dolan*? Challenging the Constitutionality of Monetary Exactions in the Wake of *Lingle v. Chevron*," *Boston University Law Review* vol. 87 (2007): 740–41.

38 The exact cost was never established. At trial, a construction expert estimated the cost of a single culvert replacement at about $9,500, and it appeared that perhaps a dozen such culverts would have to be replaced. Joint Appendix, Koontz v. St. Johns Water Management District (No. 11-1447), pp. 121–23 (on file with Pacific Legal Foundation). The district later claimed that the required repairs would have cost only $10,000. Ibid., p. 71.

39 Ibid., p. 29.

40 Ibid., p. 39.

41 St. Johns River Water Mgmt. Dist. v. Koontz, 77 So. 3d 1220, 1230 (Fla. 2011), *rev'd*, 133 S. Ct. 2586 (2013).

42 *Id.* at 1230.

43 Koontz v. St. Johns River Water Mgmt. Dist., 133 S. Ct. 2586, 2599 (2013).

44 *Id.* at 2600.

45 Christina Martin, "After 22 Years, Government Compensates PLF Client for Taking Use of Property," *PLF Liberty Blog*, Mar. 26, 2016, http://blog.pacific legal.org/after-22-years-government-compensates-plf-client-for-taking-use-of-property/.

46 *Nollan*, 483 U.S. at 833n2.

47 Richard M. Frank, "Inverse Condemnation Litigation in the 1990s – The Uncertain Legacy of the Supreme Court's *Lucas* and *Yee* Decisions," *Urban Law Journal* vol. 43 (1993): 108–09.

48 *Lucas v. South Carolina Coastal Council*, 505 U.S. 1003 (1992).

49 *Id.* at 1029.

50 *Id.* at 1032n18.

51 In Stop the Beach Renourishment, Inc. v. Florida Dep't of Envtl. Prot., 560 U.S. 702 (2010), the Supreme Court reiterated that a state court decision could qualify as a taking if it arbitrarily reinterpreted state property law, but found that the Florida courts had not done such a thing in that case.

52 Lakeview Dev. Corp. v. City of S. Lake Tahoe, 915 F.2d 1290, 1295 (9th Cir. 1990).

53 *Id.* (citations and quotation marks omitted).

54 Burke v. California Coastal Comm'n, 168 Cal. App. 4th 1098, 1105 (2008).

55 See, for instance, Town of Flower Mound v. Stafford Estates Ltd. Partnership, 135 S.W.3d 620 (Tex. 2004).

56 Lynch v. California Coastal Comm'n, 177 Cal. Rptr. 3d 654, 659, *review granted*, 339 P.3d 328 (Cal. 2014).

57 *Id.* at 662–63.

58 *Id.* at 659.

59 Evans v. United States, 74 Fed. Cl. 554, 563–64 (2006), *aff'd*, 250 F. App'x 321 (Fed. Cir. 2007).

60 Horne v. U.S. Dep't of Agric., 750 F.3d 1128, 1142 (9th Cir. 2014).

61 Gonzales v. Raich, 545 U.S. 1 (2005).

62 Horne v. Dep't of Agric., 135 S. Ct. 2419, 2430–31 (2015).

63 Abraham Bell & Gideon Parchomovsky, "Givings," *Yale Law Journal* vol. 111 (2001): 547–618.

64 Ibid., pp. 549–50.

65 Ibid., p. 552.

66 Dworkin, *Matter of Principle*, p. 199.

67 Bell & Parchomovsky, "Givings," p. 594.

68 Jianlin Chen & Jiongzhe Cui, "More Market-Oriented Than the United States and More Socialist Than China: A Comparative Public Property Story of Singapore," *Pacific Rim Law & Policy Journal* vol. 23 (2014): 42–44.

69 Griswold v. City of Carlsbad, California, 402 F. App'x 310 (9th Cir. 2010).

70 http://www.scottsdaleaz.gov/Assets/ScottsdaleAZ/Building/Prop207Waiver.pdf.

71 "Proposition 207: Could the Best Lawyers Yield a Better Downtown?" *AZ Attorney*, Mar. 21, 2013, https://azatty.wordpress.com/2013/03/21/proposition-207-could-the-best-lawyers-yield-a-better-downtown/.

72 Mike Sunnucks, "Cities Use Waivers to Dodge Prop. 207," *Business Journal*, Jan. 21, 2007, http://www.bizjournals.com/phoenix/stories/2007/01/22/story6.html?page=all.

73 Kenneth Regan, "You Can't Build That Here: The Constitutionality of Aesthetic Zoning and Architectural Review," *Fordham Law Review* vol. 58 (1990): 1013–31; Bruce A. Rubin, "Architecture, Aesthetic Zoning, and the First Amendment," *Stanford Law Review* vol. 28 (1976): 179–201; Janet Elizabeth Haws, "Architecture As Art? Not in My Neocolonial Neighborhood: A Case for Providing First Amendment Protection to Expressive Residential Architecture," *B.Y.U. Law Review* 2005: 1625–68.

74 Hurley v. Irish-Am. Gay, Lesbian & Bisexual Grp. of Boston, 515 U.S. 557, 569 (1995).

75 Cohen v. California, 403 U.S. 15, 26 (1971).

76 *Hurley*, 515 U.S. at 569.

77 Leicester v. Warner Bros., 232 F.3d 1212, 1217 (9th Cir. 2000).

78 State ex rel. Stoyanoff v. Berkeley, 458 S.W.2d 305, 310 (Mo. 1970).

79 New York Times Co. v. Sullivan, 376 U.S. 254, 270 (1964) (citing our "profound national commitment to the principle that debate on public issues should be uninhibited, robust, and wide-open, and that it may well include vehement, caustic, and sometimes unpleasantly sharp attacks").

80 Samuel E. Poole III, "Architectural Appearance Review Regulations and the First Amendment: The Good, the Bad, and the Consensus Ugly," *Urban Lawyer* vol. 19 (1987): 323.

81 Reid v. Architectural Bd. of Review of City of Cleveland Heights, 192 N.E.2d 74, 77 (Ohio, 1963).

82 *Id.* at 80–81 (Corrigan, J., dissenting).

83 *Id.* at 81.

84 Comm. for Reasonable Regulation of Lake Tahoe v. Tahoe Reg'l Planning Agency, 311 F. Supp. 2d 972, 1005 (D. Nev. 2004).

85 Rakove, *James Madison: Writings*, p. 515.

CHAPTER SEVEN

1   554 U.S. 570 (2008).

2   *Id.* at 594.

3   *Id.* at 634.

4   561 U.S. 742 (2010).

5   Staub v. City of Baxley, 355 U.S. 313, 322 (1958).

6   Alan Gura, "The Second Amendment as a Normal Right," *Harvard Law
     Review Forum* vol. 127 (2014): 223–29.

7   Appellants' Opening Brief, Kachalsky v. Cacace (2d Cir. No. 11-3642-CV-(L)),
     p. 50, http://www.scribd.com/doc/102602549/Kachalsky-v-Cacace-NY-CA2-
     Plaintiffs-Apellants-Cross-Apelless-Opening-Brief#scribd.

8   Shuttlesworth v. City of Birmingham, 394 U.S. 147, 151 (1969).

9   Appellants' Opening Brief, Kachalsky v. Cacace, p. 45.

10   Kachalsky v. Cnty. of Westchester, 701 F.3d 81, 86 (2d Cir. 2012). Shortly
     before this book went to press, a federal judge in Washington barred the city
     from enforcing a similar "good cause" law. Grace v. D.C. (D.D.C. No. 15-2234)
     (May 17, 2016).

11   *Kachalsky*, 701 F.3d at 92.

12   Richards v. Cnty. of Yolo, 821 F. Supp. 2d 1169, 1176 (E.D. Cal. 2011).

13   Peruta v. Cnty. of San Diego, 742 F.3d 1144 (9th Cir. 2014).

14   *Id.* at 1169–70.

15   Peruta v. San Diego, No. 10-569771 (*en banc*, June 9, 2016), https://cdn.ca9.
     uscourts.gov/datastore/opinions/2016/06/09/10-56971.pdf.

16   Haw. Rev. Stat. § 134-9.

17   "Murder Rate Drops as Concealed Carry Permits Rise, Study Claims," Fox-
     News.com, July 9, 2014, http://www.foxnews.com/us/2014/07/09/murder-
     drops-as-concealed-carry-permits-rise-claims-study/. Apparently all are armed
     security guards. John R. Lott Jr. et al., "Concealed Carry Permit Holders
     across the United States," Crime Prevention Research Center, July 9, 2014,
     http://crimeresearch.org/wp-content/uploads/2014/07/Concealed-Carry-Per
     mit-Holders-Across-the-United-States.pdf.

18   See L. A. Powe, "Guns, Words, and Constitutional Interpretation," *William
     and Mary Law Review* vol. 38 (1997): 1384 ("[p]ossibly the Second Amend-
     ment can best be understood to incorporate a common law rule against prior
     restraints").

19   Donald W. Dowd, "The Relevance of the Second Amendment to Gun Control
     Legislation," *Montana Law Review* vol. 58 (1997): 109–10.

20   Henry Louis Gates Jr., ed., *Frederick Douglass: Autobiographies* (New York:
     Library of America, 1994), p. 817.

21   Douglas Blackmon, *Slavery by Another Name* (New York: Anchor Books,
     2009), pp. 81–82.

22 Manning Marable & Leith Mullings, eds., *Let Nobody Turn Us Around: An African American Anthology* (Lanham, MD: Rowman & Littlefield, 2009), p. 412.

23 Dowd, "The Relevance of the Second Amendment," p. 109.

24 Akhil Reed Amar, *The Bill of Rights* (New Haven: Yale University Press, 1998), pp. 46–47.

25 James Dumas, *Tennessee Stories* (Nashville: Turner Publishing, 1998), p. 105.

26 John Egerton, *Speak Now Against the Day: The Generation Before the Civil Rights Movement* (Chapel Hill: University of North Carolina Press, 1995), p. 394.

27 Ibid.

28 Ibid.; "The Battle of Athens, Tennessee," *Guns & Ammo*, Oct. 1995, pp. 50–51; Lones Seiber, "The Battle of Athens," *American Heritage* vol. 26, no. 2 (Feb.–Mar. 1985).

29 Egerton, *Speak Now Against the Day*, p. 395. See also the excellent presentation by Matt Green: "Battle of Athens Georgia Judge Matt Green," YouTube video, 1:01:35, posted by Mobile Federalist Society, Aug. 7, 2014, https://www.youtube.com/watch?t=19&v=OmDp882eCdo.

30 Quoted in Seiber, "The Battle of Athens."

31 Eleanor Roosevelt, "McMinn: A Warning," *Daily Post-Athenian*, Aug. 7, 1946.

32 Dorr v. Weber, 741 F. Supp. 2d 993, 997 (N.D. Iowa 2010).

33 *Id.* at 1008–09.

34 Dowd, "The Relevance of the Second Amendment," p. 109.

35 Jim Walsh, "Ex-Boyfriend Sought in Woman's Slaying," *Courier Post*, June 5, 2015, http://www.courierpostonline.com/story/news/crime/2015/06/04/woman-fatally-stabbed-berlin-twp/28461361/.

36 See, for example, Town of Castle Rock, Colo. v. Gonzales, 545 U.S. 748 (2005).

37 Dowd, "The Relevance of the Second Amendment," p. 109.

38 See sources cited in Brief Amicus Curiae of International Law Enforcement Educators & Trainers Association et al., District of Columbia v. Heller (U.S. No. 07.290), pp. 19–21, http://www.americanbar.org/content/dam/aba/publishing/preview/publiced_preview_briefs_pdfs_07_08_07_290_RespondentAmCu17LawEnforceOrgsnew.authcheckdam.pdf.

39 United States v. Behrman, 258 U.S. 280 (1922).

40 See, for example, Dirk W. Lachenmeier & Jürgen Rehm, "Comparative Risk Assessment of Alcohol, Tobacco, Cannabis, and Other Illicit Drugs Using the Margin of Measure Approach," *Science Reports* vol. 5 (2014): 8126.

41 Emily Ekins, "Poll: 70% Favor Legalizing Over-the-Counter Birth Control," *Reason*, Oct. 20, 2014, http://reason.com/blog/2014/10/20/poll-70-favor-legalizing-over-the-count2; American College of Obstetricians and Gynecolo-

gists, Committee on Gynecologic Practice, Opinion No. 544, Dec. 2012, http://www.acog.org/Resources-And-Publications/Committee-Opinions/Com mittee-on-Gynecologic-Practice/Over-the-Counter-Access-to-Oral-Contracep tives. Although often referred to as "over-the-counter" availability, current reform efforts instead aim only to allow pharmacists to prescribe the Pill themselves. This would make it unnecessary for women to visit a doctor's office, but it is not true over-the-counter availability, as a prescription would still be required and the Pill would not be available for direct purchase by consumers. This is more accurately referred to as "behind-the-counter" availability.

42 Christine M. Williams, "Catholic Doctors Oppose Call for Over-the-Counter Contraceptive Pills," *National Catholic Reporter*, Jan. 11, 2013, http://ncron line.org/news/politics/catholic-doctors-oppose-call-over-counter-contraceptive -pills.

43 Amir Qaseem et al., "Screening Pelvic Examination in Adult Women: A Clinical Practice Guideline from the American College of Physicians," *Annals of Internal Medicine* vol. 161, no. 1 (2014): 67–72.

44 Stephanie Mencimer, "Holding Birth Control Hostage," *Mother Jones*, Apr. 30, 2012, http://www.motherjones.com/politics/2012/04/doctors-holding-birth-con trol-hostage.

45 Tummino v. Torti, 603 F. Supp. 2d 519, 538 (E.D.N.Y. 2009).

46 *Id.* at 548.

47 Tummino v. Hamburg, No. 13-1690, 2013 WL 2435370 (2d Cir. June 5, 2013).

48 Due process of law forbids the government from depriving a person of liberty arbitrarily – i.e., with insufficient reason and without adequate procedural protections. See Sandefur, *Conscience of the Constitution*, pp. 71–120.

49 Washington v. Glucksberg, 521 U.S. 702, 719–20 (1997).

50 Rochin v. California, 342 U.S. 165 (1952).

51 Abigail Alliance for Better Access to Developmental Drugs & Washington Legal Found. v. von Eschenbach, 445 F.3d 470, 484–85 (D.C. Cir. 2006).

52 Abigail Alliance for Better Access to Developmental Drugs v. von Eschenbach, 495 F.3d 695, 712 (D.C. Cir. 2007) (*en banc*).

53 Michael F. Cannon & Michael D. Tanner, *Healthy Competition*, 2d ed. (Washington, D.C.: Cato Institute, 2007), p. 123.

54 Julian Savulescu, "Bioethics: Why Philosophy Is Essential for Progress," *Journal of Medical Ethics* vol. 41 (2015): 28–33. See also I. Chalmers, "Regulation of Therapeutic Research Is Compromising the Interests of Patients," *International Journal of Pharmaceutical Medicine* vol. 21 (2007): 395–404.

55 Mark Flatten, "Dead on Arrival: Federal 'Compassionate Use' Leaves Little Hope for Dying Patients" (Goldwater Institute, 2016), http://goldwaterinsti tute.org/en/work/topics/healthcare/right-to-try/dead-on-arrival-federal-compas sionate-use-leaves-l/.

56   Darcy Olsen, *The Right to Try: How the Federal Government Prevents Americans from Getting the Lifesaving Treatments They Need* (New York: Harper, 2015), ch. 2.

57   Ibid., p. 23.

58   Jacob Sullum, "No Relief in Sight," *Reason*, Jan. 1997, http://reason.com/archives/1997/01/01/no-relief-in-sight.

59   Statement of Dr. Lester Grinspoon, Harvard Medical School, Medical Marijuana Referenda Movement in America: Congressional Hearing before the Subcommittee on Crime of the House Judiciary Committee, Oct. 1, 1997, Serial No. 110, pp. 95–98.

60   Pearson v. McCaffrey, 139 F. Supp. 2d 113, 117 (D.D.C. 2001).

61   *Id.* at 121–22.

62   Conant v. Walters, 309 F.3d 629, 637 (9th Cir. 2002).

63   Amarin Pharma, Inc. v. U.S. Food & Drug Admin., 119 F. Supp. 3d 196, 201 (S.D.N.Y. 2015).

64   United States v. Caronia, 703 F.3d 149, 156 (2d Cir. 2012).

65   *Id.* at 166.

66   *Id.* at 167.

67   *Amarin Pharma*, 119 F. Supp. 3d at 201.

68   Michelle Ye Hee Lee, "Sun City Medical-Marijuana Dispensary Applicant Sues Maricopa County," *Arizona Republic*, June 25, 2012, http://www.azcentral.com/news/politics/articles/2012/06/22/20120622medical-marijuana-dispensary-applicant-sues-maricopa-county.html#ixzz3ZYlUvggH.

69   Sara Goldenberg, "Maricopa County Attorney Bill Montgomery Calls Veteran 'Enemy' During Marijuana Debate," ABC 15 Arizona, Mar. 31, 2015, http://www.abc15.com/news/region-phoenix-metro/central-phoenix/maricopa-county-attorney-bill-montgomery-calls-veteran-enemy-during-marijuana-debate.

70   White Mountain Health Center, Inc. v. County of Maricopa (Maricopa County Super. Ct. CV-2012-053585, Dec. 3, 2012), http://archive.azcentral.com/ic/pdf/white-mountain-marijuana-ruling.pdf.

71   "Judge Overturns Maricopa County Zoning Law on Medical Marijuana," ABC 15 Arizona, Oct. 15, 2013, http://www.abc15.com/news/state/judge-overturns-maricopa-county-zoning-law-on-medical-marijuana.

72   One oft-cited statistic holds that one in four college women is raped during her college years. This number is simply false, based on a flawed survey that has been thoroughly debunked. See Mary P. Koss et al., "What We Didn't Learn from the American Association of Universities' Sexual Assault Report," *Huffington Post*, Sept. 23, 2015, http://www.huffingtonpost.com/mary-p-koss/association-of-american-universities-sexual-assault-report_b_8182956.html; Ashe Schow, "No, 1 in 5 Women Have Not Been Raped on College Campuses," *Washington Examiner*, Aug. 13, 2014, http://www.washingtonexaminer.com/no-1-in-5-women-have-not-been-raped-on-college-campuses/article/2551980.

73 Cal. Education Code § 67386(a)(1).

74 Cal. Education Code § 67386(a)(2)(2)(B)(3).

75 Goss v. Lopez, 419 U.S. 565, 574–76 (1975).

76 Robert Shipley, "What Ezra Klein Gets Wrong about the 'Yes Means Yes' Law in California," *FIRE Blog*, Oct. 17, 2014, https://www.thefire.org/ezra-klein-gets-wrong-yes-means-yes-law-california/.

77 Unsurprisingly, courts are already expressing increasing concern about the way laws like "yes means yes" deprive the accused of their rights to due process of law. In April 2016, for example, the California Court of Appeal held that the University of Southern California violated the constitutional rights of a male student who was disciplined for sexual misconduct without being given access to the evidence against him or being given "an adequate opportunity to defend his actions." Doe v. Univ. of S. California, No. B262917, 2016 WL 1321509, at *1 (Cal. Ct. App. Apr. 5, 2016).

78 Jenny Kutner, "Yes to 'Yes Means Yes': California's Affirmative Consent Law Is the First Step to Eradicating Campus Sexual Assault," Salon, Sept. 29, 2014, http://www.salon.com/2014/09/29/yes_to_yes_means_yes_californias_affirmative_consent_law_is_the_first_step_to_eradicating_campus_sexual_assault/.

79 Katie McDonough, "Liberals' Blind Spot on Rape: Why Jonathan Chait & Co. Miss the Real Point," *Salon*, Oct. 15, 2014, http://www.salon.com/2014/10/15/liberals_blind_spot_on_rape_why_jonathan_chait_co_miss_the_real_point/.

80 Ibid.

81 Jones v. Balkcom, 210 Ga. 262, 266–67 (1953).

82 State v. Ingram, 237 N.C. 197, 198 (1953).

83 Julie Lavonne Novkov, *Racial Union: Law, Intimacy and the White State in Alabama* (Ann Arbor: University of Michigan Press, 2008), pp. 99–101.

84 Stuart Taylor & K.C. Johnson, *Until Proven Innocent: Political Correctness and the Shameful Injustices of the Duke Lacrosse Rape Case* (New York: St. Martin's Griffin, 2008); Dorothy Rabinowitz, "The Dishonest Rewrite of the Duke Lacrosse Case," *Wall Street Journal*, May 18, 2014, http://www.wsj.com/articles/SB10001424052702304081804579558413534190406.

85 Margaret Hartmann, "Everything We Know about the UVA Rape Case," *New York Magazine*, May 13, 2015, http://nymag.com/daily/intelligencer/2014/12/everything-we-know-uva-rape-case.html.

86 Janet Bloomfield, "13 Women Who Lied about Being Raped and Why They Did It," *Thought Catalog*, Dec. 10, 2014, http://thoughtcatalog.com/janet-bloomfield/2014/12/13-women-who-lied-about-being-raped-and-why-they-did-it/.

87 Edgar W. Butler et al., *Anatomy of the McMartin Child Molestation Case* (Lanham, MD: University Press of America, 2001).

88 James Robinson, "What It's Like to be Falsely Accused of Rape," *The Telegraph*, Mar. 26, 2015, http://www.telegraph.co.uk/men/the-filter/another-mans-shoes/11494055/What-its-like-to-be-falsely-accused-of-rape.html. Similar sto-

ries are recounted in Ashe Schow, "Students Accused of Sexual Assault Speak about Their Trauma," *Washington Examiner*, Feb. 1, 2016, http://www.washingtonexaminer.com/students-accused-of-sexual-assault-speak-about-their-own-trauma/article/2582103.

89 Edward Greer, "The Truth behind Legal Dominance Feminism's 'Two Percent False Rape Claim' Figure," *Loyola of Los Angeles Law Review* vol. 33 (2000): 947–72.

90 Ibid., pp. 967–68.

91 Editorial, "When Yes Means Yes," *N.Y. Times*, Sept. 8, 2014, http://www.nytimes.com/2014/09/09/opinion/california-lawmakers-redefine-campus-sexual-assault.html?ref=opinion&_r=2.

92 Editorial, "'Ask First' at Antioch," *N.Y. Times*, Oct. 11, 1993, http://www.nytimes.com/1993/10/11/opinion/ask-first-at-antioch.html.

CHAPTER EIGHT

1 http://smvote.org/BallotMeasures/detail.aspx?id=53687092663.

2 Memo from City Councilmember Jesse Arreguin to Mayor & City Council, Oct. 28, 2014, http://www.berkeleyside.com/wp-content/uploads/2014/10/2014-10-28-Item-10-Release-of-Balloons.pdf.

3 Steve Lopez, "Out on a Limb over Trimming Fiasco," *L. A. Times*, Nov. 28, 2007, http://articles.latimes.com/2007/nov/28/local/me-lopez28.

4 *In re.* Bobrowich, No. 159/02, 2003 WL 230701, at *2 (N.Y. Civ. Ct. Jan. 6, 2003).

5 Pierce v. Society of Sisters, 268 U.S. 510 (1925); Meyer v. Nebraska, 262 U.S. 390 (1923). For background, see David Kopel, "*Meyer v. Nebraska*: As Told by the Lawyer Who Won It," *The Volokh Conspiracy*, Feb. 4, 2016, https://www.washingtonpost.com/news/volokh-conspiracy/wp/2016/02/04/meyer-v-nebraska-as-told-by-the-lawyer-who-won-it/.

6 See Clint Bolick, *Voucher Wars* (Washington, D.C.: Cato Institute, 2003).

7 People v. DeJonge, 442 Mich. 266, 292 (1993).

8 *Id.* at 290–91.

9 Hugh Lafollette, "Licensing Parents," *Philosophy & Public Affairs* vol. 9, no. 2 (1980): 182–97.

10 Buck v. Bell, 274 U.S. 200 (1927).

11 Ma Jian, "China's Barbaric One-Child Policy," *Guardian*, May 5, 2013, http://www.theguardian.com/books/2013/may/06/chinas-barbaric-one-child-policy. In 2015, China claimed it was ending the one-child policy and imposing a two-child policy instead. Parents are still required to obtain government permission before having children. Shannon Tiezzi, "China Ending Its One-Child Policy Isn't That Big of a Deal," *Diplomat*, Oct. 30, 2015, http://thediplomat.com/2015/10/china-ending-its-one-child-policy-isnt-that-big-of-a-deal/.

12 Tocqueville, *Democracy in America*, p. 692.

13 Jeffrey Hause, ed., *Aquinas: Basic Works* (Indianapolis: Hackett, 2014), pp. 333–34.

14 Cass R. Sunstein, "The Paralyzing Principle," *Regulation*, Winter 2002–03, pp. 32–37.

15 Gregory N. Mandel & James Thuo Gathii, "Cost-Benefit Analysis Versus the Precautionary Principle: Beyond Cass Sunstein's *Laws of Fear*," *University of Illinois Law Review* vol. 2006: 1052.

16 Richard Feynman, *What Do You Care What Other People Think?* (New York: Norton, 1988), p. 180.

17 The shuttle's actual failure rate, as Americans learned through tragic experience, was more like 1 in 50 – at best.

18 Jaap C. Hanekamp, "The Precautionary Principle: A Critique in the Context of the EU Food Supplements Directive," *Environmental Liability* vol. 2 (2006): 49.

19 Adam Thierer, *Permissionless Innovation* (Arlington, VA: Mercatus Center, 2014), p. 28 (emphasis omitted).

20 Peggy McIntosh, "White Privilege and Male Privilege: A Personal Account of Coming to See Correspondences through Work in Women's Studies," Wellesley College Working Paper No. 189 (1988), http://files.eric.ed.gov/fulltext/ED335262.pdf.

21 Ibid., p. 3.

22 Ibid., p. 9.

23 Ezra Rosser, "The Ambition and Transformative Potential of Progressive Property," *California Law Review* vol. 101 (2013): 134–35.

24 Ibid., p. 140.

25 Ibid., pp. 142–43.

26 Ibid.

27 Cathy Cockrell, "To Berkeley Civil-Rights Scholar, Race Is Uppercase Concern," *Berkeley News*, Dec. 11, 2012, http://news.berkeley.edu/2012/12/11/john-powell-profile/.

28 john a. powell, "Worlds Apart: Reconciling Freedom of Speech and Equality," *Kentucky Law Journal* vol. 85 (1997): 16.

29 Ibid., p. 39.

30 Ibid.

31 Ibid., p. 91.

32 Ibid., p. 92.

33 Ibid., p. 65.

34 Ibid., p. 66.

35 Harry Brighouse & Adam Swift, *Family Values: The Ethics of Parent-Child Relationships* (Princeton: Princeton University Press, 2014), p. 2.

36 Ibid., p. 135.

37 Joe Gelonesi, "Is Having a Loving Family an Unfair Advantage?" Radio

National (Australia), May 1, 2015, http://www.abc.net.au/radionational/pro-grams/philosopherszone/new-family-values/6437058.

38 Friedrich Hayek, "Competition as a Discovery Procedure," *Quarterly Journal of Austrian Economics* vol. 5, no. 3 (Fall 2002): 9–23.

39 Edwards v. D.C., 755 F.3d 996, 1006 (D.C. Cir. 2014).

40 See Milton Friedman, *Free to Choose* (New York: Harcourt Brace Jovanovich, 1980), ch. 7.

41 Department of the Treasury Office of Economic Policy, Council of Economic Advisers, and Department of Labor, *Occupational Licensing*, p. 45.

42 Carolyn Cox & Susan Foster, "The Costs and Benefits of Occupational Regu-lation" (FTC Report, 1990), pp. 43–44, https://www.ftc.gov/system/files/documents/reports/costs-benefits-occupational-regulation/cox_foster_-_occupational_licensing.pdf.

43 A.R.S. § 32-4301, *et seq.*

44 R.C.W. § 18.118.030, *et seq.*

45 C.R.S.A. § 24-34-104.1, *et seq.*

46 5 M.R.S. § 12015, *et seq.*

47 26 V.S.A. § 3101, *et seq.*

48 Colorado Department of Regulatory Agencies Office of Policy and Research: Interior Designers, 2000 Sunrise Review, p. 23, http://goo.gl/T9UZ8g.

49 A.R.S. § 41-1038.

AFTERWORD

1 *The Collected Poems of Rudyard Kipling* (Hertfordshire, UK: Wordsworth Editions Ltd., 2001), p. 307. See also Robert Jackson, Opening Statement before the International Military Tribunal, Nov. 21, 1945, http://www.roberthjackson.org/speech-and-writing/opening-statement-before-the-international-military-tribunal.

INDEX

permit system of government regulation
(*cont.*)
   knowledge problem and, 30–32, 39,
   41, 111–12, 207; lack of ability to challenge court, 35–36, 208; as proactive,
   29; *propiska* in Soviet Union and,
   42–45; rent-seeking and, 29–30, 39,
   41, 207; stifling of innovation and,
   36–39, 41, 208; superiority assumption about government, 209; used to
   restrict other rights, 160–64; vagueness of laws and, 207–08
Phillips, Michael, 240n88
physicians, professional speech doctrine
   and, 102–03, 233n55
"pie crust promises," 5, 219n12
Plan B over-the-counter contraceptives,
   prior restraint on practice of medicine and, 177–78, 248n40
Planned Parenthood v. Casey, 233n55
Pledge of Allegiance, 64–65, 68
political speech: campaign finance laws
   and "fairness," 74–83, 230n119; union
   agency fees and right to dissent, 68–74
Pollock, John C., 121
positivists, rejection of natural rights by,
   12–19
Posner, Richard, 111
powell, john a., 204–06
precautionary principle, 199–202
"preponderance of the evidence" standard, rape accusations, 188, 193
prior restraint, x, 28. *See also* businesses
   and economic transactions; freedom
   of speech; medicine; Second
   Amendment
private certification proposal, advantages of, 210–11
private investigators, professional
   speech doctrine and, 98–99
private investment, CON laws and
   supposed protection of, 110–13

private property. *See* property
Privilege Theory, 202–06
probatio diabolica fallacy (Devil's
   proof), 8, 10, 19, 69, 119, 187, 202
professional speech doctrine, licensing
   and prior restraint, 84, 98–103, 183–
   84, 233n55
Progressives: campaign finance laws and,
   74–83; eugenics movement and, 198;
   fairness doctrine and, 89–91; free
   speech as collective, not individual,
   right and, 58–63; government seen as
   source of rights, x; regulation of food
   and medicine and, 176; right not to
   speak and, 58, 63–68; union agency
   fees and right to dissent, 68–74; zoning and, 139–40
property, 134–64; agricultural crops and
   government taking of, 153–57; free
   speech seen as, 58; "givings" theory
   and, 157–60; permit fees, exactions,
   and land versus cash compensation,
   143–48; Privilege Theory and property "disobedience," 203–04; repair
   and maintenance of, 151–53; use of as
   privilege versus right, 144–45, 148–
   53; waiving of legal right in exchange
   for permits, 160–64; zoning and
   "rational" planning, 140–43; zoning
   and segregation, 135–40
propiska (residence permits), in Soviet
   Union, 42–45
protectionism. *See* Competitor's Veto
psychology professionals: occupational
   licensing and, 93–96; professional
   speech doctrine and, 101–02
"public convenience and necessity,"
   CONs and, 106–08, 235n10, 235n18
Pure Food and Drug Act (1906), 176

race. *See* African Americans; slavery
Racial Union: Law, Intimacy and the

A NOTE ON THE TYPE

THE PERMISSION SOCIETY *has been set in Darden Studio's Corundum Text, a family of types derived from the work of Pierre-Simon Fournier le jeune. Fournier's achievement as a typographer is best known in the form of Monotype's interpretation of the "Saint Augustin Ordinaire" types shown in his 1725* Manuel Typographique. *Cut under Stanley Morison's direction in 1925–26, the Monotype version – christened "Fournier" – was under development at the same time as a somewhat darker type that would eventually be given the name Barbou in honor of the publisher of Fournier's* Traité historique sur l'origine et les progrès des caractères de font pour l'impression de la musique *(1765), which provided Morison's models for the types. Morison would have preferred to release Barbou to the printing trade, but a misunderstanding during his absence from the works led to the release of Fournier. But for a handful of appearances, Barbou largely disappeared from view. The present version of the type captures the rich color of the eighteenth-century original and maintains its lively spirit, especially in the italics.*

DESIGN & COMPOSITION BY CARL W. SCARBROUGH